SOCIAL JUSTICE AND CULTURAL COMPETENCY

SOCIAL JUSTICE AND CULTURAL COMPETENCY

Essential Readings for School Librarians

Marcia A. Mardis and Dianne Oberg, Editors

Co-published with The International Association of School Librarianship

LIBRARIES UNLIMITED®
An Imprint of ABC-CLIO, LLC
Santa Barbara, California • Denver, Colorado

Copyright © 2020 by The International Association of School Librarianship

Library of Congress Control Number: 2019951045

ISBN: 978–1–4408–7120–7 (paperback)
     978–1–4408–7123–8 (ebook)

23 22 21 20 19   1 2 3 4 5

This book is also available as an eBook.

Libraries Unlimited
An Imprint of ABC-CLIO, LLC

ABC-CLIO, LLC
147 Castilian Drive
Santa Barbara, California 93117
www.abc-clio.com

This book is printed on acid-free paper (∞)

Manufactured in the United States of America

Contents

Foreword

Katy Manck

What is social justice? How do we foster cultural competence in our personal lives and professional practice? How can we help our students and teachers become better global and local citizens? Social justice can be defined as "the view that everyone deserves to enjoy the same economic, political and social rights, regardless of race, socioeconomic status, gender or other characteristics," according to the Education World website. The global importance of social justice for all is displayed in the 17 Sustainable Development Goals (SDGs) centering the 2030 Agenda for Sustainable Development adopted by all UN states. Of particular interest to libraries are the SDGs for quality education, gender equality, reduced inequalities, and peace, justice, and strong institutions.

The concept of cultural competence originated in the fields of social work and health services, referring to individuals and organizations that are respectful and responsive to beliefs, practices, cultural, and linguistic needs of diverse population groups (www.samhsa.gov).

Social justice and cultural competence both indicate an ongoing process of growth and progress, making them highly useful lenses for teacher librarians and library/information science educators of preservice librarians to use as they purposefully examine policies and procedures at their institutions, assess resource collections and representation of local voices, and consider their individual interactions with persons of other cultural groups.

Lessons bridging the academic subject curriculum are among the most valuable that school librarians can provide to our students and their teachers—empathy, seeing the world beyond their own community, cooperation, tolerance, and more. As Kofi Annan, seventh secretary-general of the United Nations, said in his 2001 Nobel Peace Prize lecture:

People of different religions and cultures live side-by-side in almost every part of the world, and most of us have overlapping identities which unite us in very different groups. We can love what we are, without hating what—and who—we are not. We can thrive in our own tradition, even as we learn from others, and come to respect their teachings. (https://www.un.org/press/en/2001/sgsm8071.doc.htm)

When the school library is viewed as "the largest classroom in the school, regardless of physical size," as I often say, it is the best place for these larger life lessons to blossom, for the social-emotional learning needed by all students and teachers to be an expected part of interactions and discussions, for all readers and listeners to experience the wider world through "books as windows, mirrors, and sliding glass doors" as Dr. Rudine Sims Bishop noted in 1990.

But how can a teacher librarian who grew up and was educated within a specific social and economic setting fairly and justly serve all the children and teachers who arrive at their school library from many different cultural backgrounds, family configurations, and lived experiences? Consulting lists of "multicultural" books or attending "diversity training" are just the smallest of steps toward that goal.

This is where intentional study of social justice and continuing development of cultural competence can enable teacher librarians and their fellow educators to teach and reach every child as the school community recognizes and celebrates the value of the diverse cultures gathered there.

For me, being part of the International Association of School Librarianship (IASL) has been vital in building up my cultural competence and turning my energies toward more active social justice. I've long said that "IASL exists because every child in the world deserves a qualified teacher librarian and a great school library." That means a teacher librarian working to recognize and reach all the cultures in their school through positive interactions and a "windows, mirrors, and sliding glass doors" school library collection reflecting the lived experience of students and staff as well as viewpoints and opinions from the world outside their neighborhood.

IASL was founded in 1971 to actively develop school librarianship, teacher librarians, and school libraries in every country of the world. Through its annual international conferences and concurrent research forums, IASL brings together practicing teacher librarians with researchers of school librarianship in an ongoing conversation aimed at educating our youth and communities for a better future through the best that our profession can offer.

To this end, IASL's peer-reviewed journal *School Libraries Worldwide* (*SLW*) has published seminal research studies, reports of action research and best practices, and targeted literature reviews since 1995 as impetus to drive school librarianship forward and upward, making them globally available to its members and through library databases.

Information seeking, reading, literacy, and instruction in research have long been topics of *SLW* articles, but focus on the larger social picture is emerging as school libraries become project-based learning centers, their collections are intentionally reflective of their students' lived experience, and educators in the library and the classroom are urged to consider the whole student and their local cultures within the context of our global society.

Second in the International Perspectives series coproduced by IASL and Libraries Unlimited, this volume highlights research studies and recent reports published in *SLW* that support IASL's mission and give evidence of best practices that teacher librarians can adopt to bring these life lessons of social justice and cultural competence not only to students but also to their entire school population. Please note that this volume doesn't headline itself with "diversity" or "multicultural" because the articles and studies here go far beyond such items that we can easily mark as completed on a list as the authors challenge us to wrestle with the idea that social justice and cultural competence aren't things that we can accomplish—they are journeys that we must undertake and habits of mind that we must continually cultivate.

Each section begins with an overview of the topic, newly written for this publication, and all article authors have added information expanding what was originally published in *SLW*.

The first two sections—Social Justice and Cultural Competency—introduce and expand on their respective concepts, while the third section—Innovative Practice—highlights school library projects that effectively supported youth and their teachers in their ongoing learning about these essential skills for navigating modern society.

My grateful thanks to our editors Dr. Marcia A. Mardis of Florida State University (USA) and Dr. Dianne Oberg of University of Alberta (Canada) for ably shepherding this volume to publication. Working with over a dozen authors is a challenge that they accomplished with gracious words despite a firm deadline.

The IASL Publications Advisory Committee worked diligently over many months with Libraries Unlimited to ascertain which topics for this second volume in the International Perspectives series would be most interesting and useful for teacher librarians and professors of library and information science. The result of their continuing efforts is now a reality, and I thank IASL PAC members Dianne Oberg (Chair), Marcia Mardis, Susan LaMarca, Hanna Lataputty, and Luisa Marquardt once again.

What pathways are you and your institution taking on your social justice and cultural competence journey? May our conversations continue and flourish for the benefit of our students and communities!

REFERENCES

Annan, K. (2001, December 10). *Nobel Peace Prize lecture*. Retrieved from https://www.un.org/press/en/2001/sgsm8071.doc.htm

Bishop, R. S. (1990). Mirrors, windows, and sliding glass doors. *Perspectives: Choosing and Using Books for the Classroom, 6*(3), ix–xi. Retrieved from https://scenicregional.org/wp-content/uploads/2017/08/Mirrors-Windows-and-Sliding-Glass-Doors.pdf

Introduction

Marcia A. Mardis

Culture includes the traditions, values, beliefs, and patterns of behavior that shape and influence participants' social identities. Race, ethnicity, sex, gender, sexual orientation, religion, socioeconomic class, ability, age, and national origin are all examples of these identities. As information professionals, we celebrate cultural diversity and help our learners understand and construct their social identities.

Social justice and cultural competence are key concepts in the conscious practice of teacher librarianship. In this volume, we operationally define cultural competence as the ability to live and work effectively in culturally diverse environments and enact a commitment to social justice. Social justice entails creating a society with an equitable distribution of resources where all people are safe, can meet their needs, and can fulfill their potential. Culturally competent practitioners employ a range of awareness, knowledge, and skills:

- Self-awareness—awareness of one's own social identities, cultures, biases, and perspectives.
- Understanding and valuing others—knowledge of and appreciation for others' social identities, cultures, and perspectives.
- Knowledge of societal inequities—understanding of how social identities and forms of oppression affect people's experiences and access to power, resources, and opportunities.
- Skills to interact effectively with diverse people in different contexts—ability to adapt to and work collaboratively with different cultural groups.
- Skills to foster equity and inclusion—ability to identify and address inequities and create environments, policies, and practices to ensure diversity and fairness.

Librarianship's commitment to promoting social justice is deep. Melvil Dewey developed and promoted the Dewey Decimal System as a social equalizer that would allow every library user a universal location system for reading material (though Dewey's cultural competence was troubled by his commitment to neutral universality) (Wiegand, 1996). Likewise, Ranganathan's Five Laws of Library Science (books are for use; every person his or her book; every book its reader; save the time of the reader; the library is a growing organism) acknowledge libraries as sites for diversity and personalization.

Cultural competence goes beyond awareness of cultures beyond the dominant; social justice is an essential counterpart to ensure that all members of a culture are recognized, supported, honored, and safe. To this point, library historian Wayne Wiegand related a social justice tale in the American Association of School Librarians' KQ Blog:

[O]ne student wrote that in the mid-1980s his high school librarian was being pressured to remove titles about homosexuality from the shelves. At the time, he was a sophomore struggling with his own sexual identity, and he needed those books. Then something unusual happened. Title by title the librarian reported the books "lost"—thus satisfying parents and school superiors protesting their presence in the collection–but, my student reported, somehow he and his gay friends soon discovered these "lost" books had actually been "misshelved" behind others in a remote part of the library. There they could access the books freely, and all understood that any book taken from the collection (which need not be checked out since it was officially "lost") had to be returned to the same place. The collection was still there—intact and including a few newer donated titles—the day he graduated. (Wiegand, 2017, n.p.)

Almost every teacher librarian has a version of this story because marginalized community members are all around us—this volume is centered on the idea that school libraries and teacher librarians can offer all learners and stakeholders opportunities to expand knowledge, gain skills, and develop expertise.

As I considered my own time as a school librarian, I wondered whether I had been a social justice warrior, whether I was culturally competent. First, I thought about Tom.

Every school librarian has a Tom. Tom was one of the kids I called my "library hounds"—students who were always in the library at the Catholic boys' high school where I had my first school librarian job. Tom was a handsome and popular grade 12 student and had a reputation for not being very bright. With his characteristic good humor, he laughed along with the jokes about his apparent lack of intelligence and even made fun of himself. Because Tom played football and wrestled, he fit in with his classmates in many other ways and never seemed to take the jibes to heart.

Quite by accident, one morning, I stumbled on Tom's secret when he was sitting at a computer in the school library looking despondently at the screen. He explained that he just couldn't look at the screen anymore, and he was so frustrated that he couldn't type fast enough. I asked him if he'd like me to type while he talked. He agreed and our daily ritual began.

Tom's grades began to improve because he was turning in more and better-quality assignments. He became more confident and participated in class more often. When Tom's teachers asked him to explain his turnaround, he credited my assistance. Tom's well-intentioned ascription landed me in the headmaster's office where I was questioned about doing Tom's homework. I explained that I didn't do his homework; I just typed what he told me to type. I also explained that Tom complained of not being able to concentrate and not always understanding what he read. Ultimately, I was cleared of all suspicion of wrongdoing, and Tom received screening and assistance for his learning challenges. By the end of the school year, he had gained strategies to help himself and visited me less often. The last day of school, Tom walked me to my car, gave me a huge beautifully wrapped box, hugged me, blushed, and ran off. In the box was set of matching bath towels and a lovely note in Tom's halting script: "I appreciate you in advance." I had never heard anyone say this strange phrase before. As I have pondered it in the ensuing 20 years, I think it means, "I appreciate that you could see who I could be." Tom is now a successful corporate lawyer. We stay in touch through Facebook. The towels are in my bathroom linen closet. I fought for Tom and taught him to fight for himself with a just result.

OUTSIDERS, OUTLIERS, SOCIAL JUSTICE, AND CULTURAL COMPETENCE

Every school library has its "library hounds" who hang around, initially to read books and magazines, but eventually just to talk to the school librarian. Many of these kids have heartbreaking stories. Their home lives are chaotic. They are new to the area or country. Their peers scorn them. Their teachers don't understand them. They are too bored or distracted to sit in class. They seek refuge in the school library and the companionship of an adult who doesn't scold them for unfinished homework or a messy room. As school librarians, we listen. We recommend books for them to read that will make them feel connected and normal. We give them jobs to do that make them feel useful (and help us get little tasks done). In short, we make them feel safe.

So profound is the feeling of safety that the Association of Superintendents and Curriculum Developers (ASCD) in the United States has a campaign called "The Whole Child" to raise awareness about children's needs to be healthy, challenged, engaged ... and safe. An ASCD Whole Child Blog post entitled "It Takes a Whole School: School Librarians' Roles in the Whole Child" includes a quote from a school librarian-to-be who said,

My definition of a library is one in which a child feels comfortable and relaxed, stimulated and challenged, joyful and creative. It contains a variety of activities and visual aids to engage students while educating them. In this library there are plenty of nooks and crannies for children to cuddle up in with a book, worry free, to allow their imaginations to soar. There are plenty of warm and friendly librarians [who] students trust and feel comfortable in asking any question that they might possibly have. A library is a space where students do not have to fret over the prospect of not being able to find what they need or do what they need to do because of proximity, bullies, an unhelpful staff, a lacking collection, or a cold and uninviting atmosphere. (Mardis, 2013, n.p.)

I cannot think of a better description of the school librarians and libraries that make library hounds feel safe and that turn outsiders into outliers. Gladwell (2008, pp. 112–113, 115) pointed to a key difference between outsiders and outliers:

[Outsiders] lacked something that could have been given to them if we'd only known they needed it: community around them that prepared them properly for the world ... no one, not rock stars, not professional athletes, not software billionaires, and not even geniuses—ever makes it alone.

ABOUT INTERNATIONAL ASSOCIATION OF SCHOOL LIBRARIANSHIP (IASL) AND *SCHOOL LIBRARIES WORLDWIDE*

The International Association of School Librarianship (IASL) is a small, voluntary, professional association, whose mission is the worldwide promotion of school-based libraries. It was founded in the early 1970s with a mission of providing an international forum for those people interested in promoting effective school library programs as viable instruments in the educational process. IASL's mission places the group within efforts to extend literacy and education to all citizens of the world. IASL supports development of school-based libraries supplied with collections reflecting local needs and staffed with professionals capable of serving as a bridge between children and access to reading material and literacy support (Knuth, 1996).

School Libraries Worldwide (*SLW*) is the official professional peer-reviewed research journal of the IASL. It is published twice yearly, in January and July, on the IASL website. The journal includes literature reviews and papers of commentary and opinion in addition to research and best practices articles. *SLW* is a refereed journal, with an editorial board drawn from 14 countries on 5 continents. *SLW* was edited by Dianne Oberg from 1995 to 2007 and by Marcia A. Mardis and Nancy L. Everhart from 2008 to the present. The journal is available to all members of IASL as part of their benefits of membership. Libraries of universities and colleges (with school librarianship programs) subscribe, as do school library service centers. Articles are indexed in a number of indexing and abstracting services (including *Bibliothek Forschung und Praxis, Children's Literature Abstracts, Contents Pages in Education, ERIC, Library Literature, and Library and Information Science Abstracts—LISA*), and the articles are available full text online through ProQuest. In addition, IASL (http://iasl-online.org) supports open access to the articles and *SLW* archives by providing access through its website.

About This Volume

The second in a special series, this volume is a collection of IASL research that includes impactful articles written by a global selection of talented researchers that have been published in *SLW*, IASL's peer-reviewed research journal. All publication royalties will be donated to IASL.

The volume documents empirical social justice and cultural competence research taking place in international school libraries. In many ways these researchers have distilled key challenges and best practices relating to promoting equitable, diverse, and accessible learning atmosphere. The intent of this volume is to show how social justice looks in the international arena, describe program and strategies that may be emulated in other libraries and schools, and depict a global perspective on the role of school libraries in education and elevate the status of teacher librarians

This volume is divided into three sections that each contain selected papers from *SLW* introduced by a newly written section overview provided by an expert researcher or researchers. The sections are as follows:

Section 1: Social Justice. The papers featured in these chapters address a range of international dimensions of equity and equality. In the section overview chapter, Dian Walster addresses the relationships among technologies and equity in school libraries. By applying the evaluative methods Walster discusses in the piece, school librarians can assess areas of equity concern, propose changes, and judge how technology programs fare in regard to equity. Extending the discussion of access and equity, Deborah Lang Froggatt positions access to effective school library programs as a social justice issue. Using theory of and model for the informationally underserved (IU), Froggatt argues that without access to high quality school libraries, disenfranchised students within a school, in a school district, or across a governmental region may experience their education without opportunities to grow into information literate, self-directed, lifelong learners. The chapter includes a study of a diverse set of American urban 15-year-old students who had learned without school libraries. In the final chapter in this section, "Using Institutional Ethnography to Explore Socioeconomic Differences in Brazilian School-Based Librarianship," Lucy Santos Green and Melissa P. Johnston explore the practices of school-based librarians in other countries, and how these practices are influenced or affected by socioeconomic structures, which foster new knowledge, contributing to global communities of practice.

Section 2: Cultural Competence. This section's papers center on understanding and celebrating cultural diversity. Section overview author is Dianne Oberg. In the next chapter, Michelle Hudiburg, Elizabeth Mascher, and Alice Sagehorn ground the need for greater awareness and appreciation for cultural diversity:

> As the cultural landscape of American classrooms change, educators have a responsibility to meet the needs of all students by embracing culturally competent teaching models. According to the U.S. National Center for Education Statistics, enrollment of White U.S. school age children decreased from 62% to 52% between 2000 and 2016. In contrast, Hispanic enrollment increased from 16% to 25% of the total public school population, and Asian/Pacific Islander showed a 2% increase. (see p. 73)

Their paper focuses on using the Purnell Model for Cultural Competence to create cultural responsive learning environments. In "What Does Cultural Competence Mean to Preservice School Librarians? A Critical Discourse Analysis," Kafi D. Kumasi and Renee F. Hill present an evaluation of the underlying ideologies exhibited by library and information students. Sandra Hughes-Hassell and Julie Stivers provide the next chapter, "Youth Services Librarians' Perceptions of Cultural Knowledge: An Exploratory Study with Implications for Practice," in which they report the findings of an exploratory study designed to explore the extent to which youth services librarians prioritize the need for cultural knowledge and awareness in developing effective programs and services for today's youth. They conclude their chapter with implications for teacher librarian practice. In the final chapter of this section, Janice Underwood, Sue Kimmel, Danielle Hartsfield, and Gail Dickinson examine preservice school librarians' experiences with booktalking multicultural literature in a mixed reality simulation environment. This environment facilitated teacher librarians' critical reflection on personal bias and systemic racism in schools and literature, an initial step toward culturally relevant librarianship.

Section 3: Social Justice and Cultural Competence: Innovative Practice. In her extensive section overview, "Fostering Resilience, Wellness, and Hope in the School Library," Meghan Harper explains that school libraries are uniquely positioned to offer resilience, wellness, and hope to children who may be experiencing or have experienced trauma. She points out that vulnerable students who have experienced trauma may need a mental, an emotional, and a physical refuge, and school libraries can foster personal growth, resiliency, and wellness in youth, in addition to supporting their academic performance. This chapter is rich with tips and resources for teacher librarians to make an immediate difference to their learning communities. The chapter "Fostering Information Competence in a High-Poverty Urban School: An I-LEARN Project" recounts two teachers and 49 students at a high-poverty elementary school who worked with Delia Neuman, Allen Grant, Vera Lee, and M. J. Tecce DeCarlo to complete an inquiry-based project using a learning model developed for struggling learners. Rita Reinsel Soulen and Lois D. Wine address the need for teacher librarians to develop their own strengths in "How School Librarians Contribute to Building Resilience in New and Beginning Teachers." In this chapter, they noted,

> Development of teacher resilience is critical to classroom success and teacher retention ... Personal resilience of new teachers may be bolstered through caring and supportive relationships that create trust, provide role models, and offer encouragement and reassurance. (see pp. 127–128)

Sabrina Carnesi then provides a chapter that uses the language of social justice along with school library standards and guidelines in which she provides a study providing indications for highly effective partnerships for implementing literature discussion circles and Socratic seminars as platforms of expression for seldom heard young adult voices. The final chapter in the volume, "Practicing a Critical Stance to Research Ethics in Global Contexts: Challenges and Ways Forward," Marlene Asselin and Ray Doiron leave IASL community members with a poignant thought:

> As an international association representing libraries supporting teaching and learning for children and youth throughout the world, IASL needs to seriously take renewed responsibility to ensure ethical research for their global membership and for the larger library community ... is time for IASL to step forward for the global school library community. (p. 170)

CONCLUDING THOUGHTS

This volume is meant to both reflect and lead the practice of teacher librarianship. The new *National School Library Standards* (American Association of School Librarians, 2018) are based on six shared foundations inherent to our profession; while cultural competence and social justice are woven throughout the standards, two shared foundations, "include" and "engage," provide teacher librarians with a road map for their own practice as well as their work with learners and their creation of learning spaces. To embody "include," learners and school librarians "demonstrate an understanding of and commitment to inclusiveness and respect for diversity in the learning community," and to demonstrate "engage," learners and school librarians "demonstrate safe, legal, and ethical creating and sharing of knowledge products independently while engaging in a community of practice and an interconnected world."

Likewise, the IFLA *School Library Guidelines* (Schultz-Jones & Oberg, 2015) emphasize that teacher librarians,

put the rights of library users before their own comfort and convenience and to avoid being biased by their personal attitudes and beliefs in providing library service. They deal with all children, youth, and adults on an equal basis regardless of their abilities and background, maintaining their right to privacy and their right to know. (p.7)

Social justice and cultural competence are no longer abstract concepts—they are very really, very necessary components of learning and teaching today. We sincerely hope that the papers in this volume provide you with tools and insight to ensure equity, diversity, and accessibility in your own learning environment.

ACKNOWLEDGMENT

This volume would not have been possible without the substantial coediting support of the IASL Publication Action Committee (PAC) Chair Dianne Oberg.

NOTE

Portions of this introduction have been adapted from "Editorial: 'I Appreciate You in Advance': Outsiders, Outliers, and Safety in the School Library" by Marcia A. Mardis, published in *School Libraries Worldwide, 19*(1), i–iv.

REFERENCES

American Association of School Librarians. (2018). *National school library standards for learners, school librarians, and school libraries.* Chicago, IL: American Library Association.

Gladwell, M. (2008). *Outliers: The story of success.* New York, NY: Little, Brown and Company.

Knuth, R. (1996). An international forum: The history of the International Association of School Librarianship. *School Libraries Worldwide, 2*(2), 1–32.

Mardis, M. A. (2013, February 3). It takes a whole school: School librarians' roles in the whole child. Retrieved from http://www.wholechildeducation.org/blog/it-takes-a-whole-school-school-librarians-roles-in-the-whole-child

National Center for Education Statistics (NCES). (2017). Population distribution. Retrieved from https://nces.ed.gov/programs/raceindicators/indicator_raa.asp

Schultz-Jones, B., & Oberg, D. (Eds.). (2015). *IFLA school library guidelines* (2nd ed.). Retrieved from https://www.ifla.org/files/assets/school-libraries-resource-centers/publications/ifla-school-library-guidelines.pdf

Wiegand, W. A. (1996). *A biography of Melvil Dewey: Irrepressible reformer.* Chicago, IL: American Library Association.

Wiegand, W. A. (2017, May 30). The American public school library: A history. Retrieved from https://knowledgequest.aasl.org/american-public-school-library-history/

I

Social Justice

Section Overview

Technology and Equity in School Libraries: An Issue of Social Justice

Dian Walster

ABSTRACT

This chapter addresses the relationships among technologies and equity in school libraries. An autoethnographic approach is used to examine issues that school libraries and school librarians face in the age of big data, equity concerns, and attacks on how schools support reading. It explores three specific technologies related to accessibility, reading, and online searching. Different methodologies suitable to each area inform the discussions. Social and cultural aspects of equity are presented, and examples are provided. By applying the evaluative methods discussed, school librarians can assess areas of equity concern, propose changes, and judge how technology programs fare in regard to equity.

INTRODUCTION

Some years ago I wrote a chapter on technology in school libraries that looked at historical issues and perspectives (Walster, 1998). This chapter is an extension and enlargement of those ideas particularly as regards new technologies. Our conceptualizations of how technologies interact with social and cultural concerns are complex and have significant implications for students, their families, and society. This chapter uses an autoethnographic approach to examine issues that school libraries and school librarians face in the age of big data, social equity concerns, and attacks on how schools support reading. It is done through the lens of technologies in school libraries toward supporting accessibility, reading, and online searching.

Autoethnography is a type of ethnographic research (Jones, Adams, & Ellis, 2013). It looks at how culture works through the reflection of a single individual. Throughout the chapter I use my own experiences, educational background, field notes, remembrances, and reading to examine the culture of technology and equity in school libraries. In other words, as a former school librarian and currently a professor of library and information science and teacher of school librarians, what are the issues I find critical? How, given my experiences and understandings, do I think we might effectively go about examining the problems? What are the areas, concerns, or experiences my background and beliefs may limit in terms of the culture of technology and equity? In the next paragraph, I talk about my definition of technology and I explain (in an autoethnographic way) where my knowledge came from and what else I may not be considering. The paragraph is an example of how autoethnography works.

When speaking of technology and technologies, I usually have a broader definition than others. During my PhD years, when I was completing a degree in educational communications and technology, I was introduced to a definition of technology that included both mechanical technologies (tangible things) and social technologies (processes and systems). This definition came from a class I took on women and technology with Phil Bereano at the University of Washington. Although I know in broad strokes where the ideas came from, I do not know the actual origin of the definition. In trying to track it down, I found similar definitions but none exactly the same as I recalled (see Wahab, Rose, & Osman, 2012, for a variety of definitions of technology). In terms of missing information, there is a lack of international perspective. My experiences have been with the U.S. public school system, and that is reflected in the examples and ideas discussed. It is within this framework of the U.S. educational system and my understandings of mechanical and social technologies that I discuss technology concerns in this chapter.

As a way of explaining how social and mechanical technologies can interact in school libraries, consider reading as an example. Reading is a social technology (teaching reading processes) and uses technological objects (books, computers, laptops, etc.). A book is an example of a mechanical technology, but the way we are taught to read a book (e.g., using phonics to sound out words) is an example of a social technology. A mechanical technology is a tangible, solid, and real object. A social technology is a process or way of doing or being that is culturally constructed. The outcomes of social technologies can be accomplished through different processes or systems. In this scenario, another social technology to teach reading would be through holistic rather than phonetic methods.

For this chapter, I focus on one aspect of social justice: the differences between equity and equality. In general, equality is about treating everyone in the same way. This works if everyone is starting from the same point, position, or educational background. Equity is about providing what is needed to have each individual or group reach similar levels or attainments. Equity may mean that multiple approaches and diverse resources are provided for individuals and groups who start in different places. Equity as a type of social justice within library and information science (e.g., the typology of Mehra, Rioux, & Albright, 2010) would suggest providing the needed resources, strategies, and approaches to help all students, for example, attain appropriate reading skills for their age or grade.

There are many technologies, both social and mechanical, related to school libraries and school librarians that I could address in this chapter. I am going to focus on three that I believe are particularly relevant in the present social and technological climate:

- accessibility of information resources,
- reading from print and online sources, and
- search processes in online environments.

I chose these three areas because of conversations I have had with colleagues and friends and my own reading, thinking, and experiences. I will address the reasons for these choices in each section. Each of these areas is combined with a different methodological perspective to examine how mechanical and social technologies interact in creating situations school librarians can evaluate to attain social justice outcomes. The methodologies are also approaches school librarians can use to find out what is happening in their schools regarding equity and technology.

ACCESSIBILITY

Access to information is a critical component of the training and background of all librarians. In schools, helping students learn to access information is a standard piece of the library curriculum. Information literacy is a social technology factor in knowing how to access information, but having and using a computer effectively is a mechanical technology element. Although access is incredibly important, this section is *not* about access. It is about accessibility as an aspect of social justice (Dadlani & Todd, 2016). Accessibility is a variation of access tied to social and cultural issues. It is not only about how to access information but also about which conditions are necessary for individuals and groups with unique physical, cultural, and behavioral characteristics to access information effectively. The focus is on equity rather than equality.

For many years my School of Information Sciences has been struggling with providing closed captioning of media materials (such as videos and PowerPoint presentations) for our online students. It wasn't that we didn't think it was important. It was simply that the extra time, money, and effort needed seemed excessive based on the needs of one or two students. There also are conflicts across universities regarding who should be providing these services (Farkas, 2016). Although support for students with disabilities is a government mandate (Jaeger, 2018), the financing of these mandates (Americans with Disabilities Act, 1990; Rehabilitation Act, 1973; Twenty-First Century Communications and Video Accessibility, 2010) is not supported to the needed levels for education. What opened my eyes was a conversation with a director of Disability Services who clearly indicated that the uses of closed captioning went far beyond students with hearing impairments. Closed captioning was helpful for second language learners, students with other types of learning disabilities, and in environments that were noisy or loud. In addition, other learners who didn't have recognized disabilities could also benefit from closed captioning (Morris et al., 2016). Visual learners might be provided with more information from words and speech than just from oral communication. In other words, it was more than one or two students who could benefit from closed captioning of videos in online instructional environments.

In school libraries, similar considerations will arise. Often school librarians are asked to provide the variety of materials needed to create accessibility for the range of students served in a school. For example, a student with hearing problem may need different hardware and software than a student with perfect hearing. However, students with good hearing may need visual as well as audio clues because of different learning styles or modes. Students with good hearing, able to process standard visual and reading clues, may need materials with closed captioning in English if they are early second language learners. Accessibility is about making sure that each student or group of students has appropriate mechanical tools and social processes to meet needed educational outcomes.

One of the ways to look at accessibility issues is through the lens of a series of theories put forward by Elfreda Chatman (1991, 1999) and Gary Burnett (Burnett, 2015; Burnett, Besant, & Chatman, 2001) and variously called small works, life in the round, and a theory of normative behavior. These are sociological approaches that have in common the position that all of us are part of many "small worlds" with specific information characteristics. These characteristics include ideas related to normative behavior such as social norms, worldview, social types, and information behavior. When small worlds come into contact, one or more of these concepts may be interpreted differently across the worlds.

In the earlier example regarding closed captioning, there are a number of small worlds that may affect choices made in schools. Accessibility experts such as those in disability services, special education, and second language learning see closed captioning of mediated visual instructional materials as essential to providing equity of access for a wide range of students. Administrators may see the cost/benefit ratio as unacceptable. In an administrator's view, special services provide interpreters for certain students, and these are acceptable costs. However, having videos with closed captioning made by teachers for students may be considered by some administrators to be worth neither the time nor the effort. Another group, such as teachers, may not believe it is their job to provide the closed captioning. Rather in terms of job priorities and job allotment, it is disability services, special education, or second language teachers who should be responsible if closed captioning is needed. Another approach is to relegate the task to the school librarian. It becomes the job of the school librarian to ensure all materials in a collection are accessible by all types of students who do not fall within the "average" label.

These are multiple small worlds, with multiple perspectives, roles, responsibilities, and priorities. Clashes such as these can easily mean no one accepts responsibility to support students who need closed captioning or for whom closed captioning could be useful. In some schools one group of students (e.g., hearing impaired) may be helped whereas others are not (e.g., second language learners). Everyone in the school may be trying to help, but their perspectives and priorities are not the same. Differing worldviews can result in a variety of accessibility approaches across the student population and a variety of equity concerns that arise from these approaches. Using the Chatman model of small worlds can help us identify not only the various small worlds that may be colliding but also specifically what the information behaviors or social norms are that result in conflicts of values and beliefs.

READING

I've been concerned with reading and school libraries for many years. The National Reading Panel's (2000) recommendations in the early part of this century that resulted in the No Child Left Behind Act (2001) and the resultant flurry of standardized testing have long been of interest to school librarians (Cleveland, 2007). The changes that have occurred with the more recent legislation (i.e., Every Student Succeeds Act, 2015) still leave considerable concern regarding how school libraries support student reading and student reading achievement. For this section, the technologies I'm going to look at are the mechanical technology of the book and the computer as "machines" that students read from. The social technology I will examine is something we don't often consider in regard to this dichotomy. My interest in this topic actually comes from my husband's dissertation (Yeaman, 1984) where he looked at reading from screen and reading from print materials. Line length was a critical variable in print materials, and he wanted to see how this played out in an online reading environment. It is his experience not only with his dissertation but also with his online reading that created my focus on line length. Often when he is reading from a computer screen, he will complain about his discomfort with long lines. He says it makes it more difficult to understand the text.

Often reading research is about whether students do "better" reading books or reading online materials (Picton, 2014). This section is about a factor that provides a substantive difference between reading print materials and reading online: line length. This may seem like an odd choice, but in fact it brings into play a number of mechanical and social technology considerations that we often do not think about regarding reading and effects of equity in reading.

Line length research for printed books typically suggests 45 to 75 characters, with 66 characters (including spaces) considered optimal for legibility, fluency, and comprehension. As we know, line length in the online environment can vary dramatically depending on size of screen, size and type of font, and how many windows are being used. This affects the ability of a reader to recognize, process, and internalize not only the words but also concepts. In other words, it affects readability, fluency, and comprehension. How does this impact equity in reading? Readers who are beginners, readers with certain types of reading disabilities, and second language readers may have a more difficult time processing both words and concepts with long lines. These students may already have reading problems, and certain types of online reading may exacerbate or minimally impede their developing reading skills. The current trend to provide more and more instructional materials through online, electronic, and digital resources without having print options may cause reading deficiencies not only for the students indicated here but for all students. A balanced approach to print and electronic reading resources may be particularly needed in educational settings. In addition, teaching students how to use the technology to customize an appropriate line length with a reasonable font size to match their needs may be an approach school librarians could use.

The methodological approach I am suggesting for examining reading in print and online in your school library is autoethnography. I suggest this method for two reasons. First, I find it to be a particularly useful technique when there is a need to establish relationships between culture and practice. It is both a good exploratory method and an excellent research inquiry method.

Second, it is an approach that could be used effectively by school librarians. Autoethnography can be used to collect information, write interpretations, and draw on librarians' background and experiences as filters for understanding social and cultural experiences in schools. As school librarians, we see and experience a wide range of educational processes and instructional strategies. We often are responsible for helping not only students but also teachers learn to use technological resources and materials. We definitely are the experts in both online and printed information resources, including reading processes associated with access, retrieval, evaluation, and use. Our insights are valuable in understanding how technology affects equity in reading in public schools. By helping others understand what we see and know, we can consider how to create equity across students. This could be achieved by providing multiple reading strategies and differentiated approaches for students with different learning styles, experiences, backgrounds, reading skills, and cultures related to their online reading habits and the mechanical technologies used.

ONLINE SEARCHING

Toward the end of last year, a colleague suggested I read a book called *Algorithms of Oppression* (Noble, 2018). At the time I thought it sounded interesting, but I couldn't fit reading it into my schedule. As I was thinking about what I wanted to put into this chapter, I kept thinking I needed something regarding big data, digital data, information policy, and student privacy, security, and safety online, but I couldn't figure out how to roll all of that into one easily explainable, interesting, and useful section. As often happens when I struggle to put ideas together, I end up reading something. Sometimes it is directly related to what I want to write about. Sometimes, as it was in this instance, it's just a book I've been meaning to read.

Algorithms of Oppression led me to a topic that has bothered me for years. One of the courses I teach is Research Methods in Library and Information Science. For many of my students (and students of my colleagues who also teach this class), the statistics component of research methods is incredibly challenging. Trying to understand the underlying concepts, applications, uses, and interpretations of the data analyses goes well beyond even those students who have taken basic statistics classes. What we often end up doing is hoping the authors of the research reports knew what they were doing and that their choices and interpretations are close enough to be useful. This is not exactly a phobia or an anxiety but perhaps a learning task that is just too difficult and takes too much time for the perceived benefits.

This same trusting thinking process can occur when people conduct an online search. We assume the algorithms used to retrieve and produce "relevant" results are somehow meaningful and developed appropriately (Sandvig, Hamilton, Karahalios, & Langbort, 2015). If you try to find out what specific analyses or algorithms are used in a search engine, either you may go down a rabbit hole of infinite links or you simply may not be able to find how the results you see are chosen. Rather than spending hours, days, or months trying to find out how Google, Yahoo, Bing, or even a government agency's website conducts your search, you spend your time plowing through the search results trying to find things that work for you. Students conduct their online searching in a similar way, but they may be even less discriminating in the results they believe to be reliable, authentic, or useful. If they believe the first items they see are the most "relevant," then those first sets of results become their view of that topic. As librarians, we need to help ourselves and our students find out whether the complex and somewhat mysterious algorithms used in online searching put forth results that represent people, cultures, and ideas in equitable ways.

As Noble (2018) discovered when she conducted a Google search on the phrase "Black girls" in 2010, the first site listed was a pornography site. Two years later when she found the same results, she wrote an article. Later that year when she searched again, the porn sites had been suppressed. This tweaking of search results, however, does not minimize the problems that arise regarding how the algorithms that created the results were initially conceived and how they were changed. As Noble (2018) so eloquently states,

There is a missing social and human context in some types of algorithmically driven decision making, and this matters for everyone engaging with these types of technologies in everyday life. It is of particular concern for marginalized groups, those who are problematically represented in erroneous, stereotypical, or even pornographic ways in search engines and who have also struggled for nonstereotypical or nonracist and nonsexist depictions in the media and in libraries. (p. 17)

The method I propose for this section is critical data studies: "Critical data studies examine the impacts of big data and algorithmic tools on culture, society, policy, law, and more. Their work investigates the who, what, where, why and how data is collected and used to inform decisions once made by humans" (Cornell CIS, 2019, n.p.). Critical data studies often use a critical theory perspective to "unpack some of the ways that data assemblages do work in the world with respect to dataveillance and the erosion of privacy, profiling and social sorting, anticipatory governance, and secondary uses and control creep" (Kitchin & Lauriault, 2014, n.p.). Critical data studies offer a perspective and viewpoint regarding looking beyond surface considerations and trying to figure out what is going on underneath the umbrella or behind the curtain. In other words, who and/or what is the Great and Wonderful Oz?

In the context of school libraries and equity, critical data studies might help us look more deeply at the algorithms (social technologies) that we use in retrieving information not only from online and internet sources but also from our public access catalogs. What are possible inherent biases in results obtained or in the underlying subject headings used for access? What effect does it have on students if the only faces they see in pictures of scientists are White men? Or nurses are White women? Or in a search I just completed of the terms "professional" (White man), "beauty" (White woman), and "student" (White man). Similarly, a search for "maids" resulted in predominantly images of Black women. These stereotypes are being proliferated through algorithms used to produce search results. As librarians, we can understand and help our students realize that search results can be and often are biased, stereotyped, and unreliable. We can teach them how to sort through results and look for authoritative, reliable, and responsible information. We can provide them with alternatives and examples that create equity for all students.

WHAT ACTIONS CAN SCHOOL LIBRARIANS TAKE IN MANAGING TECHNOLOGY AND EQUITY CONCERNS?

In this chapter I have looked at three technological issues with implications for equity in school libraries: accessibility, reading, and online searching. For each of these issues, I have narrowed the discussion to one area that addresses both a mechanical and a social interaction of technology. I looked at accessibility through considering closed captioning (a social technology) as applied to video productions (a mechanical technology). I examined reading in print and online as it is affected by line length. In this case, reading was the social technology and mechanical technologies were the book and the reading device (e.g., computer, laptop, smart phone). Finally, I reflected on the relationship between algorithms used in online searching and equity concerns related to the results. In this section, the mechanical technology was the computer but only in the broadest sense. This was mostly about the social technology of search and retrieval mechanisms.

In addition, I proposed methodologies that might help us understand the equity concerns for each of the technology areas: Chatman's small worlds framework, autoethnography, and critical data studies. Each of these methods, to some degree, has at its core a semblance of wanting social justice as an outcome of applying the method.

These methods can be applied without a social justice direction, but generally each one is more likely to be used to examine social issues and to recommend changes that have social justice implications.

The social justice component I focused on in this chapter is equity. Equity emphasizes the importance of not assuming everyone is starting at the same place. It considers the unique characteristics, abilities, and dispositions of each individual or group. It makes certain that resources, instructional strategies, and support systems are equitable across the board. In other words, equity gives students the mechanical tools and social processes needed so that each one can reach the goal or outcome.

At this point, if I were a school librarian, I would be asking the question: Okay, so these problems and issues exist, but what can I actually do?

Awareness

One of the simplest and most straightforward responses is that first you need to be able to see that there is something that might need to be done. Being aware is not as easy as it sounds. Perhaps the thinking might be, "Well, I read this article; therefore I am aware of a number of issues or problems that I didn't know about before, or that I didn't think about before. That meets the criteria of awareness." In fact, awareness has different facets and is about identifying not only problems or issues but also how you feel about things and why. It also concerns what others are doing regarding these issues and problems and why.

What might you do to sharpen your awareness of technology and equity issues? First of all, try to determine if these issues and questions are meaningful and important to you. Perhaps there are other areas of social justice or educational commitment that are more important. If so, you will want to figure out why. What do you want to accomplish, and where do you want to spend your time? There are also other chapters in this book that may help you clarify and refine your thinking regarding social justice and what you want to do.

Universal Design of Instruction

One of the most straightforward approaches for librarians and other educators is to become familiar with and to apply the principles of Universal Design of Instruction (UDI). Many of you may already have experience and familiarity with this approach, but, if you don't, then it would be worthwhile to become familiar with it. It is one way to address accessibility issues and create equity within the instruction you provide for students and also to help teachers address these issues.

Some of the principles of UDI include equitable use, flexibility in use, and simple and intuitive use (Connell et al., 1997). Another important consideration relates to the physical environment (Burgstahler, 2015). These principles are not just for students with disabilities. One of the most shocking examples I have heard of a physical environment problem impacted most first and second graders in a school. The computers with the library's online catalog were placed on a lovely cherrywood semicircular station that had been built for the library and stood in the middle of the room. Unfortunately, the station placed the computers so that they were too high for most of the lower elementary kids to reach. Plastic boxes were placed for the shorter kids to stand on. An accommodation had been made, but the plastic boxes were serious safety problems not only for the students using them but for other students as well. Either providing a lower station that would have been acceptable to taller students or providing two levels of computer stations would have been more acceptable and equitable choices.

Collecting Information for Making Changes and for Understanding the Difference Changes Make

Earlier I spoke about autoethnography as a tool, technique, and research methodology that I use on a regular basis. Interestingly, autoethnography is both a data collection process and a data analysis process. This makes it complicated to explain and use. The way one collects autoethnographic information as data is to write field notes, reflect on past experiences, and analyze current understandings. The way one writes up an autoethnographic account is to take notes, reflections, and other "data" from the environment (i.e., documents, processes, experiences, etc.) and create an analysis of what you have seen, heard, and experienced. You are looking at culture through your own eyes. What does it mean to you? This is one way to go about collecting and using information to create an analysis and suggestions for changes you might consider related to technology and equity.

Other information is already collected for you (e.g., testing scores, learning management system data, and online public access catalog data). You just need to figure out how you might use it and what the biases in how the data were collected or analyzed might affect your interpretations. What do you do with the information/data once you have it? If you are trying to decide on actions to take, then the data become a way of figuring out where inequity might exist and suggesting strategies for helping. If you have implemented a change or a new program, then you collect data to find out what the impact was. What really happened? Was it worth the time, effort, and cost?

Social justice requires active participation. Identifying a problem does nothing to move forward a social justice agenda. As a school librarian, you can help your school, district, and community address issues of concern to you and others. You can identify an area to improve by collecting information and drawing conclusions; then you can propose a course of action to take, and you can evaluate what impact that course of action had. A few examples of other explorations of social justice by school librarians are provided next.

In a special issue of *Qualitative and Quantitative Methods in Libraries* on social justice and social inclusion, Dadlani and Todd (2014) discovered that a "process of moving between different principles of egalitarianism and utilitarianism based on resource availability was used by teachers and school librarians" (p. 39) in seven exemplary high school libraries in New Jersey. They proposed a qualitative method that addressed sustainability.

Froggatt (2015) used a theory of and a model for the informationally underserved that shows "a social justice research methodology and findings that demands advocacy" (p. 54). She looked at diverse students in their teens who learned *without* school libraries.

Carnesi (2018), in a study looking at collaboration between a teacher and a school librarian and using a qualitative research method, concluded,

By taking a social justice perspective and providing and using materials that represent the lived experiences of underrepresented youths in an instructional context, school librarians and teachers can foster an educational environment that can begin to address the educational issues facing underrepresented youths and empower them to engage in their own education. (p. 113)

Another approach to examining equity and technology is through looking at the policy arena and policy agendas. Hoffman and Mardis (2009) speak more broadly about policy related to school libraries, but they also touch on equity and technology concerns.

REFERENCES

Burgstahler, S. (2015). Universal Design of Instruction (UDI): Definition, principles, guidelines and examples. Retrieved from https://www.washington.edu/doit/universal-design -instruction-udi-definition-principles-guidelines-and-examples

Burnett, G. (2015). Information worlds and interpretive practices: Toward an integration of domains. *Journal of Information Science Theory and Practice, 3*(3), 6–16. Retrieved from http://dx.doi.org/10.1633/JISTaP.2015.3.3.1

Burnett, G., Besant, M., & Chatman, E. A. (2001). Small worlds: Normative behavior in virtual communities and feminist bookselling. *Journal of the American Society for Information Science and Technology, 52*(7), 536–547.

Carnesi, S. (2018). A platform for voice and identity: School library standards in support of YA urban literature's transformative impacts on youth. *School Libraries Worldwide, 24*(1), 99–117.

Chatman, E. A. (1991). Life in a small world: Applicability of gratification theory to information-seeking behavior. *Journal of the American Society for Information Science, 42*, 438–449.

Chatman, E. A. (1999). A theory of life in the round. *Journal of the American Society for Information Science, 50*, 207–217.

Cleveland, L. (2007). Surviving the reading assessment paradox. *Teacher Librarian, 35*(2), 23–28. Retrieved from http://proxy.lib.wayne.edu/login?url=http://search.ebscohost.com/login.aspx?direct=true&db=lls&AN=502929371&site=ehost-live&scope=site

Connell, B. R., Jones, M., Mace, R., Mueller, J., Mullick, A., Ostroff, E., . . . Vanderheiden, G. (1997). The principles of universal design. Retrieved from www.ncsu.edu/ncsu/design/cud/about_ud/udprinciplestext.htm

Cornell CIS. (2019). Critical data studies. Retrieved from https://www.infosci.cornell.edu/research/critical-data-studies

Dadlani, P. T., & Todd, R. J. (2014). Information technology services and school libraries: A continuum of social justice. *Qualitative and Quantitative Methods in Libraries, 39–48.* Retrieved from https://scholar-google-com.proxy.lib.wayne.edu/scholar?hl=en&as_sdt=0%2C23&q=dadlani+social+justice&btnG=

Dadlani, P., & Todd, R. J. (2016). Social justice as strategy: Connecting school libraries, collaboration and IT. *Library Quarterly: Information, Communication and Policy, 86*(1), 43–75. doi:10.1086/684143

Farkas, M. (2016). Accessibility matters. *American Libraries, 47*(9/10), 54. Retrieved from http://proxy.lib.wayne.edu/login?url=http://search.ebscohost.com/login.aspx?direct=true&db=lls&AN=117705082&site=ehost-live&scope=site

Froggatt, D. L. (2015). The informationally underserved: Not always diverse, but always a social justice advocacy model. *School Libraries Worldwide, 21*(1), 54–72. Retrieved from https://doi-org.proxy.lib.wayne.edu/10.14265.21.1.004

Hoffman, E. S., & Mardis, M. A. (2009). A decade of promises: Discourses on twenty-first-century schools in library policy and research. *Library Trends, 58*(1), 109–120. Retrieved from https://muse-jhu-edu.proxy.lib.wayne.edu/article/361475/pdf

Jaeger, P. T. (2018). Designing for diversity and designing for disability: New opportunities for libraries to expand their support and advocacy for people with disabilities. *International*

Journal of Information, Diversity and Inclusion, 2(1/2), 52–56. Retrieved from https://publish.lib.umd.edu/IJIDI/article/viewFile/462/264

Jones, S. H., Adams, T. E., & Ellis, C. (2013). *Handbook of autoethnography.* Walnut Creek, CA: Left Coast Press.

Kitchin, R., & Lauriault, T. P. (2014). Towards critical data studies: Charting and unpacking data assemblages and their work. *The programmable city.* Working Paper No. 2. Retrieved from http://www.nuim.ie/progcity/

Mehra, B., Rioux, K. S., & Albright, K. S. (2010). Social justice in library and information science. In M. J. Bates, & M. N. Maack (Eds.), *Encyclopedia of library and information science* (3rd ed., pp. 4820–4836). Boca Raton, FL: CRC Press. doi:10.1081/E-ELIS3-120044526

Morris, K. K., Frechette, C., Dukes III, L., Stowell, N., Topping, N. E., & Brodosi, D. (2016). Closed captioning matters: Examining the value of closed captioning for all students. *Journal of Postsecondary Education and Disability, 29*(3), 231–238. Retrieved from https://files.eric.ed.gov/fulltext/EJ1123786.pdf

National Reading Panel. (2000). Teaching children to read: An evidence-based assessment of the scientific research literature on reading and its implications for reading instruction. Retrieved from https://www.nichd.nih.gov/sites/default/files/publications/pubs/nrp/Documents/report.pdf

Noble, S. U. (2018). *Algorithms of oppression.* New York, NY: NYU Press.

Picton, I. (2014). *The impact of e-books on the reading motivation and reading skills of children and young people.* London: National Literacy Trust. Retrieved from https://files.eric.ed.gov/fulltext/ED570688.pdf

Sandvig, C., Hamilton, K., Karahalios, K., & Langbort, C. (2015). *Can algorithms be unethical?* San Juan, Puerto Rico: International Communication Association. Retrieved from http://social.cs.uiuc.edu/papers/pdfs/ICA2015-Sandvig.pdf

Wahab, S. A., Rose, R. C., & Osman, S. I. W. (2012). Defining the concepts of technology and technology transfer: A literature analysis. *International Business Research, 5*(1), 61–71. Retrieved from http://dx.doi.org/10.5539/ibr.v5n1p61

Walster, D. (1998). The impact of technology: Change and innovation. In K. H. Latrobe (Ed.), *The emerging school library media center: Historical issues and perspectives* (pp. 239–257). Englewood, CO: Libraries Unlimited.

Yeaman, A. R. J. (1984). *Electronic books and legibility: A microcomputer simulation* (Unpublished doctoral dissertation, University of Washington). ProQuest Dissertations, 8419205.

A Social Justice Advocacy Model: The Informationally Underserved and Equitable Access to School Libraries

Deborah Lang Froggatt

ABSTRACT

Inequitable access to effective school library programs is a social justice issue. Disenfranchised students within a school, in a school district, or across a governmental region may experience their education without opportunities to grow into information literate, self-directed, lifelong learners. The theory of and model for the informationally underserved (IU) suggest that deficient school library programs and resources adversely impact academic achievement and independent learning dispositions that empower student inquisitiveness and critical thinking. These elements are components of an IU research study, conducted with a diverse set of American urban 15-year-old students who had learned without school libraries. The process and results of the research offer the global library and information science (LIS) community, including school library practitioners, LIS instructors, and their students, approaches for enlarging understandings of and advocating for equitable access to effective school library programs through a social justice lens.

A ROOM WITH NO VIEW

Imagine growing up in a comfortable and secure room. A caring adult provides for all of your needs. Maybe only a few books and a television surround you, but you still learn to read, write, and solve math problems and have ample time to play. You feel loved; your basic emotional needs are met. Meet Jack, the main character of Emma Donoghue's (2010) *Room*. Jack is innocent. He has no knowledge of the outside world. Slowly the reader realizes that Jack and his mother are being held in a place by a man who limits their world to a single room. When Jack leaves the room at last, he is overwhelmed. Making sense of his new environment brings extreme anxiety and uncertainty. However, this injustice is assuaged by family and professional counselors who help Jack cope with entering his new world. He begins to encounter new everyday situations with increasing fortitude.

Jack's experience of his room serves as a metaphor for the IU. IU students learn without school library access and are trapped in an educational environment in which they are constrained to the classroom. They possess little cognizance of from where their information resources come. Limited resources may curb their knowledge of the world and restrict their opportunities to access, synthesize, use, and share information. When the IUs leave their "room," they encounter a confusing, intense information world (IW) (Jaeger & Burnett, 2010). Information overload may impede their ability to navigate through the rigor of high school and the workplace. However, when students have access to effective school library programs, they acquire lifelong learning skills and the social capital (Bundy, 2008) to participate in our global community.

The theory of the IU (Froggatt, 2014, 2015) underpins a pragmatic, social justice research methodology that emphasizes the "ethical consideration" that "lead(s) to actions based on principles of equitable access to information, balance in library collections, and mediation between information seekers and content" (Budd, 2001, p. 314). When LIS professionals integrate social justice theory (Froggatt, 2014; Rioux, 2010) with advocacy efforts, powerful data are generated for understanding the impact of an effective school library program and for striving for equitable access within their teaching, studies, and practices. An effective school library program is one that provides students with a foundation comprised of Rioux's (2010) social justice assumptions. This includes participatory learning where a teacher librarian collaboratively plans inquiry-focused academic and extracurricular learning activities (Western Australia Department of Education, 2013). Students are provided opportunities to choose resources, determine their relevance, synthesize the information, and share new knowledge, all key information literacy skills (Todd & Kuhlthau, 2005). Rioux (2010) suggests that "social justice metatheory ... offers new, robust ways of articulating the long-held altruistic stances of LIS to new generations of professionals, while reminding current researchers and practitioners of the field's roots" (p. 14).

The findings of the school library impact studies (SLIS) (Baughman, 2000; Lance, 2000; Library Research Service, 2018) suggest a strong correlation between student access to effective school library programs and higher scores on standardized tests. The theory of the IU suggests the opposite: little or no access to effective school library programs prior to age 14 shows a relationship with poor standardized English language arts test performance administered during the year before high school. Descriptions of the IU research subjects' lifeworlds and their internal information seeking, information use, and information sharing practices (Jaeger & Burnett, 2010) suggest that, when learning with limited resources, students encounter a confusing, intense IW and their knowledge of this world is curbed due to restricted opportunities to access, synthesize, use, and share information. Information overload may impede their ability to navigate through the rigor of high school and the workplace.

THE RIGHT TO EQUITABLE ACCESS TO INFORMATION

A foundational principle of a democratic society (American Association of School Librarians [AASL], 2007; Jaeger & Burnett, 2010) is literacy, "the fuel for freedom ... a right," (Theodore Sizer, cited in Plaut, 2009, p. x).

Rioux (2010) offers an LIS social justice metatheoretical discourse, which incorporates the following five assumptions:

1. All human beings have an inherent worth and deserve information services that help address their information needs.
2. People perceive reality and information in different ways, often within cultural or life role contexts.
3. There are many different types of information and knowledge, and these are societal resources.
4. Theory and research are pursued with the ultimate goal of bringing positive change to service constituencies.
5. The provision of information services is an inherently powerful activity. Access, control, and mediation of information contain inherent power relationships. The act of distributing information is itself a political act. (p. 13)

The lack of access to effective school library programs denies the IU the liberty to enrich their lives as independent, information literate, and self-directed, lifelong learners. They deserve the right to a library's social capital building (Bundy, 2008), to glean the benefits of the richness of a library's body of knowledge. Effective school library programs provide students with a foundation comprised of Rioux's (2010) social justice assumptions. This is "where resource-based learning, constructivism . . . the development of thinking skills . . . and practice come together" (Farmer & Henri, 2008, p. viii). Effective school library pedagogical practices cultivate "self-reflection, self-correction, and self-regulation" (Gordon, 2009b, p. 63) to "craft connections between new information and existing knowledge" (Gordon, 2009a, p. 21).

Without these opportunities, whether diverse or homogenous, or whether urban, suburban, or exurban, there are two alternatives for the IU: accessing public library resources or learning within the confines of classroom resources. Public library access may be the only professional LIS service available to guide "everyday life information seeking" (Agosto & Hughes-Hassell, 2006, p. 1395). One of the eight students interviewed for the IU study, when asked about public library access, said, "I didn't use a library. The school didn't tell me about libraries. They would bring a cart of books but that wasn't enough" (Froggatt, 2014, p. 117)

Learning without an effective school library program is a social justice issue. Due to the ubiquity of devices and internet access, there is an assumption that students can access educational resources and that school libraries are irrelevant. The IU theory and model provide an advocacy argument for why this is not so. One needs knowledge about a given subject to locate and create new knowledge about it. If students are without the vocabulary to access digital content, "they do not know what they do not know" (McKenzie, 2008). Without a rich and culturally relevant library collection, they are denied access to a learning environment that gives advantages to their academically successful counterparts.

LITERATURE REVIEW

Jaeger and Burnett's (2010) theory of IWs situates the IU's IW in a metaphorical "sink of bubbles" (p. 38) consisting of their small worlds of everyday life comprised of normative forming groups including family, the school classroom, and other immediate cultures; their meso world of mediating, public sphere social institutions including their school district or public library; and their lifeworld, society's collective values, and norms produced and controlled by the media, government, and commercial enterprises. For example, students learning in schools without libraries are situated within an educational system that creates and controls this lack of access.

The day-to-day patterns and actions of information use within the IU's diverse, social-cultural context reflect Savolainen's phenomenological and pragmatic theory of everyday information practices (EIP) (2008). EIP theory offers an information behavior "how" component that can be applied across physical and virtual situational contexts. One's EIP include "specific information actions" (Savolainen, 2008, p. 65) situated in an "information orientation (or) . . . a set of attitudes and dispositions toward information seeking and use in certain problem situations" (Savolainen, 2008, p. 53). Thus, the IU's "information source horizon" (Savolainen, 2008, p. 91) perhaps includes family members, friends, teacher's aides, YouTube, online databases, the school computer lab, or public library situated within the small/meso/lifeworlds of their IW (Jaeger & Burnett, 2010).

Information seeking process (ISP) theory is a psycho-internal portrayal of an information seeker's thoughts, feelings, and actions (Kuhlthau, 2004). ISP research focuses on the informationally served, those with school library access, and describes the internal processes rather than contextual (Budd, 2001). Kuhlthau (2004) suggests that for those who successfully employ information literacy skills and locate appropriate resources, "knowledge states shift to more clearly focused thoughts, a parallel shift occurs in feelings of increased confidence" (Kuhlthau, 2004, p. 103). The uncertainty of locating and evaluating relevant information triggers anxiety and lack of confidence. Whether or not there is school library access, students move through ISP and the uncertainty it may cause. Observations of the IU 15-year-old cohort engaged in resource-based learning (Neuman, 2004) showed three levels of engagement (Gross, 2004): fully connected to the work, moderately connected with some interruptions, and disconnected from the learning; within each level, engagement ranged from strong to weak (Froggatt, 2014). Perhaps those who were disengaged never shifted to confidence (Kuhlthau, 2004). This approach to the cognitive demand of project-based learning, and the uncertainty therein, may reflect a lack of information literacy and resource-based learning opportunities, which influences confidence and the ability to locate and access critical, relevant information (Kuhlthau, 2004) to "resolve conflicting viewpoints, or synthesize facts to create new meaning" (Gordon, 2009a, p. 57).

Three foundational theories—IW, EIP, and ISP—support Shenton's (2007) paradox that one needs to have knowledge to search for more. A student's small world (Jaeger & Burnett, 2010) and the information horizon therein may not include access to an effective school library program for developing EIP (Savolainen, 2008) that allow for confident information search process skills (Kuhlthau, 2004). This information paradox may impact a student's curiosity and academic success due to a lack of information literacy skills and the overwhelming amount of information. Teachers (and librarians) who design research projects need to be mindful that some high school students have lacked school library access and information literacy learning prior to high school.

Buckland (1988) describes retrieving information as a cognitive system prompted by gaps in one's prior "personal knowledge." This knowledge is dominated by one's environmental context and by the "signals" a person depends upon when using library services (p. 175). "One's view of the world is an important structural determinant of one's view of what knowledge there is and where to find it" (Buckland, 1988, p. 49). Akin to Jack's room (Donoghue, 2010), the IU's classroom may offer limited educational resources. A library's body of knowledge offers young learners a tangible, visual display of information, but due to the nature of "intangibility" of information (Buckland, 1991, p. 352), the IU need and "deserve information services that help address their information needs" (Rioux, 2010, p. 13).

UNCOVERING THE IU AND THEIR DEMOGRAPHICS

The students participating in the IU research, who, prior to high school, had limited or no access to a school library, reflected the diverse population of public school students in an urban school district of over 54,000 students. At the time of the study, 58 out of 134, or 43%, of the public schools in the district lacked a library. Of the 33 professional librarians, a few worked in schools for 5- to 15-year-olds (pre-K-grade 8 schools). The racial breakdown for the district is 40.4% Latino, 35.5% Black, 8.6% Asian, 13.6% White, and 2.9% other races (Massachusetts Department of Elementary and Secondary Education, 2014). Latino and Black students are members of cultures that historically perform low on standardized tests and the population from which the subjects for this study performed similarly. Standardized test results for eighth-grade English language arts indicated that 40% of the school district's 14-year-olds or rising ninth graders scored "needed improvement" (27%) or "failed" (13%) (Boston Globe, 2011). Although 73% of all racial groups passed the state standardized English language arts test, the Latino and Black students scored substantially lower than White and Asian students: 70% of White and 69% of Asian students reached "proficiency" or "advanced," whereas only 41% of Black students and 40% of Latino students achieved that level (Massachusetts Department of Elementary and Secondary Education, 2014).

At the start of the school year, students in the researcher's school represented two familiar camps: readers and nonreaders. The readers navigated the library and appreciated the breadth and depth of the collection. This set seemed to have accessed libraries in their former schools. The nonreaders conveyed limited knowledge of library organization and tended to come from schools lacking libraries. However, when a subject of interest was discovered occasionally, the nonreaders became engaged with what the library offered. Similarly, some struggled with resource-based learning (Neuman, 2004), exhibiting frustration and weak information literacy dispositions (AASL, 2007). The prevalence of disinterest in digging deeply into their studies or evaluating retrieved information was palpable. Opportunities to understand the "intangibility" of information (Buckland, 1991, p. 352) and the process of knowledge making appeared to be lacking from their previous academic learning. An interviewee in the IU study, a strong student, shared that "for the debate project there were a lot of books on government and the president. I didn't know books like this existed" (Froggatt, 2014, p. 132).

DESIGN OF THE INFORMATIONALLY UNDERSERVED
RESEARCH STUDY

These concerns brought to mind the SLIS (Baughman, 2000; Lance, 2000; Library Research Services, 2018). Unfortunately, despite the SLIS evidence on the importance of school libraries to student learning, schools in the district were inequitably resourced, akin to America's overwhelmingly underfunded school libraries (Ballard, 2012, p. 86). Were the students who did not like to read and who appeared disinterested in library resources and struggled with research the same students who had learned without libraries? These concerns and observations crystallized into the following research questions:

- Is academic performance compromised if students are without an effective school library program?
- Do students without access to school libraries in elementary and middle school perform significantly less than proficient on standardized tests?
- How, if at all, do students without effective school library programs characterize their IWs (Jaeger & Burnett, 2010), EIP (Savolainen, 2008), ISPs (Kuhlthau, 2004), and academic performance?
- In what ways does the lack of library use prior to ninth grade impact a student's intellectual curiosity for new knowledge?

Concurrent, mixed methods research was used to collect and analyze quantitative and qualitative data to investigate equitable access to information (Rioux, 2010) in school libraries. The intention of the researcher was to bridge theory and practice (Benoit, 2002; Crowley, 2005) and to contribute to IU theory and an IU model.

Quantitative Analysis

The following quantitative analyses are applicable in a variety of intraschool and interschool contexts. IU nonparametric research hypothesis compares the nominal independent variables with an ordinal dependent variable (Leedy & Ormrod, 2005).

The null hypothesis is that the response variable, IU standardized test scores, stays the same as students with effective school library programs. In this case, μ is the population mean of students scoring proficient or better on standardized tests. The alternative hypothesis is that without effective school library programs, student academic performance will be weaker than that of their counterparts.

A Likert scale survey instrument was employed to compare ordinal independent variables or student characterizations with a scalable dependent variable (Norusis, 2008), a standardized test score. A convenience sample of 119 from the researcher's school provided data to examine a range of factors including school library availability from age 5 to 14, frequency of use, school library instruction, public library access, and cell phone utilization. These variables were tested against student standardized test results. Of these variables, three showed modest to weak negative correlations: access to a school library in the middle grades, amount of use of students with a middle school library, and public library use.

The research results are not statistically significant but indicate that one can reject the null hypothesis: little or no access to school libraries prior to high school standardized tests show a weak, negative relationship with student standardized test achievement.

Of the 86 eligible responses, Table 1 shows that 66 had a middle school library and 20 did not. Their respective standardized test scores, the "yes" and "no" responses, were assigned numerical values of 1 and 2, respectively. The responses were compared

Table 1

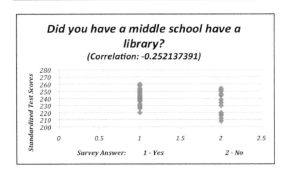

Table 2

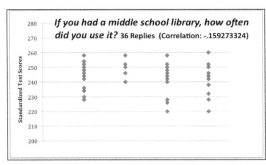

1 – 1 X Week (12) ** 2 - 1 X Month (5) ** 3 – 2 X Year (11) ** 4 - Never (10)

Table 3

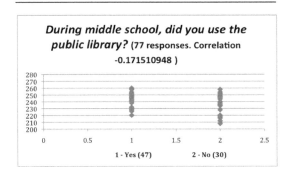

with the standardized test scores and plotted in chart form. The data points show a negative trend in the test scores associated with those without middle school library access. The Pearson correlation coefficient of −0.252137391 shows a negative modest to weak relationship between the two variables, suggesting that the standardized test scores of students without school library access in middle school tend to be lower than those of their counterparts with access.

The sample in Table 2 had middle school library access: 36 responses were given values of 1 through 4 for once a week, once a month, twice a year, and never, respectively. The data plots express a weak, negative Pearson's correlation coefficient of −0.159273324 (University of Strathclyde, n.d.) and suggest that the fewer times that students used their middle school libraries, the more poorly they scored on standardized tests. There are two high-scoring outliers in the twice a year and never categories that skew the significance of the negative correlation. Though there are not enough responses to omit outliers (Norusis, 2008), when omitted, the Pearson's correlation coefficient is −0.21977936, a modest to weak negative relationship.

Table 3 shows 77 responses regarding public library use in middle school: 47 students did use the public library; 30 did not. The "yes" and "no" responses were given the numerical values of 1 and 2, respectively. There is a downward trend in the data plots. Research on a larger sample may have indicated a more significant relationship between access to and use of public library resources and standardized test performance. The qualitative findings show that many IU rely on the public library for critical information resources.

Qualitative Analysis

The qualitative module investigated the phenomenon of the possible marginalization of those students educated without libraries. The 30-minute, semistructured interviews queried eight students whose schools lacked libraries. Coding themes included EIP (Savolainen, 2008); information use within the "small world" of the school classroom, and the "meso world" of access to school information literacy learning resources; and IWs, the situated, interrelated contexts that constantly interact and are impacted by social norms, social types, information value, information behavior, and boundaries (Jaeger & Burnett, 2010).

All but one of the respondents had entered high school without consistent school library access, "the underlying construct" (Leedy & Ormrod, 2004, p. 92). Like Donoghue's Jack (2010) in *Room*, the opportunity for the IU to acquire a cognizance of the world is limited by classroom walls, school resources, and lifeworld information boundaries (Jaeger & Burnett, 2010). The IU students in the study described learning in classrooms with mostly inadequate resources and little information literacy instruction. Classroom information availability was portrayed as "sets of books," "a few shelves," "books on a cart," the "same books," "there wasn't a lot of choice," and "there was a tiny section of literacy books." Classroom collections tended to include teacher preferences, not what the students needed.

The IU students had experienced little guided practice with and formative discussions about evaluating information and practicing purposeful information use. Their learning had included textbooks, guided reading books, and limited free reading books. Access to technology was intermittent. Little or no information literacy instruction was offered. Family members, public libraries, and bookstores serve as information go-tos.

The eight students interviewed shared an earnestness for finding and using information for personal interest and school success. However, IU information horizons (Savolainen, 2008) of the classroom and school had inhibited opportunities to explore new ideas and acquire and practice information literacy skills for information seeking and sharing. Their IU schools, intentionally or not, had created information barriers (Jaeger & Burnett, 2010) that inhibited knowledge about and access to information literacy skills for locating and using appropriate resources and information. Further research on the IU, especially those who lack positive community or family support, may further expose the injustice of learning without school libraries.

Figure 1

Model of the theory of the informationally underserved

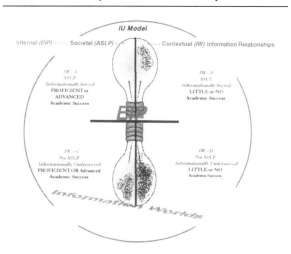

The IU model (Figure 1) expresses a dynamic problem that equates "social justice" with "intended consequences" (Creswell, 2003, p. 12). IU research in "praxis refers to action in the social and ethical sense" (Budd, 2001, p. 279).

Figure 1 is a visual account of the IU theory. The circle represents the IU contextual IWs: the small world of the classroom, the "meso" school worlds of school and the public library, and the lifeworld influences such as media, politics, and the economy. The two light bulbs represent student academic success and internal EIP situated within IW contexts. The bulbs' connected bases are the internal, invisible EIP core. This is where one's stock of knowledge (Savolainen, 2008, p. 26) activates a profile of information seeking, where use and sharing reside, and where the ISPs occur. The quantitative data are plotted across the IU four-quadrant model's light bulb symbol. The trending bottom right data points show the slight negative, but not significant, correlation between students without school libraries and low standardized test scores. This may be due to the nature of the IU research convenient sample. Testing a broader, randomized sample is warranted. The quadrants depict four small world classroom scenarios as follows:

1. *IW-A* or the informationally served: This set of students experienced effective school library programs (ESLP) access and academic success.
2. *IW-B* or the informationally served: They experienced ESLP access but had little or no academic success. The scope of this research does not include this cohort. They may have a range of other learning issues requiring different research.
3. *IW-C* or the IU: This set of students had little or no ESLP access yet had academic success. The qualitative findings suggest that family support and public library access contribute to this success.
4. *IW-D* or the IU: This set of students had little or no ESLP and poor academic success.

This triangulation of IW, EIP, and ISP theories with SLIS findings "explores and explains" (Creswell, 2003, p. 208) the IU dilemma. Compromised student academic success, due to learning without libraries, is confirmed. This emerging worldview fosters a reflection of practice in the situated context of the IU.

SOCIAL JUSTICE IMPLICATIONS FOR EDUCATING AND ADVOCATING

The lived experiences of the IU in this study offer these striking findings: the knowledge/learning conundrum for those in classrooms with limited resources, and the relationship between students' lack of school library access with poor standardized test performance. Rioux (2010) suggests that findings such as these must provoke the LIS community to integrate the social justice metatheories within daily library and archives practices. Why does this matter for LIS instructors and students? The IU are potential, future library users and advocates; thus, LIS instructors must incorporate issues of information access and advocacy practices (Rioux, 2010) in their research and teach about relevant, practical theoretical social justice models, igniting social justice information access understandings in local, national, or international LIS work places and professional organizations.

After the initial IU research and publications, this author now serves as the director of library services for the same school district where she strives to apply LIS social justice metatheories (Rioux, 2010) and transfer to a range of educational "ecosystems" (Ballard, 2012, p. 16). For example, the first and fifth social justice metatheory assumptions serve as beacons for discourse and collaborative work when serving on district- or school-based committees; uninformed colleagues must learn that all "deserve information services that help address their information needs" or that "the provision of information services is an inherently powerful activity. Access, control, and mediation of information contain inherent power relationships" (Rioux, 2010, p. 13).

Thus, self-reflection and sharing one's own personal history of information access (Rioux, 2010) are imperative for understanding the significant role libraries play in one's well-being. Conversations with stakeholders on the impact that information access and libraries had on their own learning may enlarge an understanding of how information access is an inherent right and brings social capital (Bundy, 2008). For instance, most educators attended schools with libraries, some say how their graduate studies were successful due to their university's reference library staff, and some are active public library users. Many are unaware of the SLIS findings and the social justice issues surrounding library access. Thus, when appropriate in discourse, committee work, or in presentations for district leadership, this author is armed with the IU theoretical findings and related data points described next. The stakeholders are increasingly aware of their inherent power relationship surrounding IU access, control, and mediation of information, which includes effective school library programs.

Similarly, school principals, parents, and teacher colleagues often are unaware of the significance of information literacy skills and dispositions (AASL, 2007) essential for the rigor of high school research assignments and college and career readiness. Some assume students can search and retrieve information from a range of resources and give little consideration to the cognitive demand integral to the information search process (Kuhlthau, 2004). Along with the district library resources, when presenting to school faculties, or academic support committees, this researcher includes the ISP model and showcases how librarians serve as academic deans for all students within a school.

When this discourse integrates the notion from Assumption 2, "people perceive reality and information in different ways," and Assumption 3, "there are many different types of information and knowledge," (Rioux, 2010, p. 13) with the knowledge paradox of the IU, a powerful consideration of the "societal resources . . . and cultural life role contexts" (Rioux, 2010, p. 13) fuels the goal of equalizing the information access in diverse and homogeneous communities alike. Sharing a relevant impact study research finding about school leadership serves as an opening for conversation. The findings from impact studies suggest that students garner academic success and show stronger academic performance in schools where administrators value school libraries (Lance, Rodney, & Schwarz, 2010). Partnering findings such as this with one's local IU findings strengthens political conversations about funding and access to effective school library programs.

Using IU research methodologies provides data for district- and school-wide discourse. For instance, in this researcher's district, a comparison of graduation rates with library circulation data showed that high schools in the district with the highest graduation rates also reflected the highest circulation. These same schools offer students effective school library programs; schools with little or no school library program tended to have lower graduation rates. This eye-opening comparison mirrors the results of the SLIS. The earlier examples of IU application endeavor to generate data "with the ultimate goal of bringing positive change to service constituencies," Metatheory Assumption 4 (Rioux, 2010, p. 13). Recently, this researcher used metrics from the *Massachusetts School Library Study: Equity and Access for Students in the Commonwealth* (Gordon, Cecchetti, Todd, & Li, 2018) to compare her district's student access to school library resources with others across the state. The salient disparities, when presented to the school district's Office of Opportunity Gaps committee, prompted serious discussions regarding equitable school library access for the IU. Studying similar social justice inequities within school contexts or governmental jurisdictions can harness data to jumpstart conversations about the impact of learning without a library.

The LIS social justice metatheories (Rioux, 2010) and the IU theory and model (Froggatt, 2014, 2015) highlight dynamic problems that equate "social justice" issues with "intended consequences" (Creswell, 2003, p. 12) with examples of how "social entities" such as effective school library programs "aid in the iterative unmasking of distortion, . . . further rational discourse, . . . have a positive role in this line of thinking, [and how] "the press, social movements, educative institutions and libraries" (Buschman, 2010, p. 162) contribute to a person's understanding of world. In this case, equitable access to effective school library programs develops literate, self-directed, lifelong learners who develop the social capital (Bundy, 2008) to make informed decisions and purposefully act upon them (Jaeger & Burnett, 2010).

Public school fiscal leaders and administrative decision makers must be made aware of the impact the "transformational-formational challenge of learning through the school library" (Todd & Kuhlthau, 2005, p. 86). School library professionals must continue to ask all of their stakeholders: Is social justice served when some students experience effective school library programs and many others do not? How do we ensure that, as teenage students complete their studies, they continue to have equitable access to LIS resources into adulthood? Where in our LIS practices do we see equitable information access compromised? How can we address these inequities? In regard to the IU, as the access divide grows larger, so must the conversation and advocacy efforts.

NOTE

The content of this chapter was drawn from two sources, the author's doctoral dissertation (Froggatt, 2014) and a previously published article (Froggatt, 2015).

REFERENCES

Agosto, D. E., & Hughes-Hassell, S. (2006). Toward a model of the everyday life information needs of urban teenagers, Part 1: Theoretical model. *Journal of the American Society for Information Science and Technology, 57*(10), 1394–1403.

American Association of School Librarians (AASL). (2007). *Standards for the 21st century learner.* Chicago, IL: American Library Association. Retrieved from https://www.alastore.ala.org/content/standards-21st-century-learner

Ballard, S. (2012). ALA presidential task force: Focus on school libraries. *School Library Monthly, 28*(6), 15–17.

Baughman, J. (2000). Symposium paper presented to the Graduate School of Library and Information Science. School Libraries and MCAS Scores. Retrieved from http://web.simmons.edu/~baughman/mcas-school-libraries/Baughman%20Paper.pdf

Benoit, G. (2002). Toward a critical theoretic perspective in information systems. *Library Quarterly, 72*(4), 441–471.

Boston Globe. (2011). MCAS results. Retrieved from http://www.boston.com/news/special/education/mcas/scores11/results/boston.htm

Buckland, M. K. (1988). *Library services in theory and context* (2nd ed.). Oxford: Pergamon Press.

Buckland, M. K. (1991). Information as thing. *Journal of the American Society for Information Science, 42*(5), 351–360.

Budd, J. M. (2001). *Knowledge and knowing in library and information science: A philosophical framework*. Lanham, MD: Scarecrow Press.

Bundy, A. (2008). *Joint use libraries in Western Australia, part two: The future*. A report for the State Library of WA and the WA Department of Education and Training. Retrieved from http://pls.liswa.wa.gov.au:3080/pls/noticebd.nsf/22ea2ccd139e6f3f48256bdf001ef4d9/ea23e7289c907dc3c825751d0008c57f/$FILE/JOINT%20USE%20LIBRARIES%20WA%20STAGE%202.pdf

Buschman, J. (2010). The social as fundamental and a source of the critical: Jürgen Habermas. In G. Leckie, L. Given, & J. Buschman (Eds.), *Critical theory for library and information science*. Santa Barbara, CA: Libraries Unlimited.

Creswell, J. (2003). *Research design: Qualitative, quantitative and mixed methods approaches* (2nd ed.). Thousand Oaks, CA: Sage Publications.

Crowley, B. (2005). *Spanning the theory-practice divide in library and information science*. Lanham, MD: Scarecrow Press.

Donoghue, E. (2010). *Room*. New York, NY: Little Brown.

Farmer, L. S. J., & Henri, J. (2008). *Information literacy assessment in K-12 settings*. Lanham, MD: Scarecrow Press.

Froggatt, D. L. (2014). *The theory of the informationally underserved: A pragmatic model for social justice* (Unpublished doctoral dissertation, Simmons College, USA). Available from ProQuest Dissertations & Theses Global (1564232316).

Froggatt, D. L. (2015). The informationally underserved: Not always diverse but always a social justice advocacy model. *School Libraries Worldwide, 21*(1), 54–72.

Gordon, C. (2009a). An emerging theory for evidence based information literacy instruction in school libraries, Part 1: Building a foundation. *Evidence Based Library and Information Practice, 4*(2), 56–77.

Gordon, C. (2009b). An emerging theory for evidence based information literacy instruction in school libraries, Part 2: Building a culture of inquiry. *Evidence Based Library and Information Practice, 4*(3), 19–45.

Gordon, C., Cecchetti, R., Todd, R., & Li, X. (2018). *Massachusetts school library study: Equity and access for students in the Commonwealth*. Retrieved from https://mblc.state.ma.us/programs-and-support/youth-services/school-libraries/ma-sls-2018.pdf

Gross, M. (2004). Children's information seeking at school. In M. K. Chelton & C. Cool (Eds.), *Youth information seeking behavior*. Lanham, MD: Scarecrow Press.

Jaeger, P., & Burnett, G. (2010). *Information worlds: Social context, technology, and information behavior in the age of the Internet*. New York, NY: Routledge.

Kuhlthau, C. (2004). *Seeking meaning: A process approach to library and information services*. Westport, CT: Libraries Unlimited.

Lance, K. C. (2000). *How school librarians help kids achieve: Standards—The second Colorado study*. San Jose, CA: Hi Willow Research & Publishing.

Lance, K., Rodney, J., & Schwarz, B. (2010). The impact of school libraries on academic achievement: A research study based on responses from administrators in Idaho. *School Library Monthly, 26*(9), 14–17.

Leedy, P., & Ormrod, J. (2004). *Practical research: Planning and design*. Upper Saddle River, NJ: Pearson Education.

Library Research Service (LRS). (2018). School library impact studies. Retrieved from https://
    www.lrs.org/data-tools/school-libraries/impact-studies/

Massachusetts Department of Elementary and Secondary Education (ESE). (2014). Boston:
    Enrollment data. Retrieved from http://profiles.doe.mass.edu/profiles/student.aspx?
    orgcode=00350000&orgtypecode=5&fycode=2014

McKenzie, J. (2008). Embracing complexity. *The Question Mark, 3*(4). Retrieved January 27,
    2013 from http://questioning.org/feb08/wp.html

Neuman, D. (2004). Learning and the digital library. In M. K. Chelton & C. Cool (Eds.), *Youth
    information seeking behavior*. Lanham, MD: Scarecrow Press.

Norusis, M. (2008). *SPSS statistics 17.0 statistical procedures companion*. Upper Saddle River,
    NJ: Prentice Hall.

Plaut, S. (Ed.). (2009). *The right to information literacy*. Newark, DE: International Reading
    Association.

Rioux, K. (2010). Metatheory in library and information science: A nascent social justice
    approach. *Journal of Education for Library & Information Science, 51*(1), 9–17.

Savolainen, R. (2008). *Everyday information practices*. Lanham, MD: Scarecrow Press.

Shenton, A. (2007). The paradoxical world of young people's information behavior. *School
    Libraries Worldwide, 13*(2), 1–17.

Todd, R. J., & Kuhlthau, C. C. (2005). Student learning through Ohio School libraries, Part 1:
    How effective libraries help students. *School Libraries Worldwide, 11*(1), 63–88.

Western Australia Department of Education. (2013). Research: The value of school libraries in
    learning. *School Library Support*. Retrieved January 27, 2013 from http://
    www.det.wa.edu.au/education/cmis/eval/library/value/val2.htm

Using Institutional Ethnography to Explore Socioeconomic Differences in Brazilian School-Based Librarianship

Lucy Santos Green and Melissa P. Johnston

ABSTRACT

Exploring the practices of school-based librarians in other countries, and how these practices are influenced or affected by socioeconomic structures, fosters new knowledge, contributing to global communities of practice. In this chapter, researchers describe an institutional ethnography (IE) study of school-based Brazilian librarianship in the southern region of Brazil. Themes identified are collaboration, literacy, instruction, technology integration, and the learning environment. Themes reflect common challenges faced by Brazilian school libraries such as institutional barriers to collaboration, division of instructional duties, access to materials, and staffing. Themes also speak to distinct ways in which Brazilian school libraries reflect the social and economic disparity between private schools and government-funded public schools, as well as Brazilian society at large.

INTRODUCTION

The need to equip today's youth with complex twenty-first-century information literacy and knowledge construction skills is galvanizing educators all over the world to question professional foundations and change traditional practices. Brazil, a rising global economic leader and the largest country in South America, is no exception:

Thanks to an incredible amount of institutional advancement, and a rare combination of factors, the nation burst on the global stage bolstered by its diversified exports, the success of ethanol and a recent conquest in the growth of investment, distinctions usually associated with economies classified as solid and trustworthy. (Guandalini, 2008, p. 2)

In spite of its explosive growth and economic stabilization, Brazil still struggles with high illiteracy rates and extreme poverty. School-based Brazilian librarianship reflects the social and economic disparity visible between middle- and upper-class private schools and government-funded public schools, as well as within Brazilian society at large. Although the field faces unique challenges related to culture, government structures, and the history of Brazilian education, many of the issues confronted by school-based Brazilian librarians are quite similar to challenges faced by school-based librarians in other countries.

In this chapter, we use the term *school-based librarians* to refer to Brazilian librarians who work in primary and secondary schools. We use this term in an attempt to accurately identify this library professional's role within Brazilian educational culture and context. The majority of Brazilian librarians who work in primary and secondary schools are not certified teachers, have not completed teacher education coursework, and do not self-identify primarily as educators.

In the summer of 2013, the authors of this chapter spent eight days in Florianópolis, Santa Catarina, Brazil, attending sessions at a school library forum, connecting with school library practitioners, accessing key government documents, and conducting multiple school site visits in order to answer the following research question: "What are the experiences, practices, and challenges of school-based Brazilian librarians in efforts to meet the needs of 21st century learners?"

BRAZILIAN GOVERNMENT INITIATIVES AND THE SCHOOL LIBRARY

In the fall of 2003, President Lula instituted a national policy that set parameters for the commercialization, distribution, and access to reading materials, particularly print books, the Política Nacional do Livro, Law no 10.753. This law describes the book as the main, irreplaceable vehicle for dissemination of culture, transmission of knowledge, fostering of social and scientific research, conservation of national identity, and social edification as well as improvement in quality of life. The goal of this policy was to promote and support a nation of readers. Several sections of the law directly affect Brazilian school libraries. Chapter 4, article 13, section 2, for example, claims the federal government is responsible, through appropriate agencies, for creating and expanding programs that stimulate the habit of reading in both public and private venues, introduce dedicated reading time in schools, and guarantee the existence of a basic collection of books for all school libraries (Presidência da República do Brasil, 2003).

In 2005, a national census identified 108,500 schools and over 13 million primary and secondary students with no access to a school library (Campello et al., 2011). A 2006 environmental study conducted by the Programa Nacional Biblioteca da Escola (National Library of the School Program) found that the majority of spaces identified as school libraries were nothing more than a reading room or a small corner with a stack of books. Schools that included the school library space in architectural planning were rare. The scan found that the majority of school library collections were not catalogued to standard (electronically or otherwise), and that it was common to find books still in original packaging or locked away. As a result, in 2008 the Federal Council of Librarianship (CFB) established the School Library Project: The Construction of an Information Network for Public Education (CFB, 2014). The project aimed to raise public awareness and government support for the establishment of school libraries in every Brazilian public and private school.

The most direct result of this effort was that in May of 2010, the Brazilian Congress passed Law 12.244, referred to as "Universalização das Bibliotecas" (Libraries in all Brazilian Educational Institutions). The law contains three articles. Article one states that all educational institutions, whether public or private, must have a library. Article two requires that this library contains a minimum of one title per student enrolled at the institution, and article three gives all institutions ten years (until 2020) to meet the requirements of this law (Presidência da República do Brasil, 2010). In order to help schools with the implementation of Law 12.244, the Institute of Studies on School Librarianship at the Federal University of Minas Gerais (in Portuguese, referred to as "GEBE") adapted *Information Power* (the American publication), creating standards appropriate to the present realities and political and educational climate of Brazilian education titled *The School Library as a Space for the Creation of Knowledge* (Campello et al., 2011). The GEBE Institute and the Federal Council of Librarianship continue to advocate for a strong and vibrant school library program, staffed by a professionally trained librarian, for every Brazilian public and private school. The resulting government mandates described in this section, although unfunded, respond to a growing awareness of the importance of school libraries among the Brazilian public at large.

REVIEW OF LITERATURE

School-Based Brazilian Librarians as Pedagogues

Brazilian education distinguishes between the pedagogue and the librarian, differentiating the expertise in each field (Martucci, 2000). "Pedagogues" is a term used in Brazilian librarianship research as well as professionally among Brazilian educators. The term is used in this chapter to preserve authenticity and accuracy in translation.

While the pedagogue's expertise comprises content area knowledge and pedagogical practices that help students master content, the librarian's expertise centers on the process of information transfer: production, distribution, curation, storage, cataloging, retrieval, and access (Campello, 2003). Even so, educational and library science researchers began advocating for the instructional role of the library professional, perceiving teaching to be firmly anchored in reference activities (Martucci, 2000). Mueller (1989) clearly positioned Brazilian librarians as educators when explaining that, like most pedagogues, librarians concern themselves with "guiding people in the acquisition of knowledge, preparing them so that they might, on their own, find the information they need at the moment it is needed" (p. 66). Despite this call for an expansion of the instructional role of the librarian, and continued discussions among school-based librarians regarding this role, Campello et al. (2007) claimed the instructional role was still weakly applied. An in-depth analysis of the work occurring in school libraries across the country found the instructional role to be "conducted in an inconsistent and simple manner, consequently contributing little to the process of learning, resulting in libraries isolated in the school environment and a weakening of the dialogue between the librarian and classroom teachers" (p. 228).

Valadares da Silva and Moraes (2014) observed a continued separation of school libraries from other school spaces in a case study on the experiences of the school library coordinator for a public school network in Vitória, Espírito Santo. These researchers noted that the most commonly held view (by the general public and by educators within the network) was that the school library was a "space of silence, for the storage and lending of books, disconnected from daily school activities, and ignorant of curricular and pedagogical practices" (p. 18). The researchers suggested the lack of awareness might be due to the relative newness of librarians (added to the network in 2005). However, the school library coordinator interviewed for this study admitted that there is still much work to be done in establishing the pedagogical function of the school-based librarian, citing the complete absence of any reference to the school library or librarian in curricular directives and curriculum materials provided by the Brazilian Ministry of Education.

The School Library's Role in Reading Promotion

The perception of a library as a source of reading material for research and learning is established early, as evidenced by the Parâmetros Curriculares Nacionais (National Curricular Parameters) documents that provide the curriculum framework for all Brazilian schools. The documents identify school libraries, in conjunction with classroom libraries and reading activities, as primary in the development of good readers (Campello et al., 2007). Given this situation of the library in the school, it is not surprising that the library as a cultural or an entertainment space does not figure in the mind of the Brazilian reader. Additionally, the concept of building a nation of readers against the backdrop of higher illiteracy rates has long been a key concern and tension within Brazilian education. Reading promotion holds a prominent place in the plans, policies, and mandates of government agencies and public organizations developed over the last ten years (Moreira & Duarte, 2014).

Many school-based librarians identify reading promotion and support as the field's most crucial role (Campello et al., 2007). However, Moreira and Duarte (2014) explained that Brazilian librarians have yet to differentiate between reading for learning (didactic reading) and reading for pleasure, a confusion they attribute to the absence of a reading curriculum developed specifically for the school library. Regardless of the lack of precise nomenclature, the importance of reading for learning, and the educators chiefly responsible for its development, is well established in Brazilian education. Classroom teachers, leaders in this movement, embedded reading instruction in the study of other content areas. Resources for this instruction oftentimes are pulled from classroom libraries (in large part donated by book publishers) that include textbooks, supporting tests, and, in upper grades, classic literature. Many school libraries were originally (or still are) maintained by classroom teachers so that pedagogical practices that support reading for learning are still viewed by many as the domain of classroom teachers and not school-based librarians (Moreira & Duarte, 2014).

Even so, a shift in public perception may be on the horizon, as highlighted in a recent article by a nationally syndicated news columnist. The columnist noted, with concern, a pattern of significant drop in library use between the grades of 5 and 9 (Weiszflog, Cavalcante de Queiroz, Windholz, & Failla, 2011). Some government officials interviewed for the column attributed this drop to teachers who do not have enough time to plan didactic reading activities to take place in the library. However, other stakeholders interviewed blamed the singular use of school libraries for research.

These stakeholders contend that if books are used for research purposes only, then the internet will likely replace them. Instead, Gois (2014) expressed, school administrators should avail themselves of school library professionals who can help promote lifelong reading for pleasure through other means, including but not limited to cultural activities. This shift is also reflected in the results of Brazilian academic research on librarianship with many researchers (Almeida Júnior, 2007; Carvalho & Souza, 2012) concluding that librarians should be recognized as information experts who encourage reading for pleasure to help learners develop intellectually as information users and information creators.

RESEARCH DESIGN AND RESEARCH QUESTION

Institutional ethnography (IE) is a method that enables researchers to connect issues across multiple (and unfamiliar) sites, uncovering how institutional factors shape practice in sometimes unrecognized ways. Therefore, it served as a strong approach for investigating the practices of librarians in a different country and context. In IE, an institution is defined as the coordination of people through broad organized practices, working across time and geographic spaces. IE researchers attempt to explain problematic situations by investigating how people's actions are coordinated and how people's experiences are organized within an institution by focusing on actual people, their work, and the conditions of their work (Given, 2008). IE work-setting research studies are often developed in response to a vague, persistent concern about a situation and the people it affects (Stooke, 2010). In the case of this study, this concern was voiced in the research question: "What are the experiences, practices, and challenges of school-based Brazilian librarians in efforts to meet the needs of 21st century learners?"

Data Collection and Analysis

In order to explore the experiences, practices, and challenges of school-based librarians in Brazil in their efforts to meet the needs of twenty-first-century learners, the researchers utilized the methods of participant observations and structured and semistructured interviews. Participant observation occurs when the researcher participates in the culture while still maintaining the status of an observer (Creswell, 2009). This approach allows the researcher access to the participant's culture while still maintaining objectivity. Utilizing an observation protocol adapted from Johnston (2013), researchers recorded observations and verbal exchanges concerning school library policies, procedures, and practices; the school library collection and facility; types of activities taking place in the library; technology usage; and the roles of teachers and the librarian. Approximately eight structured and semistructured interviews were conducted with school-based Brazilian librarians and classroom teachers at three separate school site visits, locations purposively selected for offering the most learning opportunities for intense study due to their accessibility. All verbal and textual data collected were transcribed and entered into a spreadsheet for translation and coding. The researchers utilized inductive qualitative content analysis to analyze interview transcripts, notes from presentations, and the observation questionnaires, culling emerging themes from the data (Glaser, 1965; Zhang & Wildemuth, 2009). In the following descriptions, pseudonyms are used to protect the identity of all participants.

Description of Sites and Participants

The first site, a private Catholic Montessori primary school, was located in an afflu-ent neighborhood and averages an enrollment of 500 students in grades prekindergarten through year 8. The library was located near the entrance of the school. A large, airy and inviting space, it was separated into visually distinct areas: a storytelling or theater corner, a workroom, a kitchen, a circulation center, a reading corner, low shelving for younger grades, and high shelving for older grades. In addition, the library housed an updated computer lab with 25 student computers, a projector, and a television. The librarian, Edvania, supervised seven other library employees: three library assistants for the morning shift, three library assistants for the afternoon shift, and one library as-sistant responsible for the computer lab. The school also employed a full-time book restoration specialist who maintained all school print materials. Edvania held a degree in library science but was not a certified teacher.

The second site, a public primary school, was located in downtown Florianópolis and housed 2,868 students in grades kindergarten through year 8. Classrooms were located on the first and second floors and opened to a large courtyard. The library was somewhat difficult to locate and took up space equivalent to two classrooms. This space was sunny and cramped, with book carts, magazines, toys, and textbooks vying for room on mismatched shelves. The librarian, Giselle, alternated between the morning and afternoon shift, supervising one other library employee. During Giselle's absence, the library remained open when there was a probationary teacher available to staff it. The reading specialist, Laura, worked a few doors to the right, and the technology lab, a room with 20 computers, was found a few doors to the left. Library employees had no access to the computer lab, and there was no technology present inside the library. Giselle held a library science degree but was not a certified teacher.

The third site, a public secondary school, was also located in downtown Florianópo-lis, housing 3,082 students in years 9 through 11. The library took up two floors of a large room inside a Portuguese colonial-style building—one of the remaining original buildings on the century-old campus. A metal spiral staircase connected the bottom floor to the top floor where the fiction collection was shelved. The first floor comprised a teacher lunchroom/breakroom, a bank of 8–10 nonfunctioning computers, a small cir-culation desk, several large tables, and high shelving for textbooks and didactic books. The library remained open during all three shifts. However, the librarian, Adriana, who was part-time, was only present for the afternoon shift. Probationary teachers manned the morning and evening shifts. Adriana was a former classroom teacher who obtained a library science degree.

IMPLICATIONS FOR PRACTICE AND LESSONS LEARNED

The five themes and lessons learned that are described next reflect common practices and challenges faced by Brazilian school library programs, such as institutional barriers to collaboration; the division of instructional duties between classroom teachers, read-ing specialists, technology teachers and librarians; access to reading materials or tech-nology; and the use of probationary teachers for school library staffing. All themes speak to distinct ways in which Brazilian school libraries reflect the social and eco-nomic disparity visible between middle- and upper-class private schools and government-funded public schools.

Theme 1: Collaboration

The theme of collaboration includes practices related to partnering with teachers to teach information literacy skills, supporting content acquisition, and working with other professionals in the building, such as the technology specialist. This theme, as voiced by one of the participants, emerged from descriptions of the struggle to develop collaborative partnerships with classroom teachers who do not consider the school-based librarian a pedagogue: "I have one of the strongest [fiction] collections in the area but the teachers have no interest in using them or working with me. They don't think I know how to teach." This perception is exacerbated by both the fact that school-based Brazilian librarians are not typically credentialed teachers and a recent Brazilian legislative move that will enable librarians to obtain licensure after a two-year associate's, or technical, degree. Edvania described the results of collaborative efforts at the private school as mixed:

Most of the time, the teachers send kids down in small groups to do research. If the kids are completing projects on a topic, they turn in the topic to me and I prepare a file of different resources on their reading level for them to use. I do try to partner with teachers occasionally, but not many of them are open to that. One of my biggest collaborators is the art teacher. We work together on all kinds of projects, and these projects tend to bring in more kids even after school.

Giselle and Adriana described the extent of their collaboration as the pulling of resources and materials for teachers or students. Adriana mentioned that previously, when the *rede* (network) could afford to support a reading specialist and librarian at the secondary school for all three shifts, true collaboration occurred between these two professionals and the music and art teachers:

When we had people here, we could recruit more volunteers and the library was always packed. We put together this incredible program for 6th grade that integrated music, art, literature and the library. They even created materials on the computer, but now, we don't have the manpower.

Giselle highlighted the impracticality of collaboration when librarians were inconsistently staffed for one or two of three school shifts: "If I start something, there is no one here to finish it. So what's the point?"

Lesson Learned: Despite the difference in scheduling between the private and public schools, it is interesting that of all the themes culled from the data, collaboration distinguished itself as the one area in which all librarians interviewed for this study experienced a significant struggle. This suggests that collaboration may not be as dependent on resources, space, or scheduling, as much as it is tied to how librarians are perceived by other educators in the building.

Theme 2: Literacy

The Literacy in Learning Exchange (LILE) defines literacy as an ability that moves beyond reading and writing: "It has always been a collection of cultural and communication practices shared among members of particular groups [so that] as society and technology change, so does literacy" (LILE, 2014). The three sites visited during this study presented starkly contrasting pictures. The ways definitions of literacy and

Brazilian government initiatives impacted reading and the materials available in library and classroom collections seemed to be different at each site.

Much of Edvania's work in reading instruction emphasized discovery and personal enjoyment (an approach in line with the Montessori philosophy of the school). Edvania pointed to a display in the storytelling corner. Several paper flowers with small quotes were hung from the ceiling on long strings. She explained this display was used formally and informally to encourage student reading:

Edvania: I wanted this project to introduce them to the different poetry books we have here in the library. Each flower hanging from the ceiling has a quote from a poem and the call number so they can look for the book if they become curious.

Researcher: Can the students look at these anytime they want to?

Edvania: Oh yes! Anytime. I've even added a few based on student suggestions.

Researcher: Is this part of a formal lesson you deliver in the library?

Edvania: Yes. I read several poems and introduced them to different books that we had. These flowers are a mystery for them to solve because if they like the quote, they have to hunt for the book and find the poem that the quote is from.

In the primary public school, Giselle clearly stated she did not deliver instruction, a detail further explored in the next theme. She led a scheduled storytelling time for younger grades (prekindergarten to year 4). However, the purpose of this activity was to introduce students to reading materials available in the collection. Adriana, the librarian at the secondary public school, did not identify or describe any instructional activities led by the library other than supporting teacher-led student research.

None of the librarians interviewed were given a budget for book purchases, but while Edvania had autonomy in selecting titles and turning in that list to administration for purchase, Giselle and Adriana made do with books that were donated or provided by the *rede*. Not once did Giselle or Adriana mention having control over the development of the collection itself. The age of the collections also varied greatly. Although the private school boasted newer books, title variety, and strong library binding, the public schools struggled with maintaining paperbacks, photocopied spiral-bound books, and out-of-date reference materials.

Lesson Learned: Inequality and disparity was particularly evident when comparing and contrasting the collections at all three sites. To follow through its support of reading initiatives and legal mandates, the federal government infrequently ships boxes of textbooks and didactic materials to public and private school libraries. Book publishers also donated class sets of classic Brazilian literature as well as other translated young adult titles. In the case of the primary private school, these materials made up a small portion of the overall collection. In fact, Edvania frequently sold duplicate and worn books at the end of the year as a quick fundraiser. However, in both public schools, the majority of books available for student use were these donated didactic texts and class sets. Unlike the financially secure private school library, the public school libraries were negatively impacted by the donated books. This finding suggests that well-intentioned donations by public or private entities (or even the lack of weeding books) can create a false impression of a well-stocked library, minimizing a school's ability to appropriately fund and curate its library collection.

Theme 3: Instruction

Data collected at the sites visited reflected a preference for flexible scheduling for research, fixed scheduling for checkout, and a unique Brazilian approach to division of labor. The typical duties associated with school-based librarianship in the United States, technology integration, reading enrichment, and collection development, for example, are divided among the classroom teacher, the reading specialist, the technology/computer teacher, and the school-based librarian. This division is fiercely protected in some of the schools we visited, where one interviewee was warned by her principal (before speaking with us) to "not complain or share negative information because this is democratic rationing."

As mentioned in the previous section, Giselle, the librarian at the public primary school, led storytelling times in the library. She gave out awards for the student who checked out the most books, the student who took the best care of his or her books, and the student who logged the most books read. However, any literacy or reading enrichment units or activities were the purview of the reading enrichment specialist. In fact, one of the reading activities the specialist recently completed was on *The Napping House* (Wood, 2000), a common elementary school library teaching activity in the United States. Giselle and the reading specialist had a strong working relationship and seemed to genuinely enjoy each other's company. They agreed that oftentimes their work overlapped and that they were happy to partner on reading projects if the opportunity presented itself.

Edvania had a bit more flexibility in defining her pedagogical role. She frequently taught research skills, small units on different genres, and as previously mentioned, collaborated with other teachers at the school. When asked about the division of labor observed, Edvania described it as a strength:

You know, a lot of libraries complain that they have no money or no way to host activities, but there are ways when you divide the work. You can recruit volunteers, establish partnerships ... I've established partnerships with a retirement home, with an artist organization, with the city, with anyone who wants to work with me. I may not be able to do it all, but there is someone who is better at it than me and can help me.

Lesson Learned: It is not difficult to understand why the division of labor is readily accepted. It is present in other facets of Brazilian society such as retail settings, where an individual sells the item, another logs the purchase, a third rings up the purchase, a fourth wraps up the purchase, and a fifth delivers the purchase to the customer. Edvania's ability to supersede this structure and her willingness to partner with others may be due to her working at a school that is much smaller, better funded, and structured around the Montessori philosophy that fosters community.

Theme 4: Technology

The private school had access to a state-of-the-art computer lab housed within the school library, wireless internet, and a computer lab instructor that operated under the supervision of the librarian. The school offered off-campus access to library databases and online resources curated by the librarian. Technology instruction was delegated to the computer lab instructor and did not consist of a formal technology curriculum.

Rather, technology skills were taught on an as-needed basis, tied to research or homework assignments, or personal projects students were interested in pursuing. Regarding technology for administrative purposes, the library catalogue was fully automated with a checkout desk that included a scanner and monitor.

In contrast, both public school librarians described their technology as outdated and unusable. The primary public school library had one computer available for the librarian. However, at the time of our visit, the computer was not working, and Giselle had been waiting for it to be fixed for quite some time. Other than this computer, there was no other technology visible or available. The technology lab, housed in a separate classroom, was inaccessible to Giselle, who did not have a key. At the secondary school, a bank of older computers, located at the back, was deemed unusable. There was no wireless internet available in either the primary or secondary campus. Administratively speaking, none of the public school libraries had online or offline catalogues. Adriana explained that the books were not catalogued, and that she was one of the few individuals who knew how to locate books in the collection. Neither library had a web presence nor did they provide online materials for students to access outside of school hours.

Lesson Learned: The fourth theme was the second thread that most clearly reflected the economic disparity witnessed between public and private schools. This disparity echoes the recent struggles in Houston, Texas, where Houston Independent School District schools in poorer areas are lacking in resources compared to same-district schools in affluent neighborhoods (Richart, 2018). It is due to the lack of access to technology that school libraries in lower socioeconomic areas are most hampered in their mission to help students develop the twenty-first-century skills needed for college and career readiness.

Theme 5: The Learning Environment

Data were collected on displays of instructional projects and school library programs developed and maintained by the librarians interviewed for this study. Neither of the public school libraries visited had space to accommodate a full class of students. At the secondary school, this was an especially challenging issue, because class sizes averaged 48–50 students. Many of the instructional projects displayed, as well as school library programs established, reflected a strong, nationalistic focus, an intentional threading of Brazilian culture and local folklore, rich integration with fine arts such as drama and puppetry, and inclusion of materials provided by the federal government. Students explored different elements of state culture, including figures from folklore, traditional musical instruments, and indigenous art and storytelling. Much of the effort put into displays and programs served to promote the library to students and parents. Edvania explained as follows:

I always tie displays to the overall theme of the school [changes monthly]. Some of the projects I display here in the library, but some I display in the courtyard and at the Entrance to the school. Every display is interactive. That way, the kids have to come into the library and research for more information.

She meticulously documented every display, every guest author and speaker, and every project, taking pictures and describing the efforts in detail. The documented projects were stored in large three ring binders in her office: "It's a way to justify what I do.

I have to document all of this on my own so that if anyone asks why the library is here, I can show them."

One unfortunate issue related to the learning environment theme was the placement of probationary teachers as library assistants. Probationary teachers are neither preservice teachers nor are they teachers placed on administrative leave because of disciplinary action. Rather, these are individuals who have obtained a medical release from the classroom. According to most of the educators we spoke with, probationary teachers can easily obtain this release from a general physician for reasons such as fragile nerves or ringing in the ears. For this reason, probationary teachers are generally held in a negative view. The law requires that these teachers be allowed to finish their contract with pay to be reassigned at the school administrator's discretion. Consequently, many end up as library assistants or as library clerks, with little if any training or desire to engage in library work, who staff the library during the librarian's absence.

At the public primary and secondary schools, probationary teachers were used to maintain the library when it was open during multiple shifts. The secondary school probationary teacher explained that she received no training and did not feel responsible for the collection in any way. She had a habit of writing down questions for Adriana to answer upon her return. On the other hand, Edvania implemented a formal training program with her probationary teachers:

I get a new crop almost every three months and I train them to help me. Some just want a chance to feel needed. Some don't want to work, but more often than not, they end up being a huge help to me.

Lesson Learned: The concern expressed by school library educators surrounding the presence of probationary teachers emphasized two points: (1) depending on the shift a student attended, he or she would not have access to the services of a library professional, so that there was no equity in library programming; and (2) staffing a library with probationary teachers sent the message that a library professional was not needed and not worth a school's financial investment. Paiva and Duarte described how this staffing approach leads to the de-professionalization of school librarianship and a gross misunderstanding of the school library space: "While there are spaces called libraries, they are occupied by teachers without librarian education with no school library program and there is no coordinated state action for training, the collection development, or library instruction" (2017, p. 130).

CONCLUSION

The goal of this research study was to examine the practices of school-based Brazilian librarians in order to learn about these practices, their experiences, and the challenges they face in efforts to meet the needs of twenty-first-century learners. While Mueller (1989) described Brazilian librarians as pedagogues responsible for fostering lifelong learning in their patrons, this study found the instructional role of the school-based librarian to be minimal at best. None of the librarians interviewed for this study described ongoing patterns of true collaboration as defined by Sonnenwald (2007). In the majority of sites visited, the researchers observed school library spaces that more closely resembled the isolated spaces described by Valadares da Silva and Moraes (2014), as well as the inconsistency in library-classroom collaborations identified by Campello et al. (2007).

Although many researchers (Moreira & Duarte, 2014; Valadares da Silva & Moraes, 2014) have cited suspicion of the librarian's pedagogical expertise as a common reason for this instructional isolation and inconsistency, this study found two additional reasons for the librarian's separation from instruction. First, economic and budgetary concerns at two public schools cut down on the number of employees available to staff the library during different school shifts. In one instance, cutting back on staff resulted in the dissolution of a sixth-grade interdisciplinary unit. Second, librarians observed for this study were isolated from instruction by a cultural emphasis on division of labor and the delineation of instructional duties (Moreira & Duarte, 2014), a division that kept school librarians from accessing computer labs and delivering reading or literacy activities.

Even so, it is important to note that the data collected in this study revealed only the content that participants chose to share at the time of fieldwork. The results of this present study are not intended to represent the entire field of Brazilian school librarianship; the data collected represent only the locations visited. Although IE research will not bring solutions, it offers a map of the challenges school-based librarians face, helping them to refocus their efforts. This knowledge helps school-based librarians develop a clearer view of how to work within the institution to achieve the goals of school-based librarianship: "producing successful learners skilled in multiple literacies" (American Association of School Librarians, 2009, p. 5) and responsible members of society. Ingrid Parent, president of IFLA recently stated, "We must think globally, act nationally, and deliver locally." This worldwide perspective allows us to investigate institutional factors that shape our profession, providing opportunities to learn from, share expertise with, and support one another, thus strengthening the practice of school librarianship throughout the world.

EPILOGUE

Although all themes speak to distinct ways in which Brazilian school libraries reflect the social and economic disparity visible between middle- and upper-class private schools and government-funded public schools, these themes also demonstrate the unique approaches Brazilian educators have undertaken in order to overcome challenges that are quite similar to those experienced by school libraries around the world. In the first stage of this IE research, we began to identify the institutional processes such as legislation, governing boards, professional organizations, education, and administration that were apparent in the work of the librarians. In Phase 2 of this project, the researchers returned to the northwestern region of Brazil to continue the task of understanding how institutional factors shape practice in sometimes unrecognized ways. The common practices identified as part of the institution of school librarianship indicate that as a profession, school-based librarians around the world struggle with similar challenges, although the ways these challenges are addressed differ significantly, emphasizing the need for an international exchange of practices and international communities of practice.

NOTE

This chapter was previously published as: Green, L. S., & Johnston, M. P. (2015). Global perspectives: Exploring school-based Brazilian librarianship through institutional ethnography. *School Libraries Worldwide, 21*(1), 1–18.

REFERENCES

Almeida Júnior, O. F. (2007). Leitura, mediação e apropriação da informação. In J. P. Santos (Ed.), *A leitura comoprática pedagógica na formação do professional da informação.* Rio de Janeiro, Brazil: Fundação Biblioteca Nacional.

American Association of School Librarians. (2009). *Empowering learners: Guidelines for school library media programs.* Chicago, IL: ALA.

Campello, B. (2003). O movimento da competência informacional: Uma perspectiva para o letramento informacional. *Ciência da Informação, 32*(3), 28–37.

Campello, B., Abreu, V., Caldeira, P., Barbosa, R. R., Carvalho, M., Sirihal Duarte, A., … Alvarenga, M. (2011). Parâmetros para bibliotecas escolares Brasileiras: Fundamentos de sua elaboração. *Informação e Sociedade: Estudos, 21*(2), 105–120.

Campello, B., Vianna, M., Caldeira, P., Abreu, V., Carvalho, M., & Benigno, A. (2007). Literatura sobre biblioteca escolar: Características de citações de teses e dissertações brasileiras. *TransInformação, 19*(3), 227–236.

Carvalho, M., & Souza, N. (2012). Letramento literário e mediação na escola: Algumas considerações. In M. Moura (Ed.), *Educação científica e cidadania: Abordagens teóricas e metodológicas para a formação de pesquisadores juvenis.* Belo Horizonte, Brazil: UFMG/PROEX.

CFB. (2014, August 24). *Conselho federal de biblioteconomia: Histórico.* Retrieved from http://www.cfb.org.br/historico/historico_03.htm

Creswell, J. W. (2009). *Research design: Qualitative, quantitative, and mixed methods approaches.* Thousand Oaks, CA: Sage Publications.

Given, L. M. (Ed.). (2008). *The Sage encyclopedia of qualitative research methods.* Thousand Oaks, CA: Sage Publications.

Glaser, B. G. (1965). The constant comparative method of qualitative analysis. *Social Problems, 12*(4), 436–445.

Gois, A. (2014, July 14). Sem incentivo à leitura. *Jornal O Globo.* Retrieved from http://oglobo.globo.com/rio/ancelmo/posts/2014/07/14/sem-incentivo-leitura-542650.asp

Guandalini, G. (2008, May 28). Com que asas o país vai voar? *Veja, 2062*(21), 48–54.

Johnston, M. P. (2013). Investigating an international exchange of best practices between German and American school-based librarians. *School Libraries Worldwide, 19*(1), 59–71.

Literacy in Learning Exchange (LILE). (2014, September 19). Reflections about the meaning of literacy. Retrieved from http://www.literacyinlearningexchange.org/defining-literacy

Martucci, E. M. (2000). Revisitando o trabalho de referência: Uma contribuição teórica para a abordagem interpretativa de pesquisa. *Perspectivas em Ciência da Informação, 5*(1), 99–115.

Moreira, J., & Duarte, A. (2014). Práticas educativas bibliotecárias de formação do leitor. *Biblioteca Escolar em Revista, 2*(2), 27–44.

Mueller, S. (1989). Perfil do bibliotecário, serviços e responsabilidades na área de informação e formação profissional. *Revista de Biblioteconomia de Brasília, 17*(1), 63–70.

Paiva, M., & Duarte, A. (2017). School library contribution to student achievement as measured by the Brazil Reading Test. *School Libraries Worldwide, 23*(1), 120–150.

Presidência da República do Brasil, Casa Civil. (2003). *Política nacional do livro* (Lei No. 10.753). Retrieved from http://www.planalto.gov.br/ccivil_03/

Presidência da República do Brasil, Casa Civil. (2010). *Universalização das bibliotecas* (Lei No. 12.244). Retrieved from http://www.planalto.gov.br/ccivil_03/

Richart, M. F. (2018, April 12). Uneven budget cuts further inequity in HISD. *The Houston Chronicle.* Retrieved from https://www.houstonchronicle.com/opinion/outlook/article/HISD-s-small-schools-don-t-need-a-bigger-12831531.php

Sonnenwald, D. (2007). Scientific collaboration: A synthesis of challenges and strategies. In B. Cronin (Ed.), *Annual review of information science and technology,* Vol. 41. Medford, NJ: Information Today, Inc.

Stooke, R. (2010). Institutional ethnography. In K. E. Fisher (Ed.), *Theories of information behavior.* Milford, NJ: Information Today, Inc.

Valadares da Silva, E., & Moraes, F. (2014). Biblioteca escolar como espaço de reinvenções curriculares. *Biblioteca Escolar em Revista, 2*(2), 17–26.

Weiszflog, A., Cavalcante de Queiroz, K., Windholz, S., & Failla, Z. (2011). Organização social civil de interesse público. *Retratos da Leitura no Brasil.* Retrieved from http://www.prolivro.org.br

Wood, A. (2000). *The napping house.* New York, NY: Houghton Mifflin.

Zhang, Y., & Wildemuth, B. M. (2009). Qualitative analysis of content. In B. M. Wildemuth (Ed.), *Applications of social science research to methods to question in library and information science.* Westport, CT: Libraries Unlimited.

II

Cultural Competency

Section Overview

Cultural Competence for a Culturally Responsive Pedagogy

Dianne Oberg

INTRODUCTION

Changing our practice as educators often requires changes in the way we think about the world, that is, changes in our often-unexamined assumptions about what is reality. The work of considering new-to-us theoretical frameworks and discourses is difficult and often uncomfortable. Theoretical frameworks are the interrelated theories and concepts that guide research or practice. We may not think about our professional practice in terms of theoretical frameworks, but all of us have underlying beliefs about the world and how it works or should work. And, these beliefs are evident in the language we use—our discourse.

I bring to this chapter my experiences in Alberta, a province in Western Canada, as a classroom teacher and teacher librarian and as an educator of teachers and teacher librarians. I also bring my experiences as a researcher working in Canada and in the United States and as an active member of two international associations, the International Association of School Librarianship (IASL) and the International Federation of Library Associations and Institutions (IFLA).

In 2017, I participated in the fifth conference of Treasure Mountain Canada, sponsored by the Canadian School Libraries organization. The theme of the conference focused on the theoretical framework of "a culturally responsive pedagogy" that, in the literature of library and information science (LIS), is considered more commonly within the theoretical framework of "cultural competence."

I first explored much of the content of this chapter in developing a conference paper, entitled "Theoretical Frameworks for Thinking about the Work Ahead." The "work ahead" for educators at this conference was expressed in one of the 94 Calls to Action in the Final Report of Canada's Truth and Reconciliation Commission, a six-year examination of the Indian Residential School System (*Truth and Reconciliation Commission of Canada*, 2015). Call to Action 63 specifically calls on school systems to "build student capacity for intercultural understanding, empathy and mutual respect."

MULTICULTURALISM AND DIVERSITY VERSUS CULTURAL COMPETENCE: THE CANADIAN CONTEXT

As educators in Canada, for more than three decades, one of our goals has been to create inclusive schooling systems within a pluralistic society (Zine, 2010). In Canada, these efforts have been framed by concepts such as "multiculturalism" and "diversity" and by images such as the cultural mosaic, rather than the melting pot. However, much of Canadian schooling still continues to be Eurocentric, which leaves many students feeling marginalized for a variety of reasons, for example,

- The dominant narration of history that does not include you or your community erases your identity.
- Not seeing yourself or your cultural realities represented in schools . . . reduces the wealth of your knowledge and experience.
- Being asked to "perform" your culture for others . . . puts you in the position of being the "native informant" in a tourist spectacle . . . [you are] the "Other."
- Not seeing anyone in the school administration who looks like you is a constant reminder of the glass ceilings that limit your chances. (Zine, 2010, p. 37)

Zine and her colleagues (Dei, James, James-Wilson, Karumanchery, & Zine, 2001) have proposed a multicentric model of education that actively works to de-center the Eurocentric knowledge that is dominant in Canadian education and to incorporate other worldviews throughout all aspects of teaching and learning. The model has four primary learning objectives: integrating multiple centers of knowledge; affecting social and educational change; recognizing and respecting difference; and teaching youth and community empowerment.

Currently, in Canada, our efforts as a society to develop cultural competence are being focused on learning about our history in relation to Canada's Indigenous peoples (First Nations, Metis, and Inuit peoples, formerly referred to as "Indians and Eskimos") and unlearning our attitudes of nonrespect toward them. All Canadians—Indigenous and non-Indigenous—need to be involved in the process of truth and reconciliation, learning the history of how our country was settled and acknowledging the ways in which those who settled in Canada treated the peoples who originally inhabited Canada. The history is a complicated one, and what we learned in school about the settlement of Canada did not always tell the whole story or even more than one side of the story. It takes extra effort to find the hidden and untold stories.

One part of Canada's story that was hidden for most of Canada's history was the implementation of the Indian Residential School system, a system that was designed to assimilate Indigenous children into the language and culture of a Western European Christian society. Residential schooling for Indigenous children was mandatory in Canada, as it was in other colonial societies such as Australia. In the United States, Indian Boarding Schools, established by the federal Bureau of Indian Affairs, began in the late 1870s, and a few of these schools still remained in the early years of the twenty-first century.

Residential schools in Canada, funded by the federal Department of Indian Affairs and administered by Christian churches, were in existence for well over 100 years

(1876–1996). Many successive generations of children endured the experience of them. That history became known over time, as survivors of the residential school system were able to bring their experiences to light in several thousand court cases that ultimately led to the largest class-action lawsuit in Canada's history. The 2006 Indian Residential Schools Settlement Agreement paid compensation of over $3 billion to approximately 80,000 residential school survivors. The then federal Justice Minister Irwin Cotler applauded the compensation decision, noting that the placement of children in the residential school system was "the single most harmful, disgraceful and racist act in our [Canadian] history." In 2008, Prime Minister Stephen Harper issued a formal apology on behalf of the Government of Canada, in front of an audience of Indigenous delegates, in an address that was broadcast nationally. He apologized for the governments' past policies of assimilation, for the known excesses of the residential school system, and for the creation of the system itself. Formal apologies and negotiations for compensation to the survivors of the Indian Day Schools and of the forced resettlement of Inuit peoples in northern Canada are ongoing.

One result of the Indian Residential Schools Settlement Agreement was the creation of the Truth and Reconciliation Commission, which traveled Canada for six years, gathering testimony from more than 6,000 survivors of the residential school system. Reconciliation is essential to help all Canadians to move forward to a better future together. "Reconciliation is not an Aboriginal problem; it is a Canadian one" (*Truth and Reconciliation Commission of Canada*, 2015, p. vi).

Reconciliation requires action in the form of restorative justice. In the 2015 final report of the Truth and Reconciliation Commission, there are 94 Calls to Action. These Calls to Action provide guidance to all sectors of Canadian society in addressing the wrongs done to Indigenous people in the past (and present). The lessons learned through the findings of the Truth and Reconciliation Commission have implications for an inclusive and equitable educational system that works toward improving the life and education of all members of our diverse society.

CALL TO ACTION 63 AND A CULTURALLY RESPONSIVE PEDAGOGY

Canada's Truth and Reconciliation Commission's Call to Action 63 specifically calls on school systems to "build student capacity for intercultural understanding, empathy and mutual respect." Developing a culturally relevant pedagogy is one way that schools can improve the educational experiences of students of all races and cultures.

For school library professionals, culturally responsive pedagogy supports our efforts in achieving the two foundational purposes of our work: "working in service of the *moral purpose* of school libraries (i.e., making a difference in the lives of young people) and of the *educational purpose* of school libraries (i.e., improving teaching and learning for all)" (International Federation of Library Associations and Institutions, p. 13). Increasingly, professionals in education and in librarianship have made the case for a culturally responsive teaching/pedagogy (see, e.g., Hudiburg, Mascher, Sagehorn, & Stidham, 2015; Ladson-Billings, 1994, 1995).

Lynch (2012) defines a culturally responsive pedagogy as "a student-centered approach to teaching in which the students' unique cultural strengths are identified and nurtured to promote student achievement and a sense of well-being about the student's cultural place in the world" (para. 2). Lynch identifies three dimensions of culturally responsive pedagogy: the personal dimension, the institutional dimension, and the instructional dimension.

The personal dimension addresses the process by which individuals learn to become culturally responsive, using the theoretical framework of cultural competence. The cultural competence framework is not unique to LIS: other professions in health, education, and psychology have developed and implemented cultural competence frameworks. The institutional dimension addresses the cultural factors affecting the organization of schools, school policies and procedures, through the lens of community engagement. The instructional dimension includes consideration of the strengths that inquiry-based learning contributes to a culturally responsive pedagogy.

The Personal Dimension

Canadians generally are supportive of policies and practices that support diversity and multiculturalism (and in fact we can be quite smug about our nation's reputation for integration of newcomers into Canadian society). Our reputation related to the treatment of Indigenous people, however, has earned us international criticism (Amnesty International, 2013).

In Canada, in much of our practice as educators, we avoid acknowledgment of race and culture—including our own race and culture—and sometimes we use terms such as "diversity" and "multiculturalism" without thinking deeply about our assumptions about the world that are encompassed within those terms. The LIS profession in Canada (as in the United States) is predominately White, female, middle class, and well educated, but rarely do we engage in discussions, for example, about Whiteness and White privilege or about gender politics and power. Without recognizing and understanding our own culture, it is impossible to recognize and understand in any meaningful way the culture of others. Both are essential parts of cultural competence.

Patricia Montiel-Overall, well known to teacher librarians through her work on teacher and librarian collaboration (2005), has proposed a cultural competence framework for LIS professionals. She describes cultural competence as,

The ability to recognize the significance of culture in one's own life and in the lives of others; and to come to know and respect diverse cultural backgrounds and characteristics through interaction with individuals from diverse linguistic, cultural, and socioeconomic groups; and to fully integrate the culture of diverse groups into services, work, and institutions in order to enhance the lives of both those being served by the library profession and those engaged in service. (2009, p. 190)

There are two perspectives on how humans come to know. The traditional perspective, from general psychology, holds that mind and culture are separate and that knowledge is acquired through practice, training, developing skills, and forming habits of mind. The other perspective, from cultural psychology, holds that mind and culture are inseparable and that knowledge is acquired through social interaction; that is, cultural values and norms are inseparable from the way humans think. This latter perspective underlies the cultural competence framework proposed by Montiel-Overall.

Developing cultural competence is a learning process, often not an easy process, involving self-reflective and thoughtful examination of one's own mental representations of the world and of others' mental representations of the world. Developing cultural competence occurs in three domains: cognitive, interpersonal, and environmental. Within each domain, key components contribute to increased cultural competence (Montiel-Overall, 2009, pp. 189–192).

Cognitive domain—This domain refers to the way individuals' actions demonstrate how they make meaning, think, reflect, and feel about the world around them. Two key components in the process of developing cultural competence in this domain are cultural self-awareness and cultural knowledge. Self-reflection is one way in which we can examine cultural and ethnic differences and consider the effect of these differences between ourselves as professionals and the members of the community we serve.

Interpersonal domain—This domain refers to the ways in which individuals behave toward one another and communicate within social contexts. Three key components in the process of developing cultural competence in this domain are cultural appreciation, an ethic of caring, and personal and cultural interaction. Cultural appreciation includes developing a positive emotional connection to the values, events, actions, and objects that make up people's lives. An ethic of caring involves the desire to develop cultural appreciation and personal relationships with others who differ from us (not because "I have to"). Interaction with members of minority and underserved communities provides opportunities to develop appropriate communication skills and to find the knowledge-holders within communities.

Environmental domain—This domain refers to the surroundings, conditions, and settings in which people live. Developing knowledge of environmental factors is essential to mitigating barriers to library use as well as to developing library environments that are more welcoming to people from diverse communities.

Montiel-Overall, Nunez, and Reyes-Escudero (2016, p. 24) proposed a continuum of cultural competence, from cultural incapacity to cultural proficiency:

- Cultural incapacity—the state of individuals who cannot grasp why anyone needs to understand anyone else's culture.
- Cultural blindness—the state of individuals who claim to see no differences between diverse groups and often feel it is inappropriate to discuss differences.
- Cultural awareness—the state of individuals who are able to candidly recognize cultural differences and have some knowledge of such differences.
- Cultural competence—the state of individuals able to adapt their practice to the needs of people around them.
- Cultural proficiency—the capacity to understand social justice issues and to work to eliminate inequities faced by cultural groups.

The Institutional Dimension

Earlier in this chapter, I shared some of the ways in which Canadian schools often marginalize minority students—students from nonmainstream racial and ethnic communities but also students who may be marginalized for other reasons such as social class, abilities, sexual orientation, or gender identity. Making even small changes to stable and complex institutions such as schools and libraries is not easy. However, one promising approach to developing cultural competence at the institutional level, being tried in public library contexts, is that of community engagement. Sung and Hepworth (2013) identify eight key components of community engagement:

- Accountability—the extent that the initiative conformed to or was driven by external organizational imperatives.
- Belonging—feelings of ownership and emphasis on relationship-building between the service and the community.
- Commitment—the degree of commitment to the project by the relevant stakeholders.
- Communication—the way in which the service is communicated with the community.
- A flexible approach—the variety of methods employed to engage and work in partnership.
- Genuineness—authenticity or a true reflection of what was said to be.
- Relevance—the degree of relevance or benefits to stakeholders.
- Sustainability—the impact and continuity of the project. (p. 10)

Underlying the key components of community engagement are two variables that work against each other: influence of authority (the extent to which engagement initiatives are initiated, shaped, or led by the organization, that is, the school and/or library) and willingness to learn (the extent to which the organization has the capacity to embrace the community's leadership or preferred approach). In essence, the greater the organization's willingness to learn, the more authentic and sustainable will be the engagement with the community. Revising and/or developing institutional missions, policies, and practices that are more welcoming and supportive of diverse communities requires that we be willing to learn from those communities.

The Instructional Dimension

A culturally responsive pedagogy recognizes the importance of including students' cultural references in all aspects of learning. This pedagogy has three key criteria: students must experience academic success, students must develop and/or maintain cultural competence, and students must develop a critical consciousness through which they challenge the status quo of the current social order (Ladson-Billings, 1994, 1995).

Traditionally, students have been expected to adapt to the culture of the school; a culturally responsive pedagogy demands that schools find ways to adapt and change to the cultures of the students. The Brown University website proposes Culturally Responsive Teaching (https://www.brown.edu/academics/education-alliance/teaching-diverse-learners/strategies-0/culturally-responsive-teaching-0) as a key strategy for teaching diverse learners and summarizes the what, why, and how of achieving seven characteristics of a culturally responsive pedagogy:

- Positive perspectives on parents and families
- Communication of high expectations
- Learning within the context of culture
- Student-centered instruction
- Culturally mediated instruction
- Reshaping the curriculum
- Teacher as facilitator

These characteristics align well with many aspects of inquiry-based instruction. As teacher librarians, we can enhance inquiry-based instruction with the insights that come from developing cultural competence. As teacher librarians, we also can play a leadership role in helping other educators become aware of the ideologies that inform their teaching philosophies and practices (Kumasi & Hill, 2013).

DISCOURSES FOR A CULTURALLY RESPONSIVE PEDAGOGY

As educators, if we intend to implement a culturally responsive pedagogy, we need to begin with examining our own ideologies and developing our cultural competence. Kumasi and Hill (2011, 2013) studied how LIS students in two American Library Association (ALA)-accredited programs in the United States perceived their levels of cultural competence, the source of their knowledge, and the importance of that knowledge. The students rated 16 cultural competence items (see Appendix) such as "Recognition of how individuals from various cultures access information" and "Understanding of the term 'literacy' including cognitive and socio-cultural perspectives." Initial analysis revealed gaps between the students' prior knowledge and the knowledge they gained while in the LIS program.

The student participants also were given the opportunity to comment on the survey and the survey topic. Analysis of the student comments suggests that within the field of LIS there are dominant and competing ideologies within cultural competence discourses (Table 1). Kumasi and Hill's competing discourse is most closely aligned with the underlying assumptions of a culturally responsive pedagogy.

The dominant discourse about cultural competence uses terminology such as "multiculturalism" and "diversity" either to be consistent with official government or

Table 1

Dominant and Competing Ideologies within Cultural Competence Discourses

Textual Theme	Dominant Discourse	Competing Discourse
Cultural competence terminology	An ideology of "political correctness" and benign pluralism translates into the use of "neutral" terms when discussing cultural competence concepts.	A critical theoretical orientation calls for naming specific modes of domination and axes of privilege when discussing cultural competence concepts.
The role of libraries/ librarians in cultural competence	A service-oriented business/ management paradigm informs how librarians talk about working with diverse library users.	A community engagement-oriented, socio-cultural paradigm informs how librarians talk about working with diverse library users.
Prior experience in relation to building cultural competence	A dominant White cultural perspective translates into prior experience meaning working in non-White or non–English-speaking cultural contexts.	A non-dominant, pragmatic perspective recognizes any library experience as valuable in a competitive, predominately White job market.

From: Kumasi & Hill, 2013, p. 135.

institutional practice or to avoid offending others. The competing discourse requires discussion of power and privilege; it requires that we name and understand our own culture as a precursor to understanding and appreciating other people's cultural contexts.

The dominant discourse about the role of libraries and librarians emphasizes service that tends to place librarians and their clientele at a distance from each other (we design the services that people may or may not use). The competing discourse emphasizes authentic interactions with people and engagement with the cultural contexts of their daily lives (we interact with people to get to know them and to develop the services they want to use).

The dominant discourse about prior experience is that cultural competence is developed by living or working in non-White environments or having educational experiences that increase awareness of multiculturalism. The competing discourse recognizes that most libraries are White, middle-class cultural environments, and that library experience of any kind would be valuable in preparation for work in that cultural environment.

DEVELOPING A CULTURALLY RESPONSIVE PEDAGOGY

One approach to developing a culturally responsive pedagogy is that taken by a group of researchers at Pittsburg State University (Hudiburg et al., 2015) as they developed a curriculum to prepare teacher librarians to be better able to address the needs of American Indian students. The researchers drew on Purnell's Model of Cultural Competence (Purnell, 2002), which describes a spectrum of cultural competence.

The lessons learned through the development of a curriculum for school library education guided by the Purnell Model help to explain the "how" of developing the cultural competence that teacher librarians need in order to support the implementation of a culturally responsive pedagogy in schools. The researchers at Pittsburg State University suggest the following:

1. **Evaluate Personal Cultural Perspectives.** Useful templates include Purnell's Model of Cultural Competence adapted for teacher librarians (Hudiburg et al., 2015, p. 141) or the Cultural Competence Survey Items (Kumasi & Hill, 2011, pp. 261–264).
2. **Be Aware of the Cultural Realities within the School Community.** Identify cultural groups represented in the school using demographic data and local informants.
3. **Promote the Value of All Cultures.** Bring culture into the classrooms and libraries through virtual field trips and guest speakers.
4. **Transform Curriculum from Culturally Neutral to Culturally Enriched.** Rather than adding a lesson or unit to the curriculum, try to transform the curriculum by weaving different cultural perspectives throughout the curriculum.

CONCLUSION

"Cultural competence does not end with knowledge about diverse cultures. It begins a lifelong process of learning" (Montiel-Overall, 2009, p. 200). Each cultural group is unique in some ways, and developing cultural proficiency is time-consuming and sensitive work (see, e.g., Montiel-Overall, Nunez, & Reyes-Escudero, 2016).

The work ahead for those wanting to develop a culturally responsive pedagogy will be difficult at times, but, in many respects, it is not entirely new to us. As I reread a chapter that I wrote two decades ago titled "A community of learning for the

Information Age" (Oberg, 1999), I recognized many of the ideas that underpin the work we need to do today. In that chapter, I drew on research to outline strategies that teacher librarians could use for building a community of learning by connecting with principals, teachers, students, parents, and the community at large.

School library professionals are well placed to contribute as leaders in the changes required to develop and implement a culturally relevant pedagogy:

They have experienced in their own field the transformation of the definition of exemplary practice, and they understand the complexity of implementing a new program vision. They understand the need for careful analysis of present practice and for the need to plan the implementation process carefully and with conscious attention to the school's previous implementation history. Without this analysis and planning, [they] know that initial efforts can flounder, even after an ambitious and enthusiastic start, and that this may mean a retreat from change efforts and a return to traditional practices. (Oberg, 1999, p. 320)

Change in schools is never easy. Most educators could identify obstacles to change, including a school culture that emphasizes the classroom as the center of learning and the teacher as an independent self-reliant professional, external demands and pressures on schools, and the lack of time for educators for analysis, reflection, and planning. However, the work of developing a culturally relevant pedagogy requires that we rethink our assumptions about the role of students and the role of parents in education and that we help parents and students in rethinking their roles as well (Oberg, 1999).

We educators also know that parents are usually not consulted about or involved in school change or in curriculum change. Rarely do we in education think about how parents define learning and how they want the schools to educate their children. Where programs of parental involvement have reached only a few parents and/or where parents have come to the school mainly when their children are "in trouble" for academic or discipline reasons, layers of distrust and disillusionment will challenge change. Some parents may have experienced a very traditional school culture in their own schooling that makes them uneasy about "interfering" in the life of the school. Teacher librarians will need to make the first step to invite parents into the life of the school. For example, a teacher librarian in my city, working in a school with a very high population of English language learners, each year organizes "A Mighty Love of Reading" family field trips where parents and children join the teacher librarian and other school educators for visits to explore local public libraries and bookstores.

We educators know that students are rarely consulted in relation to any aspect of their schooling. Research has revealed that the majority of students in elementary and secondary schools think that teachers do not understand their point of view and that principals and other administrators do not listen to their concerns. The majority of elementary and secondary students say that teachers do not ask for their ideas in deciding what and how to teach. In high school, only a few students regularly participate in class discussions or ask questions, and the majority of students feel that their classmates do not understand their point of view. Educators engaged in developing a culturally relevant pedagogy will have to find ways to meaningfully engage students in a process from which they have so far been excluded.

The theoretical frameworks presented in this chapter and throughout this book should help to strengthen our ability to do the work of building communities of learning that are inclusive of all and especially of those who feel marginalized in our schools and libraries.

NOTE

Portions of this chapter have been adapted from "Theoretical Frameworks for the Work Ahead," by Dianne Oberg (https://researcharchive.canadianschoollibraries.ca/2017/11/21/theoretical-frameworks-for-thinking-about-the-work-ahead/)

REFERENCES

Amnesty International. (2013, July 23). UN human rights report shows that Canada is failing Indigenous peoples [Press release]. Retrieved from https://www.amnesty.ca/news/public-statements/joint-press-release/un-human-rights-report-shows-that-canada-is-failing

Dei, G. J. S., James, I. M., James-Wilson, S., Karumanchery, L. L., & Zine, J. (2001). *Removing the margins: The challenges and possibilities of inclusive schooling.* Toronto, Canada: Canadian Scholar's Press. [Accompanying teachers' guide, *Inclusive schooling: A teacher's companion to removing the margins.*]

Hudiburg, M., Mascher, E., Sagehorn, A., & Stidham, J. S. (2015). Moving toward a culturally competent model of education: Preliminary results of a study of culturally responsive teaching in an American Indian community. *School Libraries Worldwide, 21*(1), 137–148.

International Federation of Associations and Institutions. (2015). IFLA school library guidelines (2nd Rev. ed.). The Hague, Netherlands: IFLA.

Kumasi, K., & Hill, R. F. (2011). Are we there yet? Results of a gap analysis to measure LIS students' prior knowledge and actual learning of cultural competence concepts. *Journal of Education for Library and Information Science Education, 52*(4), 251–264.

Kumasi, K., & Hill, R. F. (2013). Examining the hidden ideologies within cultural competence discourses among library and information science (LIS) students: Implications for school library pedagogy. *School Libraries Worldwide, 19*(1), 128–141.

Ladson-Billings, G. (1994). *The dreamkeepers.* San Francisco, CA: Jossey-Bass.

Ladson-Billings, G. (1995). But that's just good teaching! The case for culturally relevant pedagogy. *Theory into Practice, 34*(3), 159–165.

Lynch, M. (2012, February 13). What is culturally responsive pedagogy? *Huffington Post, The Blog.* Retrieved from http://www.huffingtonpost.com/matthew-lynch-edd/culturally-responsive-pedagogy_b_1147364.html

Montiel-Overall, P. (2005). A theoretical understanding of teacher and librarian collaboration (TLC). *School Libraries Worldwide, 11*(2), 24–48.

Montiel-Overall, P. (2009). Cultural competence: A conceptual framework for library and information professionals. *Library Quarterly, 79*(2), 175–204.

Montiel-Overall, P., Nunez, A. V., & Reyes-Escudero, V. (2016). *Latinos in libraries, museums and archives: Cultural competence in action! An asset based approach.* Lanham, MA: Rowman & Littlefield.

Oberg, D. (1999). A community of learning for the Information Age. In B. K. Stripling (Ed.), *Libraries and learning in the Information Age: Principles and practice* (pp. 299–323). Englewood, CO: Libraries Unlimited.

Purnell, L. (2002). The Purnell Model for Cultural Competence. *Journal of Transcultural Nursing, 13*(3), 193–196. doi:10.1177/10459602013003006

Sung, H.-Y., & Hepworth, M. (2013). Modelling community engagement in public libraries. *Malaysian Journal of Library and Information Science, 18*(1), 1–13.

Sung, H.-Y., Hepworth, M., & Ragsdell, G. (2013). Investigating essential elements of community engagement in public libraries: An exploratory qualitative study. *Journal of Librarianship and Information Science.* Retrieved from https://doi.org/10.1177/0961000612448205

Truth and Reconciliation Commission of Canada. (2015, May 31). *Honouring the truth, reconciling for the future: Summary of the final report of the Truth and Reconciliation Commission of Canada.* Winnipeg, MB: Truth and Reconciliation Commission of Canada. Retrieved from https://web.archive.org/web/20160706170855/http://www.trc.ca/websites/trcinstitution/File/2015/Findings/Exec_Summary_2015_05_31_web_o.pdf

Zine, J. (2010). Inclusive schooling in a plural society: Removing the margins. *Education Canada, 42*(3), 36–39.

APPENDIX

Cultural Competency Survey Items
(from Kumasi & Hill, 2011, pp. 261–264)

Survey participants rated each item from 1 (no or low level) to 7 (high level) to indicate prior knowledge, importance of learning, and knowledge gained.

Section I: Self-awareness

1. Awareness of ways that my culture has shaped my life
2. Awareness of cultural differences that may exist between myself and others
3. Awareness of ways that my cultural beliefs impact my understanding of individuals from other cultures
4. Awareness of ways to provide library service to patrons from various cultural backgrounds (e.g., race, ethnicity, socioeconomic status, and/or sexual orientation).

Section II: Education

1. Understanding of the term "literacy" including cognitive and sociocultural perspectives
2. Knowledge of cultural differences among ethnic populations in the United States.
3. Familiarity with the history of library service to individuals from various cultures
4. Recognition of how individuals from various cultures access information
5. Recognition of barriers to information access and use that may exist for individuals from various cultures
6. Collection development strategies that reflect the information wants and needs of individuals from various cultures
7. Recognition of the role libraries play in providing outreach and specialized services to various cultural groups in the United States.

Section III: Interactions

1. Having personal interactions with individuals from various cultural backgrounds
2. Visiting libraries that are patronized by users from a variety of cultural backgrounds
3. Collaborating with others to develop library services, programs, and outreach efforts for individuals from various cultural backgrounds
4. Knowledge of professional development events designed to share information about various aspects of culture

Section IV: Optional comments
Please use the following area to include comments about the survey questionnaire and/or the survey topic.

Creating Culturally Responsive Schools

Michelle Hudiburg, Elizabeth Mascher, and Alice Sagehorn

ABSTRACT

The Purnell Model for Cultural Competence emerged as a framework for organizing clinical assessment for student nurses (Purnell, 2002). In an effort to meet the needs of the American Indian population in the Northeast Oklahoma region, Pittsburg State University (PSU) sought to train a cohort of participants using a revised model of the Purnell Model for Cultural Competence. PSU's program focused on embedding the revised model with an American Indian audience. Results showed increased cultural awareness and a change in participants' professional practice. Lessons learned from the grant project along with implications for practice are shared.

INTRODUCTION

Every child needs to know that his or her personal culture is valued. One way to address this critical element of education is culturally responsive teaching (CRT), grounded in the principle that culture influences the way students learn. This instructional approach acknowledges and affirms students' cultures as assets in curriculum development and classroom instruction (Gay, 2010; Hollins, 2011; Nieto, 2010). CRT results in academic achievement because teaching content is given relevance through cultural context (Gollnick & Chin, 2013).

Taking time to build culture into the curriculum sends a message that who students are and where they come from is important (Schencker, 2008). For instance, consider story time in the library around Thanksgiving. After reading a book, the librarian follows up by saying, "Did you know that the Pilgrims would have starved to death if the Native Americans hadn't brought them food and taught them how to plant and grow crops?" The children shook their heads indicating they didn't know this. About that time, one little Native American boy jumped up and said, "We're the heroes! We're the heroes!"

The Purnell Model for Cultural Competence (Purnell, 2002) was chosen as the basis for transforming existing library media curriculum into a CRT curriculum and pedagogy. The Purnell Model began as an assessment tool for preservice nurses and has since transformed into a model meant to help health-care professionals consciously adapt their practices in a culturally consistent manner. The Purnell Model follows 19 major assumptions regarding important concepts of cultural awareness, including "One culture is not better than another culture; they are just different" (Purnell, 2002, p. 193). Each assumption is broad in perspective, promoting heightened cultural awareness.

Cultural awareness is vital in the health-care professions; it is just as critical in education. As the cultural landscape of American classrooms change, educators have a responsibility to meet the needs of all students by embracing culturally competent teaching models. According to the U.S. National Center for Education Statistics (NCES, 2017), enrollment of White U.S. school age children decreased from 62% to 52% between 2000 and 2016. In contrast, Hispanic enrollment increased from 16% to 25% of the total public school population, and Asian/Pacific Islander showed a 2% increase. Application of Purnell's competencies as part of CRT has promising implications for the improvement of education.

Since teacher librarians serve at the core of the school curriculum, one way to transform curriculum through CRT is teaching them to address diversity differently. Professionally trained teacher librarians act not only as facilitators in developing student literacy skills but also serve as embedded instructional leaders for the training and support of other educators (Lance, 2001). When teacher librarians possess the knowledge necessary to effectively address diversity needs through curricular transformation (i.e., developing curriculum through the lens of culture, not simply content), teacher librarians can serve as catalysts for change throughout the system. Learning to intentionally address diversity requires educators to teach within the context of traditions and language of the cultural community. Training teacher librarians to lead this endeavor facilitates a mind-shift in approach, along with an adjustment in educational practices (Demmert & Towner, 2003).

CULTURAL COMPETENCE PROJECT: EMBEDDING THE MODEL

Broader implementation of CRT has promising implications for the improvement of academic performance among American Indian students (Castagno & Brayboy, 2008). American Indian students have a dropout rate twice the national average, the highest dropout rate of any U.S. ethnic or racial group (Faircloth & Tippeconnic, 2010). According to the U.S. Census Bureau (United States Census Bureau, 2017), American Indians graduate from high school at a rate of 72%, compared with the national average of 84%. Statistically, only 14% of American Indians have bachelor's degrees, compared with 28% of the U.S. population (NCES, 2017), and the poverty rate of American Indians is almost twice that of non-Natives (USCB, 2017). Educators have a responsibility to help reverse these negative trends. Incorporating culture into the curriculum can give American Indian students a sense of pride in their education, and it is one possible way to keep them in school.

The PSU Educational Technology faculty partnered with 9 American Indian tribes, 14 public school districts, and 3 libraries and received a U.S. Institute for Museum and Library Services (IMLS) Laura Bush 21st Century Librarian Program grant in

2013. Eight of the nine partner tribes had a library or library/museum housed in the tribal headquarters, yet none had anyone on staff holding a graduate-level library media degree. The partner school districts had an American Indian population ranging from 10% to more than 70% of the total school population. All of these school districts had elementary, middle, and high school libraries, but many had only one teacher librarian serving the entire school district.

The main goals of the grant were to implement CRT by building skills, benefiting diverse constituencies, transforming practice, and sharing knowledge. The project aimed to produce teacher librarians possessing skills to work with teachers and administrators within the partnering districts, to help schools reframe their vision for American Indian students. Participants would help ensure local American Indian tribal members had librarians who could serve as advocates, maintaining an inclusive climate and curricula in public schools and their libraries.

Twenty-five participants were chosen to take part in the grant project, pursuing a master's degree in educational technology with an emphasis in library media. To be considered, applicants had to be American Indian, or work in a public school with a high population of American Indian students, or both. Of the 25 participants, 11 were American Indian. Through the two-year academic program, participants built skills and abilities through coursework based on state and national standards. Program implementation of the modified Purnell Model of Cultural Competency opened doors for participants to see benefits in serving diverse constituencies, with a primary focus on the American Indian student. Along with coursework, participants learned tribal culture firsthand through fieldwork at tribal museums, cultural centers, and libraries, along with interaction with tribal members. Furthermore, they established a professional network, and they used technology skills for preserving and locating current and past documents to the tribal libraries/museums. Once networking between school and tribe was established, the natural bridge for sharing resources was built. Participants transformed practice, understanding that change has to occur both at the school curriculum's core and in tribal libraries.

WORKING TOWARD CULTURAL COMPETENCE

Throughout the grant project, program leaders worked to transform the regular curriculum from culturally neutral to culturally enriched. Instructors worked together, creating course work imbued with projects requiring participants to consciously invest in local American Indian history and culture. In the process of embedding Purnell's model into the school library program, PSU Educational Technology program leaders modified the model's 19 major assumptions to better fit an educational audience. Modifications included changing the term "health care professional" or "caregiver" to "teacher librarian." PSU program leaders also chose to focus on 16 of the assumptions, creating its own list of Purnell's cultural competencies as shown in Table 1. Each of these competencies was then mapped onto the curriculum in each course throughout the master's degree program.

COMPETENCIES IN ACTION

Inclusion of each revised competency occurred within the master's degree program curriculum. In this section, specifics of three competencies are addressed.

Table 1

Purnell's Cultural Competencies in Teacher Librarian Education Curriculum

1. Teacher librarians need similar information about cultural diversity.
2. Teacher librarians share the metaparadigm concepts of global society, community, family, and person.
3. One culture is not better than another culture; they are just different.
4. All cultures share core similarities.
5. Differences exist among, between, and within cultures.
6. Cultures change slowly over time in a stable society.
7. The primary and secondary characteristics of culture determine the degree to which one varies from the dominant culture.
8. If students are coparticipants in their education and have a choice in education-related goals, plans, and interventions, success outcomes will be improved.
9. Culture has powerful influence on one's interpretation of and response to learning.
10. Individuals and families belong to several cultural groups.
11. Each individual has the right to be respected for his or her uniqueness and cultural heritage.
12. Teacher librarians need both general and specific cultural information to provide sensitive and culturally competent teaching methods.
13. Teacher librarians who can assess, plan, and intervene in a culturally competent manner will improve the learning of their students.
14. Learning culture is an ongoing process and develops in a variety of ways but primarily through cultural encounters.
15. Prejudices and biases can be minimized with cultural understanding.
16. To be effective, education must reflect the unique understanding of the values, beliefs, attitudes, lifeways, and worldviews of diverse populations and individual acculturation patterns.

Competency #3: One Culture Is Not Better Than Another Culture; They Are Just Different

As part of the program, participants were required to complete an advanced children's literature course. Focusing on literature about and written by American Indians, the instructor worked to provide quality works in each of seven genres, along with picture book and graphic novel formats (Hudiburg, Mascher, Sagehorn, & Stidham, 2015). Themes of nature, family, tradition, suffering, pride, and more wove through the selected stories.

Asking participants to immerse themselves in American Indian literature prompted evaluation of perspectives concerning what their personal education had taught them about American Indians. For instance, participants were asked to create a plan for integrating books read into classroom instruction. After reading *How I Became a Ghost* by Tim Tingle, one participant included an exercise asking students to examine their personal perspectives about events in the book. Reading *How I Became a Ghost* caused this participant to evaluate their perspectives and, in turn, ask their students to do the same.

I want the students to respond to the book. I want to know what they would do if they were in Isaac, or Naomi, or Joseph's shoes. I want them to list their favourite character … and explain why that was their favourite character. I want them to identify what the soldier's perspective and viewpoint toward the Native Americans was and why the soldiers felt that way toward the Indians.

Another participant read *Super Indian* by Arigon Starr and commented:

I am not a Native American but there was a lot of inside humor that I had to share with my husband [who is]. The inside jokes ranged from: hanging outside a bingo hall to commodity cheese. They just made me laugh typing this line.

Encouraging participants to read literature from diverse cultures helped promote cultural understanding. Reading stories embedded in American Indian life experiences helped this participant gain new insights into her husband, her family, and her classroom students.

Competency #5: Differences Exist among, between, and within Cultures

Because PSU project leaders wanted to instill understanding that differences exist among, between, and within cultures, participants were assigned to groups and asked to create a video project focused on one specific element of an assigned tribe. Tribes explored for this class project included the Shawnee and Miami. Participants made videos on tribal origins, tribal culture, tribal traditions, and tribal personality. To assure quality and accuracy of their projects, participants were encouraged to conduct interviews with tribal members and authenticate facts through tribal libraries and museums.

Upon completion, video projects were shared with the members of the class. American Indian participants commented on how interesting it was to note tribal differences, especially in those so close geographically. Others expressed appreciation for the experience and their newly acquired knowledge about what being an American Indian means. Personal statements and reflections demonstrated participants were beginning to understand that differences exist across all parts of culture.

Competency #9: Culture Has Powerful Influence on One's Interpretation of and Responses to Learning

Participants were asked to create a classroom, curriculum-based (e.g., algebra, science, and language arts) lesson that would be presented to an audience of American Indian students. The project's focus was experiencing how cultural differences influence learning and response to instructional practices. At the lesson's conclusion, participants were asked to reflect on the process they had completed. Reflection questions included the following:

• How did you use previous theory and research to help you?
• Did what you've learned this semester change the way you approached this assignment?
• How did specifying your audience change the way you approached teaching the lesson?
• What characteristics of the audience made you take a different approach to the lesson?

Answers to these questions revealed a change in perspective for many of the participants. For example,

During this semester, we have learned that many Native American families have been affected by poverty. Children from low income families generally require specific direction and modeling on appropriate social interaction. In addition, they require direct instruction in speaking in a formal register, asking questions, and answering in complete sentences. These specific needs and characteristics shaped the way I planned my lesson.

Another participant responded,

I did a general search of teaching Native American children. It was interesting to read some of the suggestions for teaching those students ... Prior to this course and program I would not have thought to research how to interact with Native American children.

Finally, this participant voiced how the project helped improve their vision of American Indian students:

To me the most important thing I can give an underprivileged student is a goal. Several of the students I have do not dream of getting out of their current living conditions or location. If I can get a few of them to see that there is a plan and a way to get more, then I will have done my job ... Thank you for helping making this program a possibility and increasing Native American awareness.

No longer were participants seeing their classrooms (or schools) as a group of like-minded individuals. Instead, they were beginning to understand specific needs of the American Indian student, and how those needs influenced learning. In turn, realization that everyone has different cultural influences made them reexamine personal instructional practices.

LESSONS LEARNED

Through each course in the 36-hour graduate program, participants were exposed to competencies for cultural awareness. After completing coursework at the university, these same participants spent a year working in tribal libraries, tribal museums, and tribal cultural centers. Along with working in local tribal libraries and cultural centers, participants and instructors toured American Indian art exhibits, attended cultural events, and were represented at an intertribal council meeting. Immersion in Northeast Oklahoma American Indian culture further increased awareness of how culture plays an influential role in student learning.

When looking at community connections, a clear pattern of heightened awareness of American Indian students and their needs emerged. Participating tribal libraries implemented new systems for cataloging and classifying collections as a result of collaborations with students during practicum and internship. In addition, districts were equipped with procedures to effectively establish and maintain culturally relevant collections. These data made it clear that the project made a difference in the ability to apply CRT practices to meet the library and information needs of American Indian students. With cooperation from local tribal leaders, tribal centers, and tribal libraries, participants continue to teach colleagues about the importance of American Indian culture in Northeast Oklahoma, working with, and for, the tribal libraries, cultural centers, and museums while serving in classrooms and school libraries.

As data came back from project participants, educational planners understood the critical need for embedding CRT and the revised competencies into nongrant project curriculum at the university. Along with recognition of community connections, participants were asked whether the training in the grant project had an impact on their own biases, whether their efforts to diversify in the classroom had changed, and whether key parts of the program were beneficial. Eighty-three percent of participants expressed change in their personal biases, with 51% being "very much" more aware of how those biases influenced professional practice. Experiencing cultural activities with colleagues was reported as the most beneficial (91%) way to overcome personal cultural biases and become more culturally sensitive. Results also indicated that participants were including their CRT learning in current classroom practices even before graduation (Hudiburg et al., 2015). When asked if they felt more aware of the diverse needs of their students because of participation in the program, 91% responded affirmatively. The same percentage also reported being better able to include diversity in their everyday teaching practices because of the program training.

PSU program leaders continue modifying their library media curriculum to embrace the unique abilities of students from all cultures into their libraries, and to see future librarians encourage classroom teachers to do the same, using CRT practices. Future plans focus on the growing Hispanic population in the geographic region, using CRT practices and competencies similar to those used with the American Indian project. Any new project proposed will include an initial "Jump Start" program in order to lay relevant cultural groundwork. During Jump Start, participants will be exposed to local and national speakers, events, and presentations emphasizing Hispanic cultural expectations and knowledge. These experiences will not only provide participants with a strong cultural background but will also model methods available for infusing cultural experiences within their schools along with breaking down barriers of personal bias. Combining data from the two projects would assist PSU program leaders in their process of continual program improvement, with a primary focus on diversity and promotion of cultural competence.

IMPLICATIONS FOR PRACTICE

As a result of lessons learned throughout the curriculum transformation and subsequent American Indian project, several implications for practice emerged. These are discussed next along with suggestions for implementation.

Evaluate Personal Cultural Perspectives

Culture defines the way we teach and learn, regardless of whether we are consciously aware of its influence (Gay, 2010). To effectively develop an environment of CRT, it is important to first recognize personal perspectives (Anderson, 2011). Just as silent censorship can cripple collection development practices, so too can cultural misconceptions influence curriculum transformation. Utilize the Purnell's cultural competencies to examine how personal cultural perceptions influence professional practice. In addition, continually broaden knowledge by seeking out, engaging in, and promoting opportunities for cultural experiences. Approaching the personal evaluation process with sensitivity and awareness can help break down any existing cultural misconceptions and can assist teacher librarians in encouraging and supporting fellow educators to do the same.

Be Aware of the Cultural Realities within the School Community

Once evaluation of personal perspectives has been established, awareness of the cultural realities within the school community is important. Utilizing available demographic data, as well as communication with administration and colleagues, identifies cultures represented within the school community. Knowledge of where students come from allows teacher librarians to build on those cultural realities through collection and curriculum development. Establishing the school library as a safe place where students can ask questions and explore their cultures helps further immerse them in the community (Boelens, Cherek, Tilke, & Bailey, 2015). Students who feel their culture has value within the school community are more likely to be engaged in learning experiences, both inside and outside the classroom. Bringing awareness of the school's cultural realities is a key step in successful CRT implementation.

Promote the Value of All Cultures

Promoting the value of all cultures shows students and parents that they are valued as individuals with background knowledge, experiences, and identities critical to the learning process (DeCapua, 2016). Partner with local entities offering cultural resources such as public libraries, museums, or cultural centers. Once partnerships are established through the school library, encouraging colleagues to utilize available cultural resources will help broaden the circle of influence. Collaborate with these entities to host various events for the community. Bringing culture into the classroom can also be a means of promoting culture. Virtual field trips can take students anywhere in the world, allowing them to see and experience the sights and sounds of their families' native lands, while exposing others to their classmates' rich heritage. Likewise, bringing individuals into the classroom provides students opportunities to interact with guest speakers, authors, and experts of various cultures from the local community or a country on the other side of the world. Using virtual meeting technology such as Skype, FaceTime, or Zoom opens vast possibilities for individual interaction. Finally, communicating and collaborating with families in promoting cultural events and opportunities in the community will speak volumes about the recognition of, and respect for, all cultures represented in the school.

Transform Curriculum from Culturally Neutral to Culturally Enriched

CRT distinguishes between curriculum "infusion" and curriculum "transformation." Curriculum infusion occurs when an isolated lesson or unit of study is added to the curriculum. A single lesson about female explorers added to social studies curriculum is a token response, or after-thought (Morey & Kitano, 1997). Transformation, on the other hand, weaves culture throughout the curriculum, making the content meaningful at all levels (Banks, 2014). Transforming curriculum happens after schools embrace CRT and work together to create a culturally enriched learning environment. One way this can be done is by giving course content relevance through cultural context. For instance, ensure course content is presented from a variety of cultural perspectives. Teacher librarians can support this step by developing a highly diverse collection across all genres. Another means of transforming the curriculum is encouraging individuals to read literature from diverse cultures because it helps promote cultural understanding (Hudiburg et al., 2015). A high school student can develop understanding and compassion for Afghanistan by reading *The Kite Runner,* discussing current events, examining geography, exploring history, and listening to music. In isolation, these activities teach facets of other cultures, but woven together they bring deeper insight into the human condition.

CONCLUSION

The school library profession strives to stay abreast of trends in schools, and staffing libraries with individuals well versed in CRT helps make the library a valuable asset. With the rapid increase of cultural diversity in schools, it is important to have highly qualified and diverse teacher librarians. Unfortunately, literacy, cultural, and language barriers can prevent educators from effectively engaging students and their families.

When schools become more conscious of the cultural backgrounds of their students, they are more able to connect with their cultures through literature, history, and—more importantly—their community, and school practice begins to transform. Helping educators to better support and celebrate student differences can help to close achievement gaps, alleviate classroom management issues, and improve graduation statistics. Using the CRT framework and implications for practice, teacher librarians can work to create an environment where all cultures are valued by advocating for inclusive learning climates and balanced curriculum in every educational setting.

ACKNOWLEDGMENT

The work reported in this paper was supported in part by the Institute of Museum and Library Services, Laura Bush RE-01-13-0019-13.

NOTE

This chapter was previously published as Hudiburg, M., Mascher, E., Sagehorn, A., & Stidham, J. S. (2015). Moving toward a culturally competent model of education: Preliminary results of a study of culturally responsive teaching in an American Indian community. *School Libraries Worldwide, 21*(1), 137–148.

REFERENCES

Anderson, M. (2011). Teacher and student perspectives on cultural proficiency. *Leadership, 40*(5), 32–35.

Banks, J. (2014). *An introduction to multicultural education* (5th ed.). Upper Saddle River, NJ: Pearson.

Boelens, H., Cherek, J. M., Jr., Tilke, A., & Bailey, N. (2015). Communicating across cultures: Cultural identity issues and the role of the multicultural, multilingual school library within the school community. In *The school library rocks: Proceedings of the*

44th Conference of the International Association of School Librarianship (pp. 46–62). Maastricht, Netherlands: IASL.

Castagno, A. E., & Brayboy, B. M. J. (2008). Culturally responsive schooling for indigenous youth: A review of the literature. *Review of Educational Research, 78*(4), 941–993.

DeCapua, A. (2016). Reaching students with limited or interrupted formal education through culturally responsive teaching. *Language and Linguistics Compass, 10*(5), 225–237.

Demmert, W. G., & Towner, J. C. (2003). A review of the research literature on the influences of culturally based education on the academic performance of Native American students. *Northwest Regional Educational Laboratory.* Retrieved from http://educationnorthwest.org/sites/default/files/resources/cbe.pdf

Faircloth, S. C., & Tippeconnic, J. W. (2010). The dropout/graduation crisis among American Indian and Alaska Native students: Failure to respond places the future of native peoples at risk. Retrieved from http://files.eric.ed.gov/fulltext/ED511323.pdf

Gay, G. (2010). *Culturally responsive teaching: Theory, research, and practice* (2nd ed.). New York, NY: Teachers College Press.

Gollnick, D., & Chin, P. (2013). *Multicultural education in a pluralistic society* (9th ed.). Upper Saddle River, NJ: Pearson.

Hollins, E. R. (2011). The meaning of culture in learning to teach: The power of socialization and identify formation. In A. F. Ball & C. A. Tyson (Eds.), *Studying diversity in teacher education* (pp. 105–132). New York, NY: Rowman & Littlefield.

Hudiburg, M., Mascher, E., Sagehorn, A., & Stidham, J. S. (2015). Moving toward a culturally competent model of education: Preliminary results of a study of culturally responsive teaching in an American Indian community. *School Libraries Worldwide, 21*(1), 137–148.

Lance, K. C. (2001). Proof of the power: Recent research on the impact of school library media programs on the academic achievement of U.S. public school students. *Multimedia Schools, 8*(4), 14–20. Retrieved from http://0-search.proquest.com.library.uark.edu/docview/62247683?accountid=8361

Morey, A. I., & Kitano, M. (Eds.). (1997). *Multicultural course transformation in higher education: A broader truth.* Boston, MA: Allyn & Bacon.

National Center for Education Statistics (NCES). (2017). Population distribution. Retrieved from https://nces.ed.gov/programs/raceindicators/indicator_raa.asp

Nieto, S. (2010). *Language, culture, and teaching: Cultural perspectives.* New York, NY: Routledge.

Purnell, L. (2002). The Purnell Model for Cultural Competence. *Journal of Transcultural Nursing, 13*(3), 193–196. doi:10.1177/10459602013003006

Schencker, L. (2008, April 23). Educators examine American Indian dropout rates. *The Salt Lake Tribune.* Retrieved from https://www.atlanticphilanthropies.org/news/educators-examine-american-indian-dropout-rates

U.S. Census Bureau. (2017). American Indian and Alaskan Native heritage. Retrieved from https://www.census.gov/newsroom/facts-for-features/2017/aian-month.html

What Does Cultural Competence Mean to Preservice School Librarians? A Critical Discourse Analysis

Kafi D. Kumasi and Renee F. Hill

ABSTRACT

In order to provide culturally responsive instruction to all students, school library professionals need to recognize the various discourses around cultural competence that exist in the field of library and information science (LIS) and understand the broader meanings that are attached to these discourses. This study presents an evaluation of the underlying ideologies that are embedded in the textual responses of a group of LIS students reporting on their perceived levels of cultural competence preparation.

INTRODUCTION

The notion that all students deserve quality educational experiences is a popular discourse that reflects a broader ideology about the value and importance of education to one's life success. Yet, hidden within this discourse is a common understanding that many public school students in America do not have access to a quality education because of their circumstances of birth. These students are the metaphorical "outliers" in mainstream schools in the United States, because their cultural and linguistic backgrounds often position them on the periphery of dominant White, middle class, English-speaking cultural norms and practices.

A related discourse that has emerged regarding issues of equity and diversity in schools is the notion of cultural competence. Within the field of multicultural education, cultural competence centers on helping teachers teach toward prejudice reduction, understanding ethnic group culture, and ethnic identity development (Bennett, 2001). Yet, although cultural competence has entered into mainstream discourse communities, it remains a broad concept that gets conflated with a range of associated topics. This confusion about the meaning of cultural competence may render it ineffective as a tool for engaging in culturally responsive teaching that might benefit all students, particularly those from historically underrepresented cultural backgrounds.

BACKGROUND, PURPOSE, AND SIGNIFICANCE OF STUDY

Evidence suggests that some preservice librarians are underexposed to cultural competence concepts during their preservice preparation coursework and do not feel prepared to become culturally competent LIS professionals (Hill & Kumasi, 2011; Kumasi & Hill, 2011). Acquiring knowledge of cultural competence concepts can help librarians who work in a variety of settings to develop the knowledge, attitudes, and skills needed to work in increasingly diverse library communities. Moreover, this knowledge can be particularly useful for school library professionals, who have the means to shape curricular learning outcomes in ways that address the goals and objectives of multicultural education. Yet, it is not enough to merely be aware of this discourse. It is equally important for LIS professionals to be self-reflective and to develop a sense of "cultural critical consciousness" (Gay & Kirkland, 2003) about the ideological origins of their practices and beliefs.

One way to better understand a complex topic such as cultural competence is to examine the implicit discourses that are at play while individuals talk about this concept. To that end, the purpose of this study is to evaluate the implicit discourses that are located in the textual responses of a group of LIS students, who were reporting on their perceived levels of cultural competence preparation.

Conceptualizing Discourse

While the term "discourse" has several meanings, it is used in this study to describe the conversations and the meanings behind them that a group of people or a discourse community expresses on a particular topic.

Another premise that helped to guide this analysis is the idea that there are dominant discourses that appear most prevalently within a given society. From a critical theory perspective, these dominant discourses often reflect the ideologies of those who have the most power in society (Bloome, Carter, Christian, Otto, & Shuart-Faris, 2004; Gee, 1996). Few people challenge this dominant discourse, which makes it difficult for new ideas to enter the mainstream.

The evidence used to validate the hidden ideologies within discourses may derive from conceptual or empirical forms of "data." Typically, conceptual data are drawn from secondary sources rather than firsthand accounts. Some examples of conceptual data include the ideas expressed in scholarly journal articles and/or the messages communicated via popular culture media such as television, radio, and print ads. Fairclough (2003) suggests that there is validity in tracing discourses through these types of conceptually constructed forms of "data" that are located in popular culture.

REVIEW OF RELATED LITERATURE

Tracing "Cultural Competence" in Scholarly Discourses

Cultural competence was first conceptualized and applied within social work and health care (especially nursing) as a way to move institutions and systems toward providing effective and culturally responsive patient care (Seright, 2007). However, other fields of study have contributed to cultural competence discourse, as it is both individually oriented and institutionally focused (Dee, 2012; Hernandez & Kose, 2012; Milner, 2011).

One of the earliest articulations of the term "cultural competence" came from a team of social work researchers led by Cross, whose intent was to present "a philosophical framework and practical ideas for improving service delivery to children of color who are severely emotionally disturbed" (Cross, Bazron, Dennis, & Isaacs, 1989, p. 1). The Cross research team codified the relationship between cultural competence and organizational systems when they defined cultural competence as "a set of congruent behaviors, attitudes, and policies that come together in a system, agency, or among professionals and enable that system, agency, or those professionals to work effectively in cross-cultural situations" (Cross et al., 1989, p. 13).

Montiel-Overall (2009) provided a comprehensive treatment of cultural competence as it is positioned in the LIS scholarly discourse, which contains both individual and institutional elements. She describes cultural competence as,

The ability to recognize the significance of culture in one's own life and in the lives of others; and to come to know and respect diverse cultural backgrounds and characteristics through interaction with individuals from diverse linguistic, cultural, and socioeconomic groups; and to fully integrate the culture of diverse groups into services, work, and institutions in order to enhance the lives of both those being served by the library profession and those engaged in service. (p. 190)

This definition of cultural competence recognizes the need for self-awareness, interaction, and education. While this work has helped illustrate how cultural competence concepts might be integrated into LIS education and practice, it stops short of offering a critical examination of the ideological roots of cultural competence scholarly discourse itself.

Discourse and LIS Scholarship

The concept of discourse has gained footing as a viable conceptual and analytical tool within LIS research. According to Budd (2006) discourse analysis, like other methodologies, "offers a way of seeing things, of envisioning what is happening and what has happened" (p. 80). Most LIS researchers have taken a macro-level approach to discourse analysis, which typically involves studying the ontology, or the formation of libraries as institutions and tracing the social forces that have shaped the implicit ideologies upon which libraries have been constructed (Day, 2001).

While macro-level approaches have dominated the literature, there are more micro-level phenomena that lend themselves to discourse analysis in the LIS field as well, such as the classic reference exchange in the library. Micro-level approaches to discourse analysis focus on the transactional (sentence level) elements of discourse. By contrast, macro-level approach involves studying language as a discursive practice (beyond the sentence level). The latter approach seeks to understand the situated contexts in which words are articulated and the circuitous route in which meaning is made (Budd, 2006).

Critical Perspectives on LIS Discourses

Some scholars have critically examined the discourses upon which the LIS profession has been constructed. Such analyses are viewed as helpful in exposing the conceptual blind spots and false ideologies that exist within the profession as a means of infusing more transformative and inclusive paradigms into its theoretical base of knowledge. The two main theoretical areas where scholars have focused much of the critique include examinations of race and class.

Critical Discourse on Race and Class in LIS

With regard to how issues of race have been constructed in LIS discourse, Honma (2005) articulated a sound critique in his article, "Trippin' over the Color Line: The Invisibility of Race in Library and Information Studies." In the article, Honma posits that "the issue of race has been evaded in the field of Library and Information Studies (LIS) in the United States through an unquestioned system of white normativity and liberal multiculturalism" (p. 1). The central thesis of Honma's article is that there are inherent contradictions in the purported mission of libraries as a democratizing institution and the complicit role libraries have played in the discriminatory process of racial formation in the United States.

One of the popular critiques of how race is dealt within LIS is the tendency to rely on empty, celebratory rhetoric that employs race-neutral terms such as "diversity" and "multiculturalism," which lack the ability to address structural racism (Peterson, 1996). Most critical race scholars would argue that although the racialized legacy of the American library's past continues to be transmitted in contemporary LIS discourses and practices, there is potential for positive transformation if these discourses are exposed and critiqued. This kind of critique is also levied by Christine Pawley, who has presented a class-based analysis of the emergence of LIS as a professional discourse community.

Although race and class are widely considered to be interlocking systems of oppression, there is benefit to using a singular theoretical lens to examine certain issues that might not be otherwise easily explained. For example, class-based analyses generally focus on the economic structures within society and how these systems often put capitalist owners in conflict with workers or the laboring class. As mentioned previously, Pawley offers a cogent class-based critique of the LIS profession in her article entitled, "Hegemony's Handmaid? The LIS Curriculum from a Class Perspective." In the article, Pawley (1998) traces how middle-class values and practices have been codified within the LIS profession through the concepts of managerialism and pluralism. Pawley discusses the ways in which these two paradigms have become synonymous with middle-class values, in part as a response to corporate interests.

Another of Pawley's (2006) articles identifies four dominant paradigms that are said to guide LIS teaching and practice. These paradigms are linked to middle-class and White, male epistemologies. The four paradigms that Pawley argues dominate LIS teaching and research include science/technology, business/management, mission/

service, and society/culture. Pawley situates multicultural courses within the domains of mission/service and society/culture, explaining that,

> Although they have their origins in the relatively distant past, the society/culture and mission/ services models are also home to research and teaching in newer areas, including multiculturalism. For instance, the research heading "Services to User Populations" includes a topic called "Serving Multicultural Populations," while courses in literature and services for children and young adults frequently contain units on multicultural materials. (p. 160)

Pawley distinguishes the business/management model that depicts library and information users as "consumers or customers" from the mission/service model that casts them as "clients or patrons." From this standpoint, the mission/service model enables librarians to see themselves as service providers whose job is to assess and help meet patron "needs."

Overall, this literature review reveals the complexities surrounding discourse as an area of scholarly inquiry and the nuances of using discourse as a methodological approach. Despite its complexity, discourse can serve as a powerful analytic framework for unpacking dense theoretical concepts such as cultural competence. For this reason, the research design of the current study is heavily informed by conceptual understandings of discourse.

RESEARCH DESIGN

The process of analytic induction was the primary method used in this study, which was framed by the following research question: What are the various ideologies embedded in a group of library and information students' discourses on cultural competence? According to Thomas (2003), the primary purpose of analytic induction is to "allow research findings to emerge from the frequent, dominant or significant themes inherent in raw data, without the restraints imposed by structured methodologies" (p. 2). This method is often used by researchers to arrive at general conclusions through the examination of a set of specific facts (Spurgin & Wildemuth, 2009).

The researchers used this method to identify the major themes, or discourses around cultural competence, that were embedded in the open-ended textual responses of the LIS student respondents surveyed in this study.

Data Collection

Data for this study were collected via an electronic survey questionnaire that was emailed to students during the Fall 2011 semester. The survey instrument itself contained five sections. However, this study focuses exclusively on the qualitative data collected in the fifth and final section wherein respondents were instructed to include comments about the survey questionnaire and/or the survey topic. The first section of the questionnaire requested basic demographic information about the students, while the second through fourth sections prompted students to rank themselves and their LIS coursework in terms of cultural competence preparation using a Likert scale. The results derived from the quantitative data have been reported elsewhere (Kumasi & Hill, 2011).

Study Participants

The survey respondents were all LIS students at two American Library Association (ALA)-accredited institutions. Students were eligible to complete the survey if they had completed at least 15 credit hours in their respective programs. The original survey yielded a total of 151 student respondents out of a possible 672 eligible students enrolled at both institutions (Kumasi & Hill, 2011). There were a combined total of 29 qualitative open-ended responses submitted. Within this subsample, all respondents except one were female. Three students self-identified as African American, 24 as White, and 1 as Mexican/German. One student preferred not to reveal her race/ethnicity.

Data Analysis

Using the constant comparative method (Boyatzis, 1998), the researchers identified several broad themes in the raw data. Subsequently, the researchers identified similar words and phrases that appeared most frequently in the data. The initial broad themes served as the basis for subsequent rounds of data analysis that involved cross-checking and refining the thematic categories based on the researchers' consensus. The researchers continued to refine the thematic categories by looking for confirming and disconfirming evidence. Phrases and words from a single student's response may have been grouped into one or more broad categories based on the inductive coding process.

Issues of Validity and Limitations

As a result of this amorphous nature of discourse, providing evidence to validate the claims being made about the broader ideologies embedded within a given discourse can be extremely difficult (Cho & Trent, 2006). This analysis is therefore admittedly limited to the subjective knowledge of the researchers about the concepts that are being introduced. However, an attempt has been made to validate the claims that are being made through a process of cross-checking and looking for negative cases to provide both confirming and disconfirming evidence.

Another limitation of this study is the lack of follow-up interviews with the participants to cross-check the findings from the participants' point of view. However, this limitation is offset by the overall goal of this study, which was to examine the hidden or implicit ideologies embedded in the student's remarks.

FINDINGS AND DISCUSSION

The inductive analysis yielded several broad themes that, upon further analysis, revealed that a number of competing discourses were being articulated. For each of the broad themes that were identified, Table 1 features a brief analysis of the dominant and competing discourses that were embedded within the textual themes identified within the students' responses.

Cultural Competence Terminology

LIS literature suggests that a number of words and terms have been used as substitutes for the term "cultural competence" (Helton, 2010; Mestre, 2010). It is common

Table I

Dominant and Competing Ideologies within Cultural Competence Discourses

Textual Theme	Dominant Discourse	Competing Discourse
Cultural competence terminology	An ideology of "political correctness" and benign pluralism translates into the use of "neutral" terms when discussing cultural competence concepts.	A critical theoretical orientation calls for naming specific modes of domination and axes of privilege when discussing cultural competence concepts.
The role of libraries/librarians in cultural competence	A service-oriented business/ management paradigm informs how librarians talk about working with diverse library users.	A community engagement-oriented, sociocultural paradigm informs how librarians talk about working with diverse library users.
Prior experience in relation to building cultural competence	A dominant White cultural perspective translates into prior experience meaning working in non-White or non-English-speaking cultural contexts.	A nondominant, pragmatic perspective recognizes any library experience as valuable in a competitive, predominately White job market.

for terms such as "multiculturalism," "diversity," "cultural awareness," and "cultural sensitivity" to be used interchangeably with cultural competence. However, cultural competence has a specific definition that is similar to but not synonymous with the earlier-mentioned terms.

Thirteen research participants submitted written responses that included words and terms that seemed to be used synonymously with cultural competence. Some respondents referred to "multicultural issues" or "multiculturalism." For example, one student stated, "Having been an urban educator, I had a great deal of experience and prior knowledge related to *multicultural issues*." Another student stated, "I would like to see more required courses include information about *multiculturalism*. I would also like to see more *multiculturalism* classes become required courses in the program."

Similarly, several participants included the word "diversity" in their open-ended responses. For instance, one student commented, "Most of my experience in regard to *diversity* has come from my undergrad studies or my work at [workplace name removed to protect anonymity]. So far, my classes in the MLIS program have not addressed such topics." Another student noted that, "The general and/or archival tracks do not seem to emphasize *cultural diversity* so much in the program." Moreover, at least one respondent introduced used a related term, which was phrased as "cross-cultural programs." She stated, "I think being in information specialty reduces exposure to these topics. I also think online students have less access to *cross-cultural* programs and experiences."

These presumed variations of the term "cultural competence" might not be noteworthy if not for the fact that the researchers included a specific explanation of the term as it pertained to the survey questionnaire. Additionally, the term "culture" was used consistently throughout the questionnaire. One plausible reason students may have used these terms as substitutes for cultural competence is that an ideological stance of "political correctness" was operating beneath the surface of their responses.

The notion of political correctness being described here is not meant pejoratively, but rather is used to describe the ways in which people make conscious and subconscious language choices when discussing politically and racially charged issues in public spheres based on their understanding of how these terms have been taken up in the broader social and political context throughout history (Fairclough, 2003). In this sense, the respondents may have elected to use the terms that they have come to understand as aligned with a certain a political ideology. Or, perhaps they elected to use the terms they believed had the least chance of offending an audience that is presumably situated on either side of the political spectrum. For example, a student may consciously avoid using the term "diversity," given that it has been widely critiqued as being too generic to address any substantive issues (Peterson, 1996). Yet, they may still subconsciously insert the word "diversity" into a discussion about cultural issues because of its prevalence and perceived palatability in contemporary popular discourses.

By contrast, some students seemed to consciously reject the dominant discourse of political correctness and instead chose to name specific types of privilege and oppression whenever possible. For example, two students directly acknowledged Whiteness and White privilege in their responses. One of the students stated, "Since beginning at SLIS, my awareness of cultural differences and the need for specific library services for individuals of non-dominant cultures (the dominant culture being *White, Christian, heteronormative*, etc.) has increased greatly, thanks to the effort of my professors to include these topics in their curriculum." Another student used similarly direct language when opining that, "If the SLIS is serious about developing librarians to serve cultures from various backgrounds, the best solution would be to have a librarian or other person in a community that's *not Anglo-American* conduct a lesson on the libraries of that person's culture." A final student response, which further illustrates this practice of naming states, "In the [city name] area, the *black/white dynamic* is the most prevalent, but there are many other cultures that would require specialized learning in how to best interact." Within this last response, there seems to be an acknowledgement that cultural issues extend beyond routine realm of "White vs. Black," and yet there is also a recognition that most cultural discussions in the United States continue to be framed within a Black/White binary (Perea, 1997).

The Role of Libraries/Librarians in Cultural Competence

A number of student respondents used some variation of the word "serve" to describe the role of librarians in cultural competence. In particular, 8 of the 29 respondents gave remarks that contained the words *serve, service, services*, and/or *serving*. The frequent use of these words might suggest that the dominant discourse related to the role of libraries/librarians in cultural competence is undergirded by a business/management or a mission/service paradigm (Pawley, 2006).

One problem with the dominant service-oriented ideology of the role of libraries in cultural competence is that it positions librarians at a formal distance from library users. In doing so, the library user is depicted as a somewhat powerless consumer of the goods or services that an all-knowing librarian has procured for their benefit. For example, one student stated that "it is extremely important to learn and have knowledge about *services provided* to various multicultural groups with different cultural backgrounds." Although this response extols the merits of cultural competence preparation, it leaves the impression that there is some distilled collection of "services" related to multicultural groups that librarians can "purchase," or avail themselves of, if only they become aware of this content. Similarly, one student stated that, "I'd also bet that most librarians (and those in library school) are already fairly cognizant of the need to *serve and accommodate* individuals from various cultures." This comment supports the notion that "service" is a mentality so thoroughly engrained in the collective consciousness of the LIS profession that according to this student, most librarians should be "fairly cognizant" of how it works in their everyday practices. Furthermore, the use of the word "accommodate" connotes a business-like sensibility that seems more akin to a policy mandate than an authentic sense of engagement with library users.

By contrast, there were textual responses that seemed to reflect a competing discourse, which was rooted in sociocultural view of the role of libraries in cultural competence. Some of the textual clues that signaled a sociocultural ideological stance were the use of words such as *interact, interactive, experience,* and *community-driven*. Whereas the business/management and mission/service paradigms have roots in the positivist epistemological paradigm, a sociocultural perspective draws from the interpretivist tradition, which recognizes that it is impossible to fully understand someone unless you understand his or her culture. Culture in this sense refers to the patterns of behavior, beliefs, and values that are shared by a group of people. One student articulated a sociocultural view when she stated, "I specifically chose to take classes that would allow me to *interact* with and learn about people from other cultures (Urban Libraries, Special Issues, Multicultural Services). In the classes, I particularly enjoyed and found valuable experiences that forced me *out into the community*, working with others." This statement reflects a recognition that cultural competence is not merely about knowledge acquisition or service provision but calls for having authentic interactions with people and engaging with the cultural contexts of their daily lives.

The sociocultural view of the role of libraries in cultural competence brought forth some valid concerns about the conflict between online education and the development of cultural competence. For example, one student commented that "the experiences expressed in these questions are best developed with more hands-on experience, that which comes from internships and work and career experiences. It is also more difficult to gain *interactive* experiences from a primarily distance program." It should be noted that online education is a prevalent mode of course delivery in many LIS schools, including the two institutions where this study was conducted. Yet, there were student responses that clearly recognized the conundrum of trying to foster the kind of firsthand interaction that cultural competence is predicated upon in an online educational environment.

Prior Experience in Relation to Building Cultural Competence

Having prior experience in a purportedly "diverse" environment was one of the most prominent themes that the students expressed in their open-ended responses relative to cultural competence. Students who reported having prior experience also reported that their LIS education did not enhance their level of cultural competence. The types of prior experience that the students cited most included living or working in an environment that was characterized as being diverse and having educational experiences that somehow contribute to an increased awareness of multicultural issues.

All of the students who referenced having prior experience were self-identified as White. The racial identity of these student respondents is relevant to this finding as it may help illuminate the ways in which the term "diversity" was being constructed within their remarks. In turn, this may also reveal how the concept of cultural competence was being understood. For example, one respondent cited "having prior experience working at *minirity* [sic] companies in non-library environments." This reference to minority companies presupposes a contrast between predominantly White companies and companies where the majority of employees are non-White. Other students also made comments that reflect a dominant White perspective of diversity. For instance, one White respondent noted that, "By working at a library in a *diverse population*, I entered the program working with a diverse population and pool of co-workers." Another White respondent made an implicit connection between working in an urban area and having a multicultural base of prior knowledge and experience with the following statement: "Having been an *urban educator*, I had a great deal of experience and prior knowledge related to multicultural issues. My experience in LIS has not added greatly to my *prior knowledge*—with the exception of reading Elfreda Chatman." Here the use of the term "urban" connotes some kind of cultural diversity, which one might presume refers to a non-White and/or non-English-speaking community.

By comparison, there was a competing discourse relative to the theme of prior experience that reflects a nondominant, pragmatic ideological stance concerning cultural competence. For example, one of the African American respondents stated, "I wish that library/repository tours were more a part of regular class time (field trips). This happened in only 2 of my classes. Student professional orgs would offer this, but I couldn't get off from my full-time job. I will take a multi-cultural class next semester, so my answers will be different then, I hope." There are a few contextual clues in this response, which suggest a pragmatic view of prior experience that is not predicated on working in a so-called diverse environment. For example, when this student establishes the value of the library/repository tours without mentioning what type of tour it was, there seems to be a preference for gaining any library experience, whether it is explicitly culturally based or not. When coupled with her remark about not being able to get off from her full-time job, the statement begins to reveal a nondominant, pragmatic understanding of what kind of library experience might be beneficial to a non-White preservice librarian. The response suggests an understanding that the library workforce is predominantly White, and thus gaining any kind of library experience would prepare one for future employment prospects from this situated racialized perspective.

CONCLUSION AND IMPLICATIONS

Ultimately, understanding the hidden ideologies upon which cultural competence discourses are built is important to the work of any self-reflective, critically conscious LIS professional. Although this work is tenuous and messy at best, it can have positive real world implications for students. This is especially true if teachers (including school librarians) become aware of the origins of the ideologies that inform their philosophies of teaching and particularly those ideals that they hold that might alienate or place students, who are already educational outliers, further on the periphery mainstream educational discourses. While this kind of self-reflection may seem esoteric, school librarians can translate this kind of deep analysis into a signature pedagogy that builds on the inquiry-based approaches to teaching and learning that have become a trademark in school libraries (Callison & Preddy, 2006). Following are possible areas school library professionals might engage in this work:

- Hosting professional development seminars aimed at helping fellow educators scrutinize their own beliefs and practices about students using existing school artifacts (mission statement, newsletters, suspension reports, faculty meeting minutes, etc.).
- Coteaching inquiry-based lessons that allow student to trace the origins of discourses on both sides of a controversial topic (e.g., same sex marriage, affirmative action, transgender public facilities, etc.) using popular library reference texts such as the *Opposing Viewpoints* series and articles from subscription databases.

For the critically oriented school library professional, this work can serve as a conceptual mirror upon which everyday ideas and conversations related to cultural competence might be held up to scrutiny. Too often, we rely on empty platitudes when discussing our roles as culturally competent professionals. Yet, if we can begin to trace the origins of these ideas, we can move beyond mere awareness toward critical cultural competence.

NOTE

This chapter was previously published as Kumasi, K., & Hill, R. F. (2013). Examining the hidden ideologies within cultural competence discourses among library and information science (LIS) students: Implications for school library pedagogy. *School Libraries Worldwide, 19*(1), 128–141.

REFERENCES

Bennett, C. (2001). Genres of research in multicultural education. *Review of Educational Research, 71*, 171–217.

Bloome, D., Carter, S., Christian, B. M., Otto, S. O., & Shuart-Faris, N. (2004). *Discourse analysis & the study of classroom language & literacy events a microethnographic perspective.* Mahwah, NJ: Lawrence Erlbaum Associates.

Boyatzis, R. E. (1998). *Transforming qualitative information: Thematic analysis and code development.* Thousand Oaks, CA: Sage Publications.

Budd, J. (2006). Discourse analysis and the study of communication in LIS. *Library Trends, 55*(1), 65–82.

Callison, D., & Preddy, L. (2006). *The blue book on information age inquiry, instruction, and literacy.* Westport, CT: Libraries Unlimited.

Cho, J., & Trent, A. (2006). Validity in qualitative research revisited. *Qualitative Research, 14*(1), 17–28.

Cross, T. L., Bazron, B. J., Dennis, K. W., & Isaacs, M. R. (1989). *Towards a culturally competent system of care.* Washington, DC: CASSP Technical Assistance Center.

Day, R. (2001). *The modern invention of information: Discourse, history, and power.* Carbondale, IL: Southern Illinois University Press.

Dee, A. (2012). Evidence of cultural competence within teacher performance assessments. *Action in Teacher Education, 34*(3), 262–275.

Fairclough, N. (2003). 'Political correctness': The politics of language and culture. *Discourse in Society, 4*(1), 17–28.

Gay, G., & Kirkland, K. (2003). Developing cultural critical consciousness and self-reflection in preservice teacher education. *Theory into Practice, 42*(3), 181–187.

Gee, J. (1996). *Social linguistics and literacies: Ideologies in discourses* (2nd ed.). New York, NY: Routledge, Falmer, Taylor & Francis.

Helton, R. (2010). Diversity dispatch: Increasing diversity awareness with cultural competency. *Kentucky Libraries, 74*(4), 22–24.

Hernandez, F., & Kose, B. (2012). The developmental model of intercultural sensitivity: A tool for understanding principals' cultural competence. *Education & Urban Society, 44*(4), 512–530.

Hill, R. F., & Kumasi, K. (2011). Bridging the gaps: Measuring cultural competence among future school library and youth services library professionals. *School Library Media Research, 14*. Retrieved from http://www.ala.org/aasl/sites/ala.org.aasl/files/content/aasl-pubsandjournals/slr/vol14/SLR_BridgingtheGaps_V14.pdf

Honma, T. (2005). Trippin' over the color line: The invisibility of race in library and information studies. *InterActions: UCLA Journal of Education and Information Studies, 1*(2), 1–28.

Kumasi, K., & Hill, R. F. (2011). Are we there yet? Results of a gap analysis to measure LIS students' prior knowledge and actual learning of cultural competence concepts. *Journal of Education for Library and Information Science, 52*(4), 251–264.

Mestre, L. S. (2010). Librarians working with diverse populations: What impact does cultural competency training have on their efforts? *Journal of Academic Librarianship, 36*(6), 479–488.

Milner, H. (2011). Culturally relevant pedagogy in a diverse urban classroom. *Urban Review, 43*(1), 66–89.

Montiel-Overall, P. (2009). Cultural competence: A conceptual framework for library and information science professionals. *Library Quarterly, 79*(2), 175–204.

Pawley, C. (1998). Hegemony's handmaid? The library and information studies curriculum from a class perspective. *Library Quarterly, 68*(2), 123–144.

Pawley, C. (2006). Unequal legacies: Race and multiculturalism in the LIS curriculum. *Library Quarterly, 76*(2), 149–168.

Perea, J. (1997). The Black/White binary paradigm of race: The "normal science" of American racial thought. *California Law Review, 85*(5), 1213–1258.

Peterson, L. (1996). Alternative perspectives in library and information science: Issues of race. *Journal of Library and Information Science, 37*(2), 163–174.

Seright, T. J. (2007). Perspectives of registered nurse cultural competence in a rural state—Part 1. *Online Journal of Rural Nursing and Health Care, 7*(1), 47–56.

Spurgin, K. M., & Wildemuth, B. M. (2009). Analytic induction. In B. M. Wildemuth (Ed.), *Applications of social research methods to questions in information and library science* (pp. 329–337). Westport, CT: Libraries Unlimited.

Thomas, D. R. (2006). A general inductive approach for analyzing qualitative evaluation data. *American Journal of Evaluation, 27*(2), 237–246.

Youth Services Librarians' Perceptions of Cultural Knowledge: An Exploratory Study with Implications for Practice

Sandra Hughes-Hassell and Julie Stivers

ABSTRACT

Youth services librarians in the United States face the challenge of serving a growing population of youth from diverse cultural backgrounds. Youth of color make up the majority of students attending American public schools. To effectively serve these young people, youth librarians must be culturally aware and culturally competent. This chapter reports the findings of an exploratory study designed to explore the extent to which youth services librarians prioritize the need for cultural knowledge and awareness in developing effective programs and services for today's youth. It includes implications for practice.

INTRODUCTION

For the first time in U.S. history, youth of color[1] make up the majority of students attending American public schools (Krogstad & Fry, 2014). Since 2000, all of the growth in the child population has been among groups other than non-Hispanic Whites (O'Hare, 2011).

Today, one-fourth of America's children are immigrants or children of immigrants (Annie E. Casey Foundation, 2018). If these trends continue, demographers conclude that soon there will be no single racial group that makes up more than 50% of the total U.S. population (Crouch, Zakariya, & Jiandani, 2012).

These demographic changes have implications for school and public librarians in the United States, the majority of who are middle-aged, White, English-speaking females (American Library Association, 2012). As Mestre (2009) noted,

Many librarians are now struggling to connect with a completely new set of learners, with cultural backgrounds distinctly different from each other and from educators. It may be a challenge for the [librarian] who has only used teaching strategies and examples based on his or her life experiences. (p. 9)

Marcoux (2009) agreed, stressing that the "tension between groups with an idea of 'us and them' " has the potential to negatively impact the ability of librarians to work effectively with youth with different cultures, languages, learning styles, and backgrounds (p. 6). In fact, Kumasi (2012) found that many youth of color "feel like outsiders in library spaces and deem the school library as sole 'property' of the school librarian" (p. 36). She argued that these feelings of disconnect and exclusion must be attended to if librarians want to ensure that all students feel welcome.

Much of the public discourse concerning youth of color is based on a cultural deficit model of thinking—a stance that minimizes, or even ignores, the structural forces that have led to the unequal distribution of resources, lack of opportunity, and other forms of oppression and discrimination that negatively affect the lived experiences of people of color (Cabrera, 2013; Kumasi, 2012). Youth of color report significant ethnic and racial stereotyping by teachers, administrators, and their school peers (Foxen, 2010). They often feel overlooked or excluded, and they are frequently tracked into remedial and special education classes (Foxen, 2010). Less than one-third of schools with the highest percentages of African American and Latinx students offer calculus, and only 40% offer physics (U.S. Department of Education, Office for Civil Rights, 2009–2010 http://ocrdata.ed.gov/). About one in three African American and Native students and about one in four Latinx students do not graduate high school on time, compared to one in seven White students (U.S. National Center for Educational Statistics, 2014). Cabrera (2013) argued that educators and policy-makers who do not recognize the systemic nature of the racial disparities that exist in American society and who buy into this cultural deficit viewpoint contribute to the continued marginalization of these youth.

Research exists that disrupts the cultural deficit narrative. Numerous studies have shown that youth of color bring important cultural strengths to the table that, when capitalized on, can lead to increased academic achievement, positive racial identity development, improved self-confidence and self-esteem, and increased resiliency (Boykin & Noguera, 2011; Edwards, McMillon, & Turner, 2010; Foxen, 2010; Hanley & Noblit, 2009; Ladson-Billings, 2009; Padrón, Waxman, & Rivera, 2002; Rivera & Zehler, 1991). Librarians who serve youth of color and their families need to "consider these strengths alongside the challenges to get a full and comprehensive picture" of the youth of color in their communities (Cabrera, 2013, p. 7).

To do this requires cultural awareness and cultural competence (Allard, Mehra, & Qayyum, 2007; Kumasi, 2012; Mestre, 2009; Overall, 2014). Cultural awareness refers to the ability of librarians to understand the culture of people from diverse backgrounds. Cultural competence requires librarians to act on their understandings—to "respect cultural differences and to address issues of disparity among diverse populations competently" (Overall, 2014, p. 176). As Mestre (2009) pointed out, "creating culturally inclusive teaching/learning events will not only enhance the experience of students but is one step in providing an environment that affirms, respects, and acknowledges differences in individuals and in groups" (p. 11).

But do youth services librarians recognize the need to know and respect the diverse cultural backgrounds and characteristics of the youth of color that make up the majority of students attending American public schools? Do they understand that, in order to meet the needs of youth of color, it is necessary to integrate their culture into library services, programs, and collections? In this chapter, we report the findings of a study that looked at the extent to which practicing school and public librarians perceived cultural awareness and cultural competence as key to providing library services to the increasingly racially and ethnically diverse populations they serve.

RESEARCH DESIGN

Data Collection

Data for this study were collected via an electronic survey questionnaire that was distributed through three professional library email lists during the fall of 2014 (AASL Forum, ALSC-L, and YALSA-Bk). Over 6,000 individuals subscribe to these three email lists, including public and school librarians who serve youth. The text of the recruitment letter noted that school and public libraries are impacted by societal changes and invited youth librarians to share their perceptions of the key factors they believe affect their current library practice.

The survey instrument, adapted from one used by Juliá (2000) to look at social work student perceptions of culture as integral to social work practice, contained two sections. The first section consisted of six open-ended questions devised to explore the participants' level of awareness and recognition of the need for cultural competence in their professional practice. Since our intent was to determine the degree to which librarians independently perceive and prioritize issues of cultural competence in their work environments, none of the questions specifically asked about cultural issues. Instead, the extent to which the librarians recognized the need for knowledge of cultural awareness and competence was gauged by their responses to questions that addressed the following categories: recognition of the factors affecting youth (0–18) and their parents/caregivers' perceptions and attitudes about the value of libraries and their willingness to utilize library services, collections, and programs; the characteristics librarians should possess in order to be responsive to the needs of youth (0–18) and their parents/caregivers; and the biggest challenges youth services librarians face in delivering library programs, services, and materials to youth (0–18) and their parents/caregivers. The survey also asked participants to define the role of youth services librarians.

A section on demographic information included factors that might influence their awareness and perceptions of cultural competence such as race or ethnicity, age, gender, number of years of professional practice, and whether they had a master of library science (MLS) degree. Participants were also asked to indicate the type of library in which they worked (school or public), or if they were currently in a library science program, and which term best described the community served by their library (rural, suburban, or urban), if applicable.

Data Analysis

We used the constant comparative method (Lincoln & Guba, 1985), the most common method for analyzing qualitative data, to code the responses for evidence of cultural awareness and cultural competence. We independently coded the data, specifically looking for references to concepts related to cultural awareness and cultural competency, as well as specific words such as "race," "ethnicity," "diversity," "ELL" or "English as a second language," and "multiculturalism." Using Holsti's (1969) formula, intercoder reliability was calculated to be 94.3%, well above the commonly accepted 80% benchmark.

FINDINGS

Eighty-seven of the 338 participants who began the survey completed it. While this number is admittedly low, we believe it is sufficient given the exploratory nature of the study. Forty-three of the respondents (49%) were public librarians serving children and/or teens, and 33 (38%) were school librarians ranging from elementary to high school. Five respondents (6%) who indicated "other" were public library administrators. Four respondents (5%) were enrolled currently in a library and information science (LIS) program. Sixty-five (79%) of the respondents had earned an MLS degree; over one-third had received their degree in the past five years. Participants were asked to describe the type of community they served. Forty-four selected suburban (54%), 24 chose urban (30%), and 13 (16%) indicated rural.

Of the 81 respondents who answered the race/ethnicity question, 70 (86%) respondents identified as White, 3 (4%) as Hispanic/Latinx, 3 (4%) as 2 or more races, and 1 as African American. Five (6%) chose not to identify their race or ethnicity. Eighty-one participants answered the question asking for age. The majority (65%) were 40 or over. Of the 82 respondents who answered the question regarding gender, 73 identified as female (89%), 8 as male (10%), and 1 as other (1%) (see Table 1 for demographic data).

The respondents were given the opportunity to address elements of cultural awareness, cultural competence, and culturally relevant pedagogy in six questions. As Table 2 shows, only 15 of the 87 respondents, or 17%, included any culture-related reference in their answers to any of the six questions designed to elicit this information.

Table 1
Demographic Data for Respondents

Race/Ethnicity	White	African American	Latinx/Hispanic	Two or more races	Prefer not to report
n=82	70 (86%)	1 (1%)	3 (4%)	3 (4%)	4 (5%)
Gender	Female		Male		Other
n=82	73 (89%)		8 (10%)		1 (1%)
Age	20–29	30–39	40–49	50+	Prefer not to report
n=81	14 (17%)	20 (25%)	18 (22%)	28 (35%)	1 (1%)

Table 2

Culture-Related Responses

Participant	Responses
1	• Youth services librarians provide relative outreach and programming to the diverse groups of children that patron a library[1]
2	• Librarian recognizes the culture of the community and blends in the needs of the community into the collection and programming[1]
3	• Open to diversity[2]
4	• So often librarians overlook the population of immigrants[2]
5	• Respectful of different cultural standards[2] • Multicultural understanding[4]
6	• Feeling welcomed into an institution, regardless of background, literacy, language, affluence, and experience is critical[3] • Language levels[4]
7	• Materials that reflect the needs and diversity in community[3] • Reach all socioeconomic, cultural, and other diverse backgrounds with materials and programming[4] • Not enough staff to serve all segments of our communities[5] • Publishers need to realize the diverse segments of populations and need to publish books that reflect that diversity[6]
8	• Expressions of sincere concern for learning no matter their educational, religious, or ethnic backgrounds[3]
9	• Culturally aware collection and programming[3]
10	• Language barriers can be a challenge as well[4] • More collaboration with underserved populations (ESL speakers)[6]
11	• Cultural awareness[4]
12	• Language and cultural barriers[5]
13	• Language barriers—not enough staff are bilingual[5]
14	• More multicultural offerings[6]
15	• Community awareness and embeddedness; know your community well, be connected to the people who drive it, whether church leaders, business owners, tribal leaders, and so forth[6]

Survey Questions Eliciting the above Responses

[1] Define the role of youth services librarians.

[2] List the most important characteristics you believe a librarian should possess in order to be responsive to the needs of youth and their parents/caregivers.

[3] List the factors that you believe impact youth and their parents/caregivers' perceptions and attitudes about the value of libraries.

[4] List the factors that you believe influence youth and their parents/caregivers' utilization of library programs, services, and materials.

[5] What do you think is the biggest challenge youth services librarians face in delivering library programs, services, and materials to youth and their parents/caregivers?

[6] List the changes you believe are needed to make library programs, services, and materials more responsive to youth and their parents/caregivers.

Eleven participants provided one response that included some specific indication of cultural awareness, three participants provided two culture-related responses, and one participant answered four questions with responses containing cultural content. (Although outside the scope of this chapter, it was noteworthy that there were other omissions in terms of inclusivity. No study participants mentioned any issues related to LGBTQ youth or patrons with disabilities in response to any of the study questions.)

Although we collected data on factors that might influence the participants' awareness and perceptions of cultural competence such as race or ethnicity, age, gender, number of years of professional practice, and whether they had an MLS, only race/ethnicity emerged as noteworthy. Of the seven participants who identified as Black, Hispanic/Latinx, or two or more races, 43% (n=3) included multicultural content in their answers. Of the 70 participants who identified as White, only 17% (n=12) answered with any multicultural content. Age and gender seemed to have no effect on cultural awareness. Likewise, participants without an MLS were just as likely as those with an MLS to include some specific indication of cultural awareness. The only outlier related to professional position. None of the elementary school librarians (9% of respondents) referenced multicultural content in their answers.

When the data are examined at the question level, the lack of cultural awareness or competence becomes even more visible. The survey's six questions generated 512 responses, yet only 21 responses (4%) contained any reference to culture, and 10 of those 21 responses (48%) were from the same four participants. Only one response mentioned a specific racial or ethnic community (tribal), only one response included the word "ethnic," and only five mentioned language differences (four including "language" in the response, and one mentioning "ESL speakers").

In the first open-ended question, participants were asked to define the role of youth services librarians. Empowering youth, supporting young adult development, promoting literacy development, and providing innovative programming, research assistance, technology instruction, and outreach to youth and their families were all recognized, as was providing informational and leisure reading materials in multiple formats. However, only two participants mentioned the need to consider the culture of community members in developing these programs and services.

Question two specifically asked the respondents to list the most important characteristics a librarian must possess to be responsive to the needs of youth. Of the 88 separate responses provided, only 3 (3%) included any reference to cultural awareness. As a point of comparison, the researchers checked to see how frequently knowledge of the developmental needs of youth, another important consideration identified by the profession as central to developing responsive library programs for youth (cf Gorman & Sullentrop, 2009; Young Adult Library Services Association, 2017), was mentioned in this question's responses. Twenty-one of the 88 responses (24%) indicated the need for an understanding of youth developmental characteristics.

Question three asked participants to list the factors they believe impact youth and their parents/caregivers' perceptions and attitudes about libraries. Respondents included in their responses knowledge about what libraries have to offer; previous experience with libraries; whether libraries and librarians are welcoming, inviting, and friendly; and patrons' socioeconomic status, but again, reference to culture was virtually absent.

When asked in question four to list the factors that influenced youth and their parents/caregivers' utilizations of library programs, services, and materials, culture-related responses were minimal. Again, factors related to socioeconomic status were mentioned such as "the digital divide," "poverty," and "lack of money."

In question five, the participants were asked to indicate the biggest challenge youth services librarians are facing. Even though the question asked for the "biggest challenge," survey responses were broad, with a majority of participants including at least three issues in their response. Eighty-five total responses were provided; 39 (46%) listed budget or funding issues as compared to only three (4%) responses mentioning culture. Are budget and funding issues of monumental concern for librarians? Of course. This study is not suggesting otherwise. However, to adequately serve today's youth—based on what research shows in terms of unequal access, opportunity gaps, and lack of diversity in published materials (Boykin & Noguera, 2011; Cooperative Children's Book Center, 2014; Foxen, 2010; National Assessment of Educational Progress, 2014)—the researchers maintain that issues related to culturally relevant practices must also be a critical concern for librarians. This is especially true since budget issues are disproportionately impacting library services to communities of color in the form of library closures, reduced hours, lack of quality staff, and absence of funding for collection development (Hoffman, Bertot, Davis, & Clark, 2011).

The final question asked participants to list the changes that are most needed to make library programs, services, and materials more responsive to youth and their caregivers. As with previous questions, the responses drew relatively little evidence that the participants prioritized cultural awareness. The most frequent answers were related to marketing and increased funding as compared to only four (5%) with any mention of culture.

DISCUSSION

The most prominent and revealing finding of this study was the apparent lack of cultural awareness and competence reflected by the responses. In this section, we offer possible explanations for the relatively few culture-related responses by the participants. Each of the explanations, while not generalizable, warrants further exploration and raises issues for the LIS professional community to consider.

One possible explanation for the findings is the "implicit pervasiveness of cultural ethnocentrism," which is defined as the nonconscious tendency to view one's ethnic or cultural group as centrally important, and to measure all other groups in relation to one's own (Juliá, 2000, p. 286). The majority of our study participants, like the majority of librarians, were White. Unless these librarians had engaged in meaningful and reflective study of the historical and contemporary impact of race, racism, power, and privilege in the United States, they may not understand how their ethnic, cultural, and linguistic backgrounds guide their perceptions, attitudes, and behaviors. Unaware of the historical privileges associated with Whiteness, including access to employment, housing, health care, education, and even library services, they may have a minimal understanding of how cultural differences "make radical differences to the ways people experience and understand the world" (Segall & Garrett, 2013, p. 286). The normativeness of their race, their Whiteness, thus, may be one factor contributing to their apparent lack of understanding of the importance of cultural considerations in the design and delivery of library services to diverse communities. This explanation is further supported by research that shows that "the current culture represented in many libraries is the culture of mainstream communities, even when those libraries are located in areas that are distinctly different from mainstream communities" (Overall, 2009, p. 199).

Another possible explanation for the findings is the reluctance, and even discomfort, the vast majority of Americans have about discussing issues related to race and ethnicity—two dimensions that are central to any discussion or consideration of culture in the United States (Segall & Garrett, 2013). As Pawley (2006) noted, "LIS practitioners and educators tend to avoid the *R* word" (p. 151). This tendency to avoid discussions about race or ethnicity has been attributed to "fear of controversy and attempting to avoid community criticism, the desire not to be considered racist" (Segall & Garret, 2013, p. 267); the belief that we live in a post-racial society (Hsu, 2009); or the belief that colorblindness, or not seeing race, is a "graceful, even generous, liberal gesture" (Morrison, 1992, p. 9). The plausibility of this explanation is supported by two trends we noticed in the data. First, none of the participants mentioned the word "race" and only one the word "ethnic" in their responses; this despite the fact that it is likely that many of the respondents' patrons are youth and families of color. Instead, neutral words like "multicultural," "cultural awareness," or "diversity" were used. As Pawley (2006) noted, these words are often "used as a way of referring, in particular to race and ethnicity" although the terms are far from equivalent (pp. 151–152). Second, the frequency with which the participants mentioned socioeconomics as an important factor to consider in developing programs and services shows that the participants do understand the impact that community demographics have on libraries. For example, one participant noted, "Some [patrons] would like to utilize the library's services but don't have the transportation or internet access to do it remotely. Some may have old fines—or perceived old fines—and, depending on that library's policies, may not be able to access materials or services or think they cannot." Another said, "Many of these families often lack access to the internet as well because ... of lack of money for home internet service in poor urban areas." Talking about poverty and low wealth is often seen, especially by people from the dominant culture in the United States, as safer than raising issues related to race or ethnicity (Sue, 2013).

Another explanation for the findings of this study may be the lack of LIS coursework related to diversity and inclusion. Although the 2008 American Library Association's (ALA) "Standards for Accreditation of Master's Programs in Library and Information Studies" requires that program objectives reflect "the role of the library and information services in a diverse, global society, including the role of serving the needs of underserved groups" (p. 6), researchers have shown that students graduating from LIS programs have taken few, if any, classes related to diversity. The availability of diversity-related courses varies from one LIS program to another, with iSchools offering the fewest (Subramaniam & Jaeger, 2010). Across all types of LIS programs, the vast majority of diversity-related courses are electives that are offered infrequently, if at all (Subramaniam & Jaeger, 2011). Mestre (2010) found that nearly 80% of the students graduating from LIS programs indicated that they had not taken even one class related to diversity. Thus, despite the fact that 33% of the respondents had received their MLS degree in the last five years, it is likely that few of them, if any, had taken an academic or a formal course on serving diverse populations. Their lack of culture-related responses may, thus, be attributed to the library field's apparent unwillingness to mandate diversity-related coursework for all LIS students. One final explanation may be historical. As Berry (1999) explained,

[T]he history of the profession has shown that cultural competence has rarely blessed our professional practice or even penetrated our professional consciousness. Librarians seldom learn the language, collect the literatures, or understand in any way the beliefs, traditions, morals and mores, lifestyles, or aspirations and expectations of the minority cultures in their midst. We reach out to hand them only our culture and heritage, rather than receiving and learning about theirs and respectfully adding them to our collections and personal service. (p. 14)

CONCLUSIONS AND IMPLICATIONS

The lack of culture-related responses was surprising and discouraging, especially given the national focus on issues related to race and diversity in the United States. In April 2014 the death of Michael Brown, the unarmed African American teenager killed by a White police officer in Ferguson, Missouri, brought national attention to disparities in the American justice system. One of the overriding themes that emerged in the aftermath of this tragedy was the disconnect between the local predominantly White police force and the African American community of Ferguson. In spring 2014, the Twitter sphere erupted with discussions of the lack of diverse, nondominant cultural narratives in children's literature. Fueled by the We Need Diverse Books campaign and the twitter hashtag #WeNeedDiverseBooks, this discussion brought the need for books by and about people of color to the consciousness, once again,[2] of librarians, teachers, parents, and publishers. Professional journals like *School Library Journal*, one of the journals most frequently read by youth services librarians, joined the conversation, devoting an entire issue in May 2014 to the topic of diversity. Additionally, two of the national professional associations serving youth services librarians released white papers in 2014 that focused on the need for greater cultural awareness among librarians. *The Future of Library Services for and with Teens: A Call to Action* (Braun, Hartman, Hughes-Hassell, Kumasi, & Yoke, 2014) released in January specifically recognizes the demographic shift that is occurring in the United States and notes, "Now is the time for the field of librarianship, the population of which is overwhelmingly Caucasian, to consider what these demographic changes mean to school and public library services and programs for and with teens" (p. 2). In April, the Association for Library Service to Children (ALSC) released the white paper *The Importance of Diversity in Library Programs and Material Collections for Children* (Naidoo, 2014) that explores the critical role that librarians play in helping children make cross-cultural connections and develop skills necessary to function in a culturally pluralistic society. In the new American Association of School Librarians (AASL) *National School Library Standards* (2018), one of the frameworks is "Include." Clearly, conversations about diversity and its impact on society are occurring in the United States and in the youth services profession itself. The basic question, then, is how do we encourage youth services librarians to become more active participants in these conversations and to consider the implications cultural differences have for their work with youth of color?

Fortunately, there are a number of avenues available to enable youth services librarians to become culturally aware and culturally competent. Increasingly the youth divisions of ALA are focusing specifically on topics such as culturally inclusive programming, supporting healthy racial identity development, recognizing and disrupting implicit bias, creating inclusive library collections, and implementing restorative practices in their webinars, conferences, and professional resources. More public libraries and public school systems are centering equity, diversity, and inclusion in their strategic plans and requiring library staff to participate in racial equity training. Many library administrators ask applicants to complete a diversity statement as part of the hiring process or to provide documentation that demonstrates their ability to work with culturally and ethnically diverse communities.

Researchers at the School of Information and Library Science at the University of North Carolina at Chapel Hill have developed two free online resources focused on building the cultural awareness and cultural competency skills of librarians. Project READY (https://ready.web.unc.edu/), a free online curriculum, is designed to equip librarians with the knowledge and skills necessary to reach all students equitably and powerfully, in ways that connect with and affirm their individual and cultural identities. It not only helps librarians understand the theory, rationale, and principles of cultural competence, but it also supports librarians as they enact these ideas in their communities. Foundational understandings such as the history of race and racism in the United States, implicit bias and microaggressions, and unpacking Whiteness are explored as well as concrete ideas for transforming practice. *Equitable and Inclusive Libraries for Youth: A Professional Development Resource (*https://inclusivelibraries.web.unc.edu/*)* provides resources librarians and other library staff who serve diverse youth in public and school libraries can use to gain the skills and knowledge needed to develop inclusive, bias-free, and equitable library collections, services, and programs that better meet the needs of diverse youth. The resource aligns with the ALSC, YALSA, and AASL's professional competencies and standards and includes a range of high-quality professional development resources related to diversity and equity.

Social media platforms, like Twitter, make it possible for librarians to participate in ongoing conversations with other like-minded professionals who are committed to better meeting the needs of their diverse communities. Librarians can learn from national experts, "peek in" on conferences or other events they cannot attend in person, and engage in book studies of popular titles such as *So You Want to Talk about Race* by Ijeoma Oluo (2018) and *We Got This! Equity, Access, and the Quest to Be Who Our Students Need Us to Be* by Cornelius Minor (2018). Table 3 provides a sample list of Twitter chats that focus on issues related to equity.

As Jaeger, Bertot, and Subramaniam (2013) argued, if the library community "does not evolve along with the demographic evolution of our nation, the real threat to the future of libraries ... will be the library becoming an organization that is ossified and irrelevant to much of society" (p. 246). The results of this study suggest that there is much work to be done to ensure that all young people and their families, including people of color, "see themselves in the information resources, services, and programs being made available" (Jaeger et al., 2013, p. 246).

Table 3
Twitter Chat Hashtags

#Educolor—Activists of color in education chat; every fourth Thursday, 7:30 p.m. EST
#Cleartheair—An activist reading community that delves into books related to equity; monthly, 7:30 p.m. EST
#CritLib—Critical library pedagogy chat; every other Tuesday, 9 p.m. EST
#TLChat—Teacher librarian chat; every second Monday, 8–9 p.m. EST
#EdChat—Education chat; every Tuesday, 12–1 p.m. and 7–8 p.m. EST

NOTE

This chapter was previously published as Hughes-Hassell, S., & Stivers, J. (2015). Examining youth services librarians' perceptions of cultural knowledge as an integral part of their professional practice. *School Libraries Worldwide, 21*(1), 121–136.

ENDNOTES

1. The authors use the terms "youth of color" or "people of color" to refer to Black, African American, Latinx, and Asian Americans as opposed to the terms "non-White" or "minority." The term "non-White" normalizes Whiteness and reinforces the privileged position of Whites in the United States. As the demographic data show, the term "minority" is inaccurate.

2. The lack of diverse titles and the implications this has for youth of color, as well as White youth, first received national attention in 1965 when Nancy Larrick published her landmark article, "The All-White World of Children's Books."

REFERENCES

Allard, S., Mehra, B., & Qayyum, M. A. (2007). Intercultural leadership toolkit for librarians: Building awareness to effectively serve diverse multicultural populations. *Education Libraries Journal*, 30(1), 5–12.

American Association of School Librarians (AASL). (2018). *National School Library Standards for learners, school librarians, and libraries*. Chicago, IL: American Library Association.

American Library Association (ALA). (2012). *Diversity counts 2012 tables*. Chicago, IL: ALA. Retrieved from http://www.ala.org/aboutala/sites/ala.org.aboutala/files/content/diversity/diversitycounts/diversitycountstables2012.pdf

Annie E. Casey Foundation. (2018). *National KIDS count*. Baltimore, MD: Annie E. Casey Foundation.

Berry, J. N. (1999). Culturally competent service: To women and people of colour. *Library Journal, 124*(14), 112.

Boykin, A. W., & Noguera, P. (2011). *Creating the opportunity to learn: Moving from research to practice to close the achievement gap*. Alexandria, VA: ASCD.

Braun, L. W., Hartman, M. L., Hughes-Hassell, S., Kumasi, K., & Yoke, B. (2014). *The future of library services for and with teens: A call to action*. Chicago, IL: American Library Association. Retrieved from http://www.ala.org/yaforum/sites/ala.org.yaforum/files/content/YALSA_nationalforum_final.pdf

Cabrera, N. J. (2013). Minority children and their families: A positive look. In *Being Black is not a risk factor: A strengths-based look at the state of the Black child*. Washington, DC: National Black Child Development Institute.

Cooperative Children's Book Center. (2014). *Children's books by and about people of color published in the United States*. Retrieved from ccbc.education.wisc.edu/books/pcstats.asp

Crouch, R., Zakariya, S. B., & Jiandani, J. (2012). *The United States of education: The changing demographics of the United States and their schools*. Alexandria, VA: Center for Public Education.

Edwards, P. A., McMillon, G. T., & Turner, J. D. (2010). *Change is gonna come: Transforming literacy education for African American students*. New York, NY: Columbia Teachers College.

Foxen, P. (2010). *Speaking out: Latino youth on discrimination in the United States*. Washington, DC: National Council of La Raza.

Gorman, M., & Sullentrop, T. A. (2009). *Connecting young adults and libraries: A how-to-guide* (6th ed.). Chicago, IL: American Library Association.

Hanley, M. S., & Noblit, G. W. (2009). *Cultural responsiveness, racial identity, and academic success: A review of the literature.* Retrieved from http://www.heinz.org/UserFiles/Library/Culture-Report_FINAL.pdf

Hoffman, J., Bertot, J. C., Davis, D. M., & Clark, L. (2011). *Libraries connect communities: Public library funding and technology access study 2010–2011: Executive summary.* Chicago, IL: American Library Association. Retrieved from http://www.ala.org/tools/files/initiatives/plftas/2010_2011/plftas11-execsummary.pdf

Holsti, O. R. (1969). *Content analysis for the social sciences and humanities.* Reading, MA: Addison-Wesley Publishers.

Hsu, H. (2009, January/February). The end of White America. *The Atlantic Monthly Online.* Retrieved from https://www.theatlantic.com/magazine/archive/2009/01/the-end-of-white-america/307208/

Krogstad, J. M., & Fry, R. (2014). Dept. of Ed. projects public schools will be "majority-minority" this fall. Retrieved from https://www.pewresearch.org/fact-tank/2014/08/18/u-s-public-schools-expected-to-be-majority-minority-starting-this-fall/

Jaeger, P. T., Bertot, J. C., & Subramaniam, M. (2013). Preparing future librarians to effectively serve their communities. *Library Quarterly: Information, Community, Policy, 83*(3), 243–248.

Juliá, M. (2000). Student perceptions of culture: An integral part of social work practice. *International Journal of Intercultural Relations, 24,* 279–289.

Kumasi, K. D. (2012). Roses in the concrete: A critical race theory perspective on urban youth and school libraries. *Knowledge Quest, 40*(4), 32–37.

Ladson-Billings, G. (2009). *The dreamkeepers: Successful teaching of African American children* (2nd ed.). San Francisco, CA: Jossey Bass.

Lincoln, Y., & Guba, E. (1985). *Naturalistic inquiry.* Newbury Park, CA: Sage.

Marcoux, E. (2009). Diversity and the teacher-librarian. *Teacher Librarian, 36*(3), 6–7.

Mestre, L. (2009). Culturally responsive instruction for teacher-librarians. *Teacher Librarian, 36* (3), 8–12.

Mestre, L. (2010). Librarians working with diverse populations: What impact does cultural competency training have on their efforts. *Journal of Academic Librarianship, 36*(6), 479–488.

Minor, C. (2018). *We got this! Equity, access, and the quest to be who our students need us to be.* Portsmouth, NH: Heinemann.

Morrison, T. (1992). *Playing in the dark: Whiteness and the literary imagination.* New York, NY: Vintage Books.

Naidoo, J. C. (2014). *The importance of diversity in library programs and material collections for children.* Chicago, IL: American Library Association.

National Assessment of Educational Progress. (2014). Achievement gaps. U.S. Department of Education. Retrieved from http://nces.ed.gov/nationsreportcard/studies/gaps/

O'Hare, W. (2011). *The changing child population of the United States: Analysis of data from the 2010 census.* Baltimore, MD: The Annie E. Casey Foundation.

Oluo, I. (2018). *So you want to talk about race.* New York, NY: Hachette Books.

Overall, P. M. (2009). Cultural competence: A conceptual framework for library and information science professionals. *Library Quarterly, 79*(2), 175–204.

Overall, P. M. (2014). Developing cultural competence and a better understanding of Latino language and culture through literature. *Children and Libraries, 12*(2), 27–31.

Padrón, Y. N., Waxman, H. C., & Rivera, H. H. (2002). *Educating Hispanic students: Obstacles and avenues to improved academic achievement.* Santa Cruz, CA: University of California Center for Research on Education, Diversity & Excellence.

Pawley, C. (2006). Unequal legacies: Race and multiculturalism in the LIS curriculum. *Library Quarterly, 76,* 149–168.

Rivera, C., & Zehler, A. M. (1991). Assuring the academic success of language minority students: Collaboration in teaching and learning. *Journal of Education, 173*(2), 52–77.

Segall, A., & Garrett, J. (2013). White teachers talking race. *Teaching Education, 24*(3), 265–291.

Subramaniam, M., & Jaeger, P. T. (2010). Modeling inclusive practice? Attracting diverse faculty and future faculty to the information workforce. *Library Trends, 59*(1/2), 109–127.

Subramaniam, M., & Jaeger, P. T. (2011). Weaving diversity into LIS: An examination of diversity course offerings in iSchool programs. *Education for Information, 28*(1), 1–19.

Sue, D. W. (2013). Race talk: The psychology of racial dialogues. *American Psychologist, 68*(8), 663–672.

U.S. National Center for Educational Statistics. (2014). Status and trends in the education of racial and ethnic groups. Retrieved from https://nces.ed.gov/programs/raceindicators/indicator_RDC.asp

Young Adult Library Services Association (YALSA). (2017). *Teen services competencies for library staff.* Chicago, IL: American Library Association.

Moving Toward Culturally Relevant Librarianship: Booktalking in a Mixed Reality Simulation

Janice Underwood, Sue Kimmel, Danielle Hartsfield, and
Gail Dickinson

ABSTRACT

The role of school librarians is often overlooked in advancing a respect for cultural diversity among youth, yet librarians are in key positions to champion for social justice reform in educational settings. In this chapter, we examine preservice school librarians' experiences with booktalking multicultural literature in a mixed reality simulation environment. Our purpose was to explore the booktalking experience as a means of developing preservice librarians' understanding of ways culturally relevant pedagogy (CRP), a stance concerned with developing academic success with cultural competence and critical consciousness, can be applied to library science. Our findings revealed that preservice librarians gained different levels of cultural understanding; yet, the experience provided them with an opportunity for engaging in critical reflection regarding personal bias and systemic racism in schools and literature, which is an initial step toward culturally relevant librarianship.

INTRODUCTION

A particular challenge for educators of preservice school librarians is how to promote the practice of CRP in school libraries. CRP, as popularized by Ladson-Billings (1995), is defined as teaching practices that build on the student's family dynamics, languages, ethnicities, communication discourses, value systems, and overall life experiences. Further, CRP supports academic achievement and challenges the educational and political system that was built around a hegemonic theory of oppression for students of color (Villegas, 1991; Young, 2010). Many multicultural studies cite the limitation that educators are unsure of what CRP looks like as a tool for social justice reform because they were never given the opportunity to learn, use, or model it (Kumasi & Hill, 2013; Sleeter, 2011; Villegas, 1991; Young, 2010). Hill and Kumasi (2011) demonstrated that school librarians in particular do not feel their preparation programs train them to become culturally competent pedagogues.

This chapter provides a tangible example of how school librarians and other educators can increase their propensity for cultural competency and sociopolitical teaching, using the technology of a mixed reality simulation to promote what Young (2011) calls a meaningful and safe dialogue about race and other cultural differences. Preservice school librarians enrolled in a master's level school librarianship class were asked to perform booktalks using multicultural literature in a mixed reality simulation with actors televised as avatars representing multicultural adolescents. These preservice school librarians were given the opportunity to discuss their epistemological views about cultural practices and sociopolitical teaching and to share their perceptions about the mixed reality simulation.

Research Questions

The study focused on the following research questions:

RQ1. What are the perceptions by candidates of multicultural booktalking before and after the mixed reality experience?

RQ2. How is the mixed reality simulation an effective tool for teaching CRP?

THEORETICAL AND LITERATURE PERSPECTIVES

Much of the current thought and practice about teaching to and for diversity has been influenced by the work of Ladson-Billings (1995), who is credited with the concept of "culturally relevant pedagogy" (CRP), or teaching where educators intentionally facilitate academic success with high expectations, cultural competence, and critical consciousness to prepare students to engage in lifelong learning and democratic citizenship by fighting against social injustices. According to Ladson-Billings (1995, 2000), high academic success is fostered when teaching and learning are focused on student achievement, critical thinking, rigorous learning outcomes, and real world examples that exemplify challenging concepts. Cultural competence is more than fostering personal knowledge about a cultural other; it develops when an educator has the ability to promote students' own understanding of their culture while simultaneously exposing oppressive cultures or practices. Lastly, an educator fosters critical consciousness when he or she helps students to confront systemic inequities, racist ideologies, and societal injustices perpetuated by the status quo. There has been a call to make this pedagogy more critical and to actively guide students to wrestle with issues of social injustice and power (Giroux, 2000).

Kumasi and Hill (2013) conducted a discourse analysis to investigate the perceived cultural competence of library and information science (LIS) students. They suggest there are hidden and competing discourses in LIS surrounding the role of school librarians in cultural competence because of ambiguous multicultural rhetoric, the desire to be viewed as politically correct, and conflicting ideologies or paradigms of thought.

The practice of booktalking to share literature has long been a staple of librarianship, with numerous books (Cole, 2010; Mahood, 2010; Schall, 2011) and practitioner articles extolling the practice for librarians (Chance & Lesesne, 2012; Langemack, 2010; Young, 2003). Booktalks involve short introductions to specific book titles in order to entice readers to those titles. Bodart (2010) notes that there has been little research from the library field about the outcomes of booktalking. Although teaching with multicultural literature has received attention in the literature (Hinton-Johnson & Dickinson, 2005; Landt, 2008; Lowery & Sabis-Burns, 2007), the practice of booktalking multicultural literature has been the subject of only a few articles (York, 2008, 2009). However, using multicultural literature to guide conversations about race and injustice with young students has the potential to promote CRP (Souto-Manning, 2009).

Background of the Current Study

In this study, preservice school librarians engaged in booktalking to a virtual multicultural audience and were provided with several structured opportunities to reflect and create meaning about the experience including pre- and post-booktalk chats and readings. The experience itself occurred in Teach-Live, a mixed reality teaching lab where candidates interacted with actor-controlled avatars in the roles of diverse middle school students (ages 11–14 years old). The teaching lab consisted of a room where the preservice school librarians interacted in a simulation of a small classroom. Simulation technologies such as Second Life have been the subject of research into preservice education related to teaching efficacy (Cheong, 2010) and equity (Brown, Davis, & Kulm, 2011). Such simulations offer a rich environment for candidates to apply and practice teaching in a way "that reduces real world risks, complications, costs, and ineffectiveness" (Cheong, 2010, p. 870). The mixed reality setting used in this study, Teach-Live, was mediated by an onsite technician and provided a low-risk simulation of a real classroom. The virtual simulations also provided the basis for synchronous and asynchronous discussions and self-reflections that led to a genuine critique of personal experiences, ideologies, professional philosophies, and considerations for future praxis.

METHODS

Participants and Data Collection

Participants in this study were enrolled in LIBS 678, a hybrid summer course that included selection, collection development, and materials for adolescents. Much of the course took place asynchronously online, but candidates came to campus for a two-day residency. Assignments included reading, listening, and experiencing materials for adolescents from several categories including award winners and multiple genres and formats. Among the required categories were several multicultural ones including international, African American, Latinx, or Asian American characters or themes.

A course staple, the booktalking assignment, required candidates to booktalk in front of any adolescent audience, and the preservice candidates historically chose groups with whom they were familiar and very comfortable. Therefore, in reaction to the call to reform educator preparation with antiracist teaching (Ladson-Billings, 2000), we wanted to intentionally restructure this assignment to introduce the ideals of CRP, facilitating an opportunity for the preservice librarians to wrestle with their cultural identities and biases, and in so doing, allow them to expose injustices experienced in literature to their students. The Teach-Live Lab offered such an opportunity and fit the short time available to this course with the benefit of providing every candidate with a similar controlled experience.

Candidates were told that they should prepare to deliver a five-minute booktalk of two or three multicultural titles to be given in a teaching simulation consisting of five avatars representing middle grade students (approximately 11–14 years old). The student avatars included two females and three males; two were African Americans, two Caucasians, and one Latinx. Candidates were placed in groups of three to five for pre- and post-online booktalk group chats. The pre-booktalk chat occurred synchronously using the chat feature in Blackboard, an online course management system. Chats were recorded, and the transcripts served as one data source for this study. Groups were given the following prompts for this first chat: (1) What book or books have you selected for your booktalk and why? and (2) How are you feeling as you anticipate this experience?

Candidates took turns presenting their booktalks in the Teach-Live Lab. The technician operating the lab strictly enforced the five-minute limit. All booktalks were videotaped to facilitate grading the assignment. Only the booktalks from participants who had signed consent forms were transcribed by the graduate research assistants (GRAs). The actors who operated the avatars also provided signed consent to permit videotaping.

The Teach-Live Lab provided behavioral challenges within a continuum of five levels, with the fifth level representing the most disruptive behavior from the avatars. Disruptions included avatars who called out verbal challenges such as "Why do we have to learn this?" or who were disengaged, almost asleep, in class. The preservice school librarians in this study were mostly experienced classroom teachers, and we were not concerned as much with their ability to "manage behaviors" but wanted a realistic experience of talking with an unfamiliar and diverse audience. We provided the actors remotely controlling the avatars with a copy of the assignment and the following instructions: "We would like the avatars to respond with a challenge or reaction (level 2) that includes or reflects a cultural or racial perspective about the book (which may manifest as behavioral challenges) but would like the candidates to complete their booktalks receiving honest feedback (both positive and negative)."

After the on-campus visit and virtual booktalking experience, the preservice school librarians read an article by Ladson-Billings (1995) considered a seminal work in the area of CRP and were asked to reflect on the article and the experience on their group's Blackboard discussion board. This discussion employed a threaded discussion rather than real time chat to facilitate the composition of more reflective responses. These responses were collected by the GRAs as one of the data sources.

Grades for the assignment and the final course grades were posted before the faculty members analyzed the data in order to avoid a conflict of interest and to preserve participant anonymity. Consent forms and the four data sources were handled by the GRAs. The pre-booktalk chats, transcribed booktalk videotapes, and the post-booktalk discussion forums were scrubbed of any mention of nonconsenting candidates, and pseudonyms were assigned to consenting participants. As a part of the consent form process, participants were asked to provide some demographic information, and this information was connected with the appropriate pseudonym.

Eight candidates consented to participate, but one withdrew from the course, so seven participants remained. All participants were female. One, Emily, was African American, and others identified themselves as either "Caucasian or European

American." Participants provided some information about the demographics of their school systems; this information was self-reported and varied in specificity.

Data Analysis

Transcriptions were placed in Excel spreadsheets with a separate tab for each source. The research team met as pairs consisting of a faculty member and a GRA to look at the pre- and post-booktalk chat transcripts. Statements by the candidates from these data sources served as the unit of analysis. The transcripts of the actual booktalks and field notes from the GRAs were only used to understand the context of participant comments. The entire team met subsequently to discuss and compare findings. Nieto's (2010) framework for levels of multicultural education guided further analysis of the substantial amount of data coded as "cultural."

The team met together to discuss and code each line from the chat based on the levels of (1) monocultural, (2) tolerance, (3) acceptance, (4) respect, and (5) affirmation, solidarity, and critique from the Nieto (2010) framework. When there was disagreement, the team discussed each contested code. For example, when Abby said, "It is so important for students to feel valued and an easy way to accomplish this is to be respectful to your students and their parents/guardians," the team was torn between level two (tolerance) and level four (respect) because on one hand, Abby is using the terminology of "respect." However, as one of the team members pointed out, this statement actually represents a statement commensurate with the tolerance level because while the importance of valuing students is widely accepted, it is not as "easy" as simply being respectful to them and their families. Team members then used a shared understanding of the Nieto (2010) framework to revisit the chat transcripts.

FINDINGS

Findings are presented according to the Nieto (2010) levels. In Nieto's words, "this model can assist us in determining how particular school policies and practices need to change in order to embrace the diversity of our students and their communities" (p. 249). In terms of this study, the hope was that Nieto's (2010) model would assist us in developing a continuum for considering how library practices such as booktalking might promote and support diversity.

Monocultural

Nieto described a monocultural school as one where the dominant culture's centric position is taken for granted in practices, pedagogy, materials, and curriculum (2010, pp. 249–251). Monocultural comments were present in some of the participants' responses, particularly those that treated cultural differences as monolithic or generalizable to all members of a culture. Some remarks suggested that the families and cultures of diverse students were deficient compared to the candidates themselves, "When education is neither stressed nor valued in the home, it makes our job that much harder" (Abby). Abby even went so far as to suggest a more monocultural society would be more desirable, "Maybe it would be better to be a country like Italy or somewhere that is not as diverse. Sometimes I wonder if by trying to be the so called 'Jack of all cultures,' we are the master of none."

Camilla also suggested that her booktalk choice was "a perfect example of how important an education is, how it can change your life/circumstances in a powerful way and also that everyone, if they have the discipline, can do it." Her remark is characteristic of seeing lower social class as a personal choice rather than as a result of systemic inequalities with limited opportunities for advancement and suggested her belief in a level educational playing field.

Candidates seemed sympathetic toward the difficult home lives and neighborhood conditions of their students, but they did not position themselves as activists working for these students who live in, as Camilla said, "homes barely shelter [sic] from the elements with tar paper for windows" and neighborhoods where "prostitutes and drug dealers did not even try to hide on the corners." In addition to describing a sense of pity, there were few direct references to how the library could serve as empowerment, except for Camilla who suggested, "As a librarian I would love to be able to offer them great worlds to escape to through great books!"

Tolerance

At the level of tolerance, the focus is on assimilation and the teacher's role is to be aware of cultural differences and to attempt to be sensitive to the differences of culture. Olivia represented this level: "Think about all of the students' gender, race, and interests when making selections." Kristy saw tolerance as her goal, stating, "Instead of making a general booktalk that will speak to the mainstream, the booktalk should include more about the cultures present in the room." Jessica said that she "liked the idea of celebrating different cultures."

The majority of responses fell into this category of tolerance. Candidates acknowledged the differences or otherness in the diverse students and suggested it was their role to be sensitive and demonstrate their respect. For instance, Camilla noted, "How a teachers [sic] speaks and treats a student of a race other than her own speaks volumes." Engaging the diverse students on a superficial level was viewed as a best practice in an effort to avoid difficult conversations or socially uncomfortable situations. Olivia noted the need to "encourage the students, not upset them." Camilla also commented, "If you become frustrated with their accents or prior knowledge, they feel devalued."

Additionally, the preservice librarians made statements that demonstrated diverse students were very different from them. Olivia said, "I always think I am failing as a teacher because I haven't found the perfect lesson plan to reach my diverse population." At least one school district reinforced this difference, as Abby noted: "My school put all of us new hires in a van and drove us around to every neighborhood and housing complex we draw from so we could see where our students lived." Jessica saw this difference as an educational goal, noting that "Even if you have a school that is not extremely diverse, it will be important to teach them lessons about diversity now so that they will be prepared when they are in diverse situations." For many of our participants and for many schools, Nieto's description of tolerance (2010, pp. 251–253) is considered to be "multicultural."

Acceptance

At the acceptance level, cultural diversity is acknowledged rather than marginalized. The school curriculum reflects cultural pluralism, and the educational setting is less a "melting pot" and more a "salad bowl" where cultural differences are visible and distinct (Nieto, 2010, pp. 253–255). Camilla spoke about making explicit connections between the characters in her selected books (*A Long Way Gone: Memoirs of a Boy Soldier* and *A Girl in Translation*) and the students in the audience:

If I were to repeat my booktalks to the same audience, I would structure the talk to hit on Ladson-Billings' (1995) three points in a concise manner, taking time at the end to relate the main characters to the students in the audience.

Similarly, Jessica indicated the importance of knowing about students' backgrounds and culture in order to practice cultural relevance: "First of all, in order to use the idea of culturally relevant pedagogy, I have to know something about the culture of the students." Olivia also discussed cultural relevance as knowing students and building relationships with them: "It is about relationships and understanding the students."

Samantha made the connection between CRP as described by Ladson-Billings (1995) and her future role and practice as a school librarian.

To me, as a librarian, I need to ensure academic success with my population by finding relevant, high interest, on reading level books and creating lessons that bring about success for students of all ethnicities. I need to allow students to embrace their cultural identity within my library and class settings and create lessons and find books that embrace their culture.

Remarks coded at this level demonstrated an emerging understanding of multicultural education and culturally relevant practices.

Respect

"Respect" was the next level identified by Nieto (2010, pp. 255–257) where cultural differences are highly valued and approached in a positive manner. The students and their cultural identities shape school practices and curriculum. Schools and educators operating at this level believe all children can learn.

Jessica spoke about the need for involving the community in the library as a way of demonstrating cultural relevance:

The article [by Ladson-Billings] suggests becoming a fixture in the community and being active there so that you can truly learn about their culture, and they can see you as a member of their community. In a similar situation [like the booktalk with the avatars] where I knew absolutely nothing about the kids, I might have invited a parent or community guest in to give them someone to identify with and to help me relate to them and them to relate to me.

Camilla saw her book choices as powerful in terms of their ability to help her future students exercise agency in trying situations and expressed her faith in students' abilities to rise to these challenges if they draw from a store of personal strength: "These stories were inspirational and meant to show students that no matter what your personal circumstances are, you can be in control of your life and have the ability to change your circumstances if you have the personal strength to do so."

After reading the Ladson-Billings (1995) article, Jessica spoke of the librarian's role as a provider of "encouragement and empowerment to know [students] can succeed," while Samantha commented that "learning is so much more powerful when kids take responsibility for it, rather than us directing them." This belief in empowering students relates to Nieto's (2010) belief in the success of all students (p. 256).

Sensitive topics ought to be addressed rather than avoided as Samantha commented, "I think dispelling myths and stereotypes in literature is so very important, and the younger the better." Jessica acknowledged that educators should be aware of their own presumptions and biases about cultural groups: "It is very unfair and stereotypical [*sic*] to say that since they were black their culture was exactly this way or because they were Latino their culture was another way." The preservice librarians operating at this level recognized the importance of empowering students, reaching out to the community, and being transparent about the existence of issues like racism and stereotyping.

Affirmation, solidarity, and critique

Using Nieto's multiculturalism framework, the level of affirmation, solidarity, and critique (2010, pp. 257–261) is commensurate with an affirmation of cultural, ethnic, racial, and gender differences. Educators take an active and inquiry stance toward culture and consider social injustices as areas of conflict or pain that must be addressed. Topics such as racism, sexism, and classism are not taboo, because the librarian broaches these topics in a respectful way that causes students to reflect about their own experiences and perspectives. Specifically, Abby discussed how literature can empower students to "make decisions and providing the opportunity to look critically at issues concerning them personally and the world in general, and help them overcome difficult circumstances." Camilla suggested:

I believe there is as much to learn (if not more) from characters that make the wrong choices as those that make the right ones. I would not be surprised if many students have not had personal experience with gangs (I know they have quite a presence here) and it would be interesting to hear their stories and discuss alternate paths.

Samantha specifically identified critical consciousness and was able to connect this aspect of CRP with booktalking:

Many of the books also had characters that challenged the status quo and reading them would allow students to have what she calls critical consciousness. My goal with my book selections was to bring forth books that challenged stereotypes for different ethnicities, that made students think about different cultures and to not judge a person by their ethnic cover.

As these findings illustrate, the statements from participants fell into the full continuum of Nieto's (2010) levels of multiculturalism. While many of the responses remained at the lower levels of "monocultural" and "tolerance," it was evident their consideration of CRP (Ladson-Billings, 1995) prompted increased reflection and plans for future practice. Next, we turn to participants' perspectives on booktalking in a simulated classroom setting.

The Teach-Live Lab

The Teach-Live Lab was a unique setting for the candidates. Candidates faced a screen projecting images of a classroom with the five avatars that were depicted as full bodied, somewhat realistic looking middle school students (11–14 years old). The movements and speech of the avatars were real time reactions to participants' book-talks. Much of the discussion in the debriefing following the experience honed in on the lab experience, the avatars, interactions with the avatars, and what were perceived as problems with classroom management. Several students contrasted the experience with interacting with "real students" and wondered how it would have been different to booktalk to diverse middle school students in person. Several of the candidates compared the experience to a classroom. As Abby said, "I think I would have had more control in a classroom environment where I would have asked the audience to hold all questions and comments until after the talk." Kristy yearned for a "traditional classroom set up." This reflects the general difficulty that our students, who are classroom teachers, have in making the transition toward becoming school librarians in a new setting where they may only have five minutes and may not know the students.

DISCUSSION

In this study, we explored candidates' perceptions of multicultural booktalking using a mixed reality simulation experience with reflection and readings about CRP and the efficacy of a mixed reality simulation for teaching CRP. The findings of this study revealed several challenges and opportunities as participants considered moving toward becoming culturally relevant school librarians. A major challenge faced by the group was the lack of their ability to get through their list of books in the face of an unfamiliar and a diverse audience. They reported that they did not feel in control of the booktalking experience and blamed the Teach-Live technology for some of their challenges in the booktalks as opposed to their unfamiliarity with multicultural literature and diverse students. While participants reported finding the avatars distracting and were unable to determine the connection between the avatars and actual students, they were also more open in the post-booktalk chats about describing the behavior of individual avatars than they might have been of individual students. The perceived unreality of the setting seemed to have allowed them to safely discuss their struggles with differences and stereotypes in a forthright and candid manner.

Nieto (2010) urges educators to envision ideals of "diversity, equity, and high levels of learning" (p. 261) and suggests that the scenarios she provides for each level are attainable because pieces of each level exist in our schools today. In the same way, we saw aspects of each level in the experiences and perceptions of the preservice school librarians. They drew from the assignments in the class, the readings, and their experiences booktalking to avatars to construct frank conversations about poverty, race, and culture experienced in their classrooms and our society. Their shared experience of the Teach-Live Lab provided a common ground for these discussions. While many participants critiqued the animation of the avatars as distracting and the misbehaviors of the avatars as challenging, the experience nevertheless provoked thoughtful reflection about CRP and hegemonic injustices. Therefore, the most significant implication of this study is that the participants seemed to move toward becoming culturally relevant educators when provided a mixed reality simulation where they could practice working with diverse (or unfamiliar) students and reflect on both their personal epistemology and the prospect of using multicultural literature to expose societal injustices to their students. In fact, we found several candidates moved into Nieto's higher levels after being exposed to and reflecting about the Ladson-Billings (1995) article, noting that as future librarians they perceived they had an important responsibility to show acceptance and understanding of all cultures, of using the library collection to dispel myths and stereotypes, and to work with literature to promote inquiry into cultural differences and social inequities.

The Nieto (2010) framework helped to make sense of the vast amount of cultural references found in the candidate responses. The application of this framework and the findings suggest the framework might be used to develop a continuum of culturally relevant practices for school librarians. At the levels of tolerance and acceptance, most participants made connections with selection criteria and collection development. Some mentioned displays and other features of the school library. At the level of respect, participants saw the need for the school librarian to reach out to families and the community and build those connections for students. These remarks were commensurate with Kumasi and Hill's (2013) identification of the sociocultural disposition, which recognizes that a librarian's cultural competence is not about knowledge acquisition or service to students in diverse cultures, but calls for having "authentic interactions" within "the contexts of their daily lives" (p. 137). We were especially encouraged by the responses at the level of affirmation, solidarity, and critique such as Samantha's reflective statement:

If I did it again, I'd focus more on that and also show them the importance of cultural identity in the books and how the books make you think about your place in the sociopolitical arena that we live in today.

CONCLUSION

School librarians serve everyone in a school community. Honma (2005) suggests much work needs to be done to move America's school libraries from the "unquestioned system of white normativity and liberal multiculturalism" (p. 1) toward truly helping educators and students confront the societal injustices perpetuated by the status quo. School librarians have a unique perspective regarding the intersection of social justice and literacy because they see the big picture inclusive of the whole school, the whole curriculum, and the whole child. They have much to offer a school seeking to advance toward the more transformative and emancipatory pedagogies described by Ladson-Billings (1995, 2000), Nieto (2010), and Sleeter (2011). In this chapter we seek to demonstrate a unique strategy for introducing CRP into the preparation of school librarians. The mixed reality medium offers an innovative setting for educators to safely practice genuine sociopolitical teaching to increase student learning and to encourage preservice candidates to address human rights and social injustices in classrooms and school libraries around the world.

NOTE

This chapter was previously published as Underwood, J., Kimmel, S., Forest, D., & Dickinson, G. (2015). Culturally relevant booktalking: Using a mixed reality simulation with preservice school librarians. *School Libraries Worldwide, 21*(1), 91–107.

REFERENCES

Bodart, J. R. (2010). Booktalking: That was then, this is now. *ALAN Review, 38*(1), 57–63.

Brown, I. A., Davis, T. J., & Kulm, G. (2011). Preservice teachers' knowledge for teaching algebra for equity in the middle grades: A preliminary report. *The Journal of Negro Education, 80*(3), 266–283.

Chance, R., & Lesesne, T. (2012). Rethinking reading promotion: Old school meets technology. *Teacher Librarian, 39*(5), 26–28.

Cheong, D. (2010). The effects of practice teaching sessions in second life on the change in preservice teachers' teaching efficacy. *Computers & Education, 55*(2), 868–880.

Cole, S. (2010). *Booktalking around the world: Great global reads for ages 9–14.* Westport, CT: Libraries Unlimited.

Giroux, H. (2000). Insurgent multiculturalism and the promise of pedagogy. In E. M. Duarte & S. Smith (Eds.), *Foundational perspectives in multicultural education* (pp. 195–212). New York, NY: Longman.

Hill, R. F., & Kumasi, K. (2011). Bridging the gaps: Measuring cultural competence among future school library and youth services library professionals. *School Library Media Research, 14.* Retrieved from http://www.ala.org/aasl/sites/ala.org.aasl/files/content/aaslpubsandjournals/slr/vol14/SLR_BridgingtheGaps_V14.pdf

Hinton-Johnson, K., & Dickinson, G. (2005). Guiding young readers to multicultural literature. *Library Media Connection, 23*(7), 42–45.

Honma, T. (2005). Trippin' over the color line: The invisibility of race in library and information studies. *InterActions: UCLA Journal of Education and Informational Studies, 1*(2), 1–28.

Kumasi, K. D., & Hill, R. F. (2013). Examining the hidden ideologies within cultural competence discourses among library and information science (LIS) students: Implications for school library pedagogy. *School Libraries Worldwide, 19*(1), 128–140.

Ladson-Billings, G. (1995). But that's just good teaching! The case for culturally relevant pedagogy. *Theory into Practice, 34*(3), 159–165.

Ladson-Billings, G. (2000). Fighting for our lives: Preparing teachers to teach African American students. *Journal of Teacher Education, 51*(3), 206–214.

Landt, S. M. (2008). Multicultural literature and young adolescents: A kaleidoscope of opportunity. *Journal of Adolescent & Adult Literacy, 49*(8), 890–897.

Langemack, C. (2010). Booktalk boot camp: How you can learn to stop worrying and love being "The Bomb." *Public Libraries, 49*(1), 42–51.

Lowery, R. M., & Sabis-Burns, D. (2007). From borders to bridges: Making cross cultural connections through multicultural literature. *Multicultural Education, 14*(4), 50–54.

Mahood, K. (2010). *Booktalking with teens.* Westport, CT: Libraries Unlimited.

Nieto, S. (2010). Affirmation, solidarity, and critique: Moving beyond tolerance in multicultural education. In S. Nieto (Ed.), *Language, culture & teaching: Critical perspectives* (2nd ed., pp. 247–263). New York, NY: Routledge.

Schall, L. (2011). *Value packed booktalks: Genre talks and more for teen readers.* Westport, CT: Libraries Unlimited.

Sleeter, C. (2011). An agenda to strengthen culturally responsive pedagogy. *English Teaching: Practice and Critique, 10*(2), 7–23.

Souto-Manning, M. (2009). Negotiating culturally responsive pedagogy through multicultural children's literature: Toward critical democratic literacy practices in a first grade classroom. *Journal of Early Childhood Literacy, 9*(1), 50–74.

Villegas, A. M. (1991). *Culturally responsive pedagogy for the 1990's and beyond (Trends and issues paper no. 6)*. Washington, DC: Eric Clearinghouse on Teacher Education.

York, S. (2008). Culturally speaking: Booktalking authentic multicultural literature. *Library Media Connection, 27*(1), 16–18.

York, S. (2009). What should booktalkers realize about booktalking and multicultural literature? *Library Media Connection, 27*(5), 50.

Young, T. E. (2003). Working booktalks and bookchats: Tidbits that tantalize! *Knowledge Quest, 32*(1), 62–63.

Young, E. (2010). Challenges to conceptualizing and actualizing culturally relevant pedagogy: How viable is the theory in classroom practice? *Journal of Teacher Education, 61*(3), 248–260.

Young, E. (2011). The four personae of racism: Educators misunderstandings of individual vs. systemic racism. *Urban Education, 46*(6), 1433–1460.

III

Innovative Practice

Section Overview

Fostering Resilience, Wellness, and Hope in the School Library

Meghan Harper

INTRODUCTION

School libraries are uniquely positioned to offer resilience, wellness, and hope to children who may be experiencing or have experienced trauma. Vulnerable students who have experienced trauma may need a mental, an emotional, and a physical refuge. Helping youth and fostering hope are essential if youth are to academically succeed and thrive into adulthood. Schools adopting a trauma-informed approach to education understand the immediate and long-lasting effects of childhood trauma on learning, the future outlook for children, and the overall effect on the school environment. Trauma-informed approaches require changes in how educators interact and respond at an interpersonal level with students as well as adjustments in the school's culture, policies and procedures, and facility design in order to meet the needs of traumatized learners.

What Is Trauma?

Trauma can be defined as,

an event, series of events, or set of circumstances that is experienced by an individual as physically or emotionally harmful or life threatening and that has lasting adverse effects on the individual's functioning and mental, physical, social, emotional, or spiritual well-being. (Substance Abuse and Mental Health Services Administration, 2014, p. 7)

Trauma can be caused by an actual negative event that has happened, such as violence or injury or exposure to a real or perceived threat. Trauma can include those events that are a result of racism, oppression, poverty/homelessness, ageism, or generational trauma. Individuals' responses to trauma can vary greatly; each trauma experience is unique to the individual. However, the cumulative and negative long-term effects of traumatic experiences as a youth have been well documented. It is estimated that one-half to two-thirds of all children experience trauma. When children are exposed to trauma and are responding to a negative external event, the experience surpasses the child's ordinary coping skills (McInerney & McKlindon, 2014). These experiences affect a child's behavior and intellectual processing.

EFFECTS OF TRAUMA ON THE BRAIN

The effects of trauma on the brain are significant. In some cases, trauma affects neural development resulting in the loss of IQ, affecting memory, reasoning, and neural processing, especially in regard to emotional responses. Figure 1 depicts the brain of a healthy child and one that has been affected by trauma.

The brain of the neglected child shows significant inactivity in the temporal lobe, which regulates emotion and sensory input (National Association of Counsel for Children, 2019). As a result, students may experience lack of impulse control, skewed emotional responses to ordinary situations, decreased IQ and reading ability, lack of concentration, and perceived inability to relate to others or blaming of others. The pervasiveness of untreated trauma and the subsequent ripple effect of trauma warrants a proactive approach by educators in schools.

Children who have been exposed to violence often have difficulty responding to social cues and may withdraw from social situations or bully others . . . children who have been physically abused have been found to engage in less intimate peer relationships and tend to be more aggressive and negative in peer interactions . . . students who have experienced trauma may feel that authority figures have failed to provide safety for them in the past and may therefore be distrustful of teachers. (McInerney & McKlindon, 2014, p. 4)

Trauma may be intergenerational; feelings of trauma can be passed down from one generation to the next. Even when life improves following a traumatic event, individuals can suffer from anxiety, depression, or posttraumatic syndrome or experience a decline in physical or mental health (Castelloe, 2012). If untreated, trauma can trickle down from adult caregivers to children. Many research studies have established the relationship between childhood trauma, stress, and maltreatment and health and wellbeing later in life. Adverse childhood experiences are significant risk factors leading to many causes of illness and even death. Adverse childhood experiences and toxic stress in children are a public health crisis (Centers for Disease Control

Figure 1
Brain of a healthy child and one that has been affected by trauma (National Association of Counsel for Children, 2019)

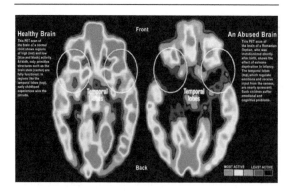

Figure 2

Negative repercussions of experienced trauma (Sandy Hook Columbine Cooperative, 2019)

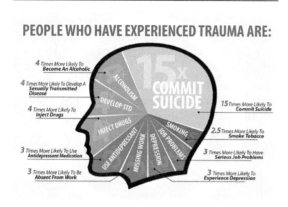

and Prevention, 2019). The quantity of adverse childhood experiences has been found to be directly correlated to at-risk behaviors and a poor quality of life. Figure 2 shows the Sandy Hook Cooperative's graphic summary of the negative repercussions of experienced trauma.

Research findings suggest that educators need to take a proactive approach with children who have experienced trauma. Although the statistics about the negative impact of trauma on children are alarming, there are equally positive statistics that suggest if trauma is addressed and if children are exposed to experiences that make them feel cared for, students may equally experience positive outcomes. Educators can implement a trauma-informed education model in schools.

Schools have an important role to play in providing stability and a safe space for children and connecting them to caring adults. In addition to serving as a link to supportive services, schools can adapt curricula and behavioral interventions to better meet the educational needs of students who have experienced trauma. (McInerney & McKlindon, 2014, p. 1)

TRAUMA-INFORMED SCHOOLS

At the heart of a trauma-informed approach is the belief that an individual's actions are affected by experienced trauma. Trauma-informed schools strive to be responsive to children who have experienced trauma and understand how trauma affects learning. Trauma-informed schools adjust the school environment to avoid the retriggering of trauma, promote resiliency in students to help them overcome trauma, and more specifically, view a students' behavior through a trauma-informed lens (Bissonette & Shebby, 2017). At the heart of trauma-informed care is a sensitivity to students' past and current adverse experiences and a deeper understanding of why they may be acting out (Dotson, 2017). A trauma-informed or trauma-sensitive school embodies the following characteristics and includes a shared understanding among all personnel about trauma. Key principles of a trauma-informed approach include the following:

- Safety (physical and psychological)—school supports all children to feel safe physically, socially, emotionally, and academically.
- Trustworthiness and transparency—between staff and families. School addresses students' needs in holistic ways, accounting for relationships, self-regulation, academic competency, and physical and emotional well-being.
- Peer support and mutual self-help—school explicitly connects students to the school community, providing multiple opportunities to develop and practice skills.

- Collaboration and mutuality—(whole school, from direct care staff to administrators). A whole-school effort: schools embrace teamwork and share responsibilities for all students.
- Empowerment, voice, and choice—(recognizing strengths and skill development). School supports children to be empowered to make choices and have self-control.
- Cultural, historical, and gender issues—(considers/leverages language and cultural traditions, is gender-responsive, addresses historical trauma. Leadership staff anticipate and adapt to the ever-changing needs of students. (Centers for Disease Control and Prevention, 2019)

Sharing these key principles will help school personnel come to a shared vision and understanding. Trauma-informed service may look differently at each school, as the needs of the stakeholders in the community are considered.

INTERNATIONAL CONTEXT

Globally, societal problems such as violence, family dysfunction, substance abuse, war, natural disasters, and poverty all create traumatic conditions for youth and have a deleterious effect on youth, on their mental stability, health, and wellness. The World Health Organization collects and shares information on health and wellness from a global perspective. Worldwide, 10–20% of children and adolescents suffer from mental disorders, and over half of mental disorders begin by age 14. Depression is the third leading cause of illness and disability among adolescents, and suicide is the third leading cause of death in older adolescents (15–19 years) (World Health Organization, 2017). Violence, poverty, humiliation, and feeling devalued increase the risk of developing mental health problems (World Health Organization, 2017). Similar findings on the struggles experienced by youth regarding the increase in mental health concerns and youth anxiety have been found in the United States in studies conducted by the National Alliance on Mental Illness. The studies show connections between childhood trauma and occurrences of mental illness, suicide, and substance abuse disorders.

RESILIENCY

Resiliency is the key to helping students overcome trauma. Resiliency is the process of adapting well in the face of adversity, trauma, tragedy, threats, or significant sources of stress (American Psychological Association, 2019). Learning about resiliency will enable the school librarian to incorporate building resilience into the school library program. Resilience can be taught. "The good news is that although some people seem to be born with more resilience than others, those whose resilience is lower can learn how to boost their ability to cope, thrive and flourish when the going gets tough" (Centre for Confidence and Well-Being, 2006). "Resilience is not a trait that people either have or do not have. It involves behaviors, thoughts and actions that can be learned and developed in anyone" (American Psychological Association, 2019).

One of the most important aspects to resilience is the availability of caring relationships with others inside and outside the family. Schools need to incorporate structures within the school that support the development of a caring relationship among students, between students and teachers, and between teachers and administrators. The positive effects of having these types of relationships and their effect on building resiliency in children should not be understated. Although the answer to helping students become more resilient may seem straightforward and simple, in reality there are seemingly an endless number of obstacles to promoting care in schools. Sometimes the very institutions designed on the premise of "caring" engage in noncare-based practices (Noddings, 1992).

THE RESILIENCY FACTOR

Research on children and how they thrive following trauma is exceedingly positive. Longitudinal studies suggest that one-half to two-thirds of children overcome trauma and go on to achieve successful and well-adjusted lives. The findings also suggest that caring adults play a remarkable and encouraging role in helping children overcome and move beyond trauma. Children who have a formal or an informal mentor are less likely to have external behavior problems such as bullying and internal problems such as depression. While caring teams of educators all work toward a common goal for individual students, a school librarian can make a huge difference in building a child's resiliency and helping a child to overcome adversity. The research findings support this conclusion: students who reported having at least *one* teacher who cares about them, helps them become more engaged in school, makes them excited for the future, or helps them build their strengths are 30 times more likely to experience academic success.

Many school librarians report that they spend a significant amount of time demonstrating caring for students. All students would benefit from a deliberate and an intentional trauma-informed school library program, proactively engaging with students who have experienced trauma and building resiliency in all students. A national study conducted in the United Kingdom asked librarians what they do to support learning. Although the study did not ask specifically about pastoral care, many of the respondents shared that demonstrating care to students was a significant and an important part of their job (Shaper & Streatfield, 2012).

FOSTERING HOPE AND RESILIENCY IN THE SCHOOL LIBRARY

School librarians need to understand the nature of resiliency and how it can be fostered in students. School librarians can provide experiences that, according to Meichenbaum (2019), create the conditions that build resiliency in children:

1. *Perceived availability of social relationships and social supports*
   Librarians can encourage opportunities for students to collaborate on shared projects with one another. Engaging activities that are likely to appeal to multiage level students such as a communal puzzle building activity encourage conversation and a common goal that is low stress. Librarians can initiate and develop a rapport with students to engage them in conversation about academic matters. Initiating interpersonal exchanges and learning students' names and interests will help students feel cared for.
2. *Focusing time and energies on tasks and situations over which they (students) have personal control*
   Librarians can offer opportunities for students to have choices of activities, setting up stations either for free-time exploratory activities, such as creativity stations and make and take stations, or more formally through the development of different products for academic assignments.

3. *The degree to which they can experience positive emotions and self-regulate negative emotions*

   Librarians when engaging with students need to be good listeners and nonjudgmental if a student expresses a negative emotion. Librarians can avoid reacting to negative behaviors with immediate punitive responses and respond with understanding and dialogue.

4. *Cognitive flexibility, using both direct-action problem-solving and emotionally palliative acceptance skills as situations call for*

   Librarians can serve as role models for analyzing problems, developing solutions, and responding to difficult topics and behavior in an appropriate manner. Librarians may vocalize their thought processes and share with students examples of how others resolve challenges and develop solutions. Librarians can specifically identify and share literature through informal readers' advisory or more formally through booktalking specific books with characters who face adversity and demonstrate emotional intelligence.

5. *The ability to engage in activities that are consistent with one's values and life priorities that reflect a stake in the future*

   As librarians interact informally or formally through instruction with students, they can encourage students to proactively engage in seeking more information about interests, careers, or plans for the future.

TRAUMA-INFORMED LIBRARY SERVICES BASED ON AN ETHIC OF CARE

School librarians should in all interactions work to address the whole child, engaging all the child's senses, whether it is during instruction, providing one-on-one guidance in use of the library's resources, or arranging the library facility so that students find it a safe, peaceful haven (Cellucci, 2017). The results of several research studies indicate that many school librarians are aware of the importance of their role in providing pastoral care to students. The findings from an action research project in a midwestern high school library revealed the importance of a facility and librarian that makes students feel cared for and safe. In this study, teachers and students were surveyed about their perceptions of the school library space. The goal of the study was focused on changing the school library to create a more useable space and making the media center/school library an indispensable part of the school. It was anticipated that survey participants would offer input on the facility design or desired changes; however, participants responded with sharing their positive perceptions of the librarian and the importance of the school library facility as a "safe space or haven for them." Comments included, "I feel safe in the library," "The best part of the library is the librarian," and, "The librarian cares about me" (Harper & Deskins, 2015, pp. 24–33).

The following principles form a foundation for librarians to plan and prioritize their day-to-day interactions and the overall school library plan. In order to demonstrate caring to students, librarians must actively engage in caring behaviors. At the heart of meeting children where they are and responding to children is the essence of an ethic of care. The main premise of the ethic of care is students who feel cared-for, learn better (Noddings, 2005). Decades of research demonstrating the importance of ethic of care in schools supports the principles of trauma-informed education. Librarians can use these three principles of caring as a foundation for developing trauma-informed strategies in the library.

1. *Caring is intentional.*
   Librarian interactions with students are thoughtful, deliberate, and planned.
2. *Caring is foundational.*
   The foundation of the library program is based on policies, procedures, and day-to-day management that represent an ethic of care.
3. *Caring is action-based.*
   Librarians take action! Engage in planned and purposeful deeds.

IMPLEMENTING TRAUMA-INFORMED LIBRARY SERVICES

Librarians as trauma-informed educators must begin by honing their interpersonal communication skills to effectively communicate and build rapport with students. Some common best practices include the following:

1. Avoid judgmental terminology and labels such as "junkie or addict."
2. Use active listening (affirm what you have heard).
3. Refer to individuals with "substance abuse disorders."
4. Ask "what has happened to you?" instead of "what's wrong with you?".
5. Reflect on personal experience, but do not necessarily duplicate it and say, "I know how you feel."
6. Get to know students and the lives they live, what they do (interest inventory).
7. Ask students for feedback.

Librarians need to consider the needs of all students who have experienced trauma and think through responses, resources, and help that can be given at a student's "point of need." This may require proactive thinking, developing a plan with your administrator or teachers to handle students who are reacting to traumatic events, gaining knowledge about available professional trauma and crisis resource individuals in your building, and identifying the protocol for seeking help for a student.

As a next strategy, librarians must engage in a continuous and systematic needs assessment of their library services. Librarians need to gather input from all stakeholders about how the library is used and the difference it makes for students in their overall learning experience. Learning about the issues facing students, the communities in which students reside, and the common experience of students will help the school librarian develop priorities in regard to instruction, collection development, and facility design. Additionally, librarians should seek out other community partners and resources that will help connect students to community resources outside the school. School librarians next begin to plan and implement trauma-informed library services, including (1) instruction, (2) collection, (3) facilities, and (4) procedures and policies.

Instruction

Through formal and informal instructions, librarians have many opportunities to promote care and resiliency for students. The following activities may be adapted to a trauma-informed approach:

1. Speed dating with books: encourage students to engage with books that have characters who have faced adversity and triumphed.

2. Booktalks: highlight specific books about common issues facing youth or those that may highlight examples of childhood trauma.
3. When providing instruction on uses of electronic databases, use preselected terms/issues, for example, eating disorders, abortion, abuse, drugs, illegal immigration, homelessness, and suicide to help student know where to find information if they need it.
4. Organize physical collections of materials, and highlight where students can find information about specific "issues"; this can be done as part of a larger orientation to the physical collection of resources.
5. Create book bundles, for example, pairing nonfiction, fiction, biographies, and memoirs with a marketing paragraph about the materials and the topic.
6. Maximize use of subject headings in the online or card catalog to assist with findability of resources on issues.

Collection

The collection of resources the school librarian curates provides many opportunities for incorporating trauma-informed services. Books, media, and resources are a powerful way to reach the hearts of students. When children are represented in literature and other media, they begin to see themselves as worthy of notice. Books are *windows* to the world, and they help children develop empathy by increasing students' understanding about how people around the world are both similar to and different from themselves. Books can demonstrate that acknowledging human differences creates unity. Additionally, research studies have found that exposure to books about people who may be different from themselves results in a positive correlation between empathy development and lowered prejudicial attitudes and behaviors (Lowe, 2009).

Promoting reading has many wonderful proven benefits to help students who have experienced trauma. Reading has been shown to be able to help people understand the issues they are experiencing, amplifying the effects of other treatment by normalizing experiences with mental health concerns and care and offering hope for positive change (American Library Association, 2012). Reading is a cost-effective and versatile option for the treatment of several mental health issues, and librarians can use readers' advisory to connect students with literature. Readers' advisory can be effective in responding to a student's immediate need for help, or it can be used as a preventative measure to help build empathy among students or to alert students to potential traumatic issues such as peer suicide.

Librarians can maximize use of the collection through the following activities:

1. Employ good signage.
2. Highlight books that address common issues and create interesting displays.
3. Connect/pair resources of different formats for use in and out of the library space.
4. Connect school library resources with community and government resources.
5. Create resource bundles that include information about resources inside and outside of school. Students may not be aware of resource people within the school.

Facilities

School librarians can consider zones of activity that foster student engagement with others, provide respite spaces, or inspire creativity. The design plan should create a versatile, flexible space for many different types of activities (quiet studying, collaborative work, private space, meditation, prayer/fasting, or peer tutoring). Activity zones can be incorporated within the facility to promote wellness and resiliency and offer opportunities for students to engage with resources and others or have a quiet space to decompress.

All library spaces should incorporate the best practices in the field such as universal design principles, and changes in the facility should be based on an evaluation of school community needs and input from stakeholders. Another consideration is to extend the facility's reach beyond the boundaries of walls with library pop-ups. These could be displays or resources made available in other areas of the school such as the offices of the guidance counselor and the nurse. Virtual spaces such as the school library web page should be considered as a 24/7 resource for students. Although the majority of library web pages are set up for passive viewing, school librarians could also consider how the school library web page could be a launch pad to other community resources or a more active space to gather input and identify issues within the school community.

Policies and Procedures

Librarians may need to reevaluate existing policies and procedures that are not trauma sensitive, increase student stress, restrict access to materials, or reduce feelings of student well-being. School librarians should consider gathering student input into library policies and procedures in order to best meet students' academic and personal needs. "Teachers' rules and consequences may be viewed as punishment by children who have experienced trauma, increasing the potential for re-traumatization" (McInerney & McKlindon, 2014, p. 4).

School librarians may need to initiate communication and dialogue with resource entities outside the school facility such as public libraries, community partners, or social service agencies in order to create collaborative partnerships to bring trauma-related resources to students and their caregivers. The following guidelines offer specific guidelines for responding to student behavior and creating an environment that is respectful of students:

1. Always empower; never disempower: Avoid battles for power with students. Students who have experienced trauma often seek to control their environment to protect themselves, and their behavior will generally deteriorate when they feel more helpless. Classroom discipline is necessary but should be done in a way that is respectful, consistent, and nonviolent.
2. Provide unconditional positive regard: As consistently caring adults, school staff have the opportunity to help students build trust and form relationships. For example, if a student tells you, "I hate you. You're mean," respond with unconditional positive regard by saying, "I'm sorry you feel that way. I care about you and hope you'll get your work done."
3. Maintain high expectations: Set and enforce limits in a consistent way. Maintain the same high expectations of a student who has experienced trauma as you do for his or her peers.
4. Check assumptions, observe, and question: Trauma can affect any student and can manifest in many different ways. Realize when you are making assumptions, and instead, talk with the student and ask questions. Make observations about the student's behaviors, and be fully engaged in listening to his or her response.
5. Be a relationship coach: Help students from preschool through high school develop social skills, and support positive relationships between children and their caregivers.

6. Provide guided opportunities for helpful participation: Model, foster, and support ongoing peer "helping" interactions (e.g., peer tutoring, support groups) (Wolpow, Johnson, Hertel, & Kincaid, 2011, p. 78).

Becoming a community link or connector for students and their families benefits the overall school environment and the school library. Instituting nonpunitive consequences for overdue library materials and nonrestrictive check-out policies is the first step to ensuring students have access to needed library resources. Evaluating policies and procedures to see which may be hindering access or negatively affecting students' use of the school library services and resources is a school librarian administrator responsibility. Likewise, the training of paraprofessionals or volunteers on trauma-sensitive responses to students will be important to ensure consistency in the application of library policies and procedures.

CONCLUSION

Worldwide, schools are struggling to address childhood trauma. School librarians can promote resiliency, wellness, and hope by implementing trauma-informed care as a foundation for the school library program. School librarians can incorporate trauma-informed practices through instruction, the collection, facility design, and implementation of policies and procedures that promote resiliency and avoid traumatization of students. School libraries should serve as information and resource-rich safe spaces where students can access information they need and want, and where students can decompress and feel cared-for. School librarians can engage interpersonally with students and promote resiliency through trauma-sensitive responses to student behavior. School librarians implementing trauma-informed practices can positively affect children who have experienced trauma and influence their future trajectory to one of well-being and hope.

REFERENCES

American Library Association. (2012, December 17). Bibliotherapy. Retrieved from http://www.ala.org/tools/atoz/bibliotherapy

American Psychological Association. (2019). The road to resilience: What is resilience? Retrieved from https://www.apa.org/helpcenter/road-resilience

Bissonette, T., & Shebby, S. (2017, December). *Trauma-informed school practices: The value of culture and community in efforts to reduce the effects of generational trauma*. Retrieved from https://www.apa.org/pi/families/resources/newsletter/2017/12/generational-trauma.aspx

Castelloe, M. (2012). How trauma is carried across generations: Holding the secret history of our ancestors. Retrieved from https://www.psychologytoday.com/us/blog/the-me-in-we/201205/how-trauma-is-carried-across-generations

Cellucci, A. (2017). The school library as a safe space. Retrieved from http://edublog.scholastic.com/post/school-library-safe-space#

Center for Adolescent Studies. (2015). Eight tools to make you a better teacher. Retrieved from https://centerforadolescentstudies.com/

Centers for Disease Control and Prevention. (2019). *Guiding principles for a trauma-informed approach*. Retrieved from https://www.cdc.gov/cpr/infographics/6_principles_trauma_info.htm

Centre for Confidence and Well-Being. (2006). *Resilience at work*. Retrieved from http://www.centreforconfidence.co.uk/flourishing-lives.php?p=cGlkPTQ4MSZpZD0xNTg1

Dotson, L. (2017). The transformative power of trauma-informed teaching. Retrieved from https://www.edweek.org/tm/articles/2017/11/22/the-transformative-power-of-trauma-informed-teaching.html

Harper, M., & Deskins, L. (2015). Using action research to assess and advocate for innovative school library design. *Knowledge Quest, 44*(2), 24–33. Retrieved from http://search.ebscohost.com/login.aspx?direct=true&AuthType=cookie,ip,custuid&custid=infohio&db=aph&AN=110493158&site=ehost-live&scope=site

Lowe, D. (2009). *Helping children cope through literature*. Retrieved from https://files.eric.ed.gov/fulltext/EJ864819.pdf

McInerney, M., & McKlindon, A. (2014). *Unlocking the door to learning: Trauma-informed classrooms and transformational schools*. Retrieved from https://www.elc-pa.org/wp-content/uploads/2015/06/Trauma-Informed-in-Schools-Classrooms-FINAL-December2014-2.pdf

Meichenbaum, D. (2019). Pathways to resilience: Important facts about resilience. Retrieved from http://www.melissainstitute.org

National Association of Counsel for Children. (2019). Your brain on trauma. Retrieved from https://www.naccchildlaw.org/search/all.asp?bst=brain+on+trauma

Noddings, N. (1992). *The challenge to care in schools: An alternative approach to education*. New York, NY: Teachers College Press.

Noddings, N. (2005). What does it mean to educate the whole child? *Educational Leadership, 63*(1), 8–13.

Sandy Hook Columbine Cooperative. (2019). *Effects of trauma*. Retrieved from http://sandyhookcolumbine.org/effects-of-trauma/

Shaper, S., & Streatfield, D. (2012). Invisible care? The role of librarians in caring for the "whole pupil" in secondary schools. *Pastoral Care in Education, 30*(1), 65–75. doi:10.1080/02643944.2011.651225

Substance Abuse and Mental Health Services Administration. (2014). *SAMHSA's Concept of trauma and guidance for a trauma-informed approach*. HHS Publication No. (SMA) 14-4884. Rockville, MD: Substance Abuse and Mental Health Services Administration.

World Health Organization. (2017). *Adolescent mental health*. Retrieved from https://www.who.int/mental_health/maternal-child/adolescent/en/

Wolpow, R., Johnson, M. M., Hertel, R., & Kincaid, S. O. (2011). *The heart of learning and teaching: Compassion, resiliency, and academic success*. Olympia, WA: Office of Superintendent of Public Instruction. Retrieved from http://www.k12.wa.us/CompassionateSchools/Resources.aspx

PROFESSIONAL RESOURCES

Further reading and annotated online professional resources are available from the author's website at http://www.meghanharper.org/.

School librarians should consider their own development and self-care as they engage in the day-to-day demands of running a library that embodies a trauma-informed approach. The following list was originally intended just for teachers was adapted for teacher/librarians from the Center for Adolescent Studies and provides strategies for helping the professional librarian hone their skills in working with youth.

Eight tools to make you a better teacher librarian

Adapted from Center for Adolescent Studies, 2015

1. **Mindfulness.** Mindfulness is the practice of being aware of your own experience with an attitude on nonreactivity. The more mindful you are, the better you'll be able to connect with, listen, and respond to youth. *(TIP: Practice mindfulness by taking 10 mindful breaths; whenever your mind wanders away from the breath, simply return your awareness to your breathing.)*

2. **Curiosity.** Teens often feel like adults aren't interested in their lives; that they just want to tell them what they can and can't do. Practice curiosity to let youth know you're actually interested in them. *(TIP: Ask youth about their hobbies and how they best like to spend their time, the music they like, the movies they're into, etc. Become interested in youth culture.)*

3. **Empathy.** Adults often don't do a good job of considering teens' perspectives, especially when it comes to youth issues like drugs, sex, and so forth. Practicing empathy will help you stand in the shoes of the youth you work with. Teens will be more drawn to you if you attempt to understand them, rather than judge them. *(TIP: Especially with the youth with whom you may feel tension, take their perspective and "live it" momentarily—visualize what it's like to be them and hold strong to that viewpoint. Do this with as many youths as necessary at least few times a week.)*

4. **Compassion.** Compassion is wanting to help youth by alleviating their suffering, stress, anxiety, depression, trauma, and so forth. When they know you want to help (with an authentic intention and not just to get what you want), they will feel more connected to you, trust you more, and ultimately be more receptive to whatever it is you're offering. *(TIP: Pick a youth you work with who is struggling in some way. Visualize him or her with compassion. Disclose to the youth that you want to help him or her when appropriate.)*

5. **Active Listening.** Often adults are conditioned to be directive with youth. We tell them what to do, but they rarely listen. When we listen, we offer an emotionally corrective experience: one in which they are heard on the rare occasion by an adult and can be fully witnessed, listened to, and understood. Practice active listening, and youth will trust you more and be receptive to what you're offering. *(TIP: While listening to a youth, use mindfulness to keep your awareness in the present moment, curiosity to keep your intention authentic, and body language [eye contact, body posture] to let the youth know you are listening undividedly).*

6. **Self-disclosure.** Skillful self-disclosure is the practice of revealing personal information for the specific sake of relationship building. Youth need to know that we are human, with opinions and experiences in order to connect with us. It's imperative that we don't overdisclose or disclose anything inappropriate, but don't be afraid to show up and be yourself. *(TIP: Fold a piece of paper in half. On one half write, "information I'm comfortable disclosing," on the other half write, "information I'm not comfortable disclosing." Write down opinions, life experiences, etc. Doing this ahead of time will help you to not be caught off guard when youth ask you about yourself.)*

7. **Tracking Skills.** These are the ability to recognize emotional tone, typically via body language, facial expressions, and so forth. When we practice tracking emotion, we can better attune to youth, which contributes to stronger relationships. *(TIP: Notice the body language—especially facial expressions—of the youth you work with as they talk to you. Try not to assume what they're feeling, but rather become curious about their body language as a window to investigate further: "I notice your brow is scrunched up right now, what are you feeling?")*

8. **Healthy Boundary Setting.** Don't be a pushover with youth, especially if you're trying to build an authentic relationship. I'm not saying you should be punitive and overly aggressive

(please don't do that!); I'm saying it's unhealthy to not set boundaries with youth when boundaries are tested. That will ultimately take away from the potential of a youth to view you as a caring, safe, and trustworthy adult relationship. *(TIP: Write out the necessary boundaries that apply to your specific setting with youth (i.e., library or classroom). Knowing these ahead of time helps you collect your thoughts on how to approach youth and set boundaries when they're tested, leading you to be less demanding and more relaxed.)*

Fostering Information Competence in a High-Poverty Urban School: An I-LEARN Project

Delia Neuman, Allen Grant, Vera Lee, and M. J. Tecce DeCarlo

ABSTRACT

Two teachers and 49 students at Fairmount Elementary School (a pseudonym) worked with a team of researchers to complete an inquiry-based project formulated around the I-LEARN model (Neuman, 2011a, 2011b). Fairmount is located in a neighborhood President Obama had designated as one of the nation's first "Promise Zones" in order to make it eligible for efforts designed to address its extreme poverty. I-LEARN is a *learning model* that extends traditional information-seeking approaches specifically to support learning with information. While one teacher—who was completing a degree in school librarianship—was more successful than the other in implementing the model, both found I-LEARN to be helpful in supporting students' information-based learning.

BACKGROUND

In the spring of 2013, the timeframe of the study, the School District of Philadelphia was in crisis: ultimately, 24 schools were closed at the end of the school year and 3,783 district employees lost their jobs (Strauss, 2013)—although some were later rehired. The Fairmount School library, which had been closed for five years but which was scheduled to reopen with a revitalized collection in a newly transformed space with new furniture and appropriate accoutrements for an elementary school library (e.g., a story area), remained closed. Ms. A, a teacher who was completing her degree in school librarianship and who had believed she would be the school's new librarian, continued in her teaching role. She was one of four teachers who had originally volunteered to participate in the I-LEARN research project and one of two who completed it. Her approach to implementing I-LEARN leads to important insights into how to foster information competence in urban schools facing similar situations.

At the time of the study, one in four children in the neighborhood lived below the poverty level (Vargas, 2014). The student body was 90% African American and 95.2% "economically disadvantaged." Only 3% of the students in grades 3–8 at Fairmount scored at the proficient level in reading and math on Pennsylvania's statewide assessment instrument (School District of Philadelphia, 2012). Against this background, the Fairmount study was designed to determine the value and utility of the I-LEARN model for improving the digital and information literacies of young urban students. The study was conducted by an interdisciplinary team of researchers—with expertise in early childhood education and technology integration, K-12 literacy, early literacy, and school libraries and information literacy—affiliated with Drexel University, which had a preexisting relationship with the school. Overall, the study results showed that using the model was beneficial to both Ms. A's five- and six-year-old kindergarten students and Ms. B's seven- and eight-year-old second graders. Ms. A's students achieved higher levels of digital/information literacy than did those of Ms. B, a veteran teacher who was widely respected but did not have any background in school libraries.

CONCEPTUAL FRAMEWORK

The primary conceptual framework for the study included the theoretical and empirical underpinnings of the I-LEARN model (Neuman, 2011a, 2011b)—a learning model that builds on and expands traditional information-seeking models specifically to address the processes and outcomes of learning with information. The model is based on the assumptions that curriculum-related learning is the primary reason for information seeking in schools and that knowing how to learn with information is a critical skill that students must acquire in order to learn in formal and informal environments throughout their lives. Ultimately, the model rests on the proposition that "expertise in accessing, evaluating, and using information is in fact the authentic learning that modern education seeks to promote" (American Association of School Librarians and Association for Educational Communications & Technology, 1998, p. 2). I-LEARN encompasses six major stages, each with three associated elements, as displayed in Figure 1.

Other scholarly areas that contributed to the study include culturally responsive teaching, digital literacy, and collaborative action research. Culturally responsive teaching involves understanding how to connect instruction to students' differing racial, ethnic, socioeconomic, and linguistic backgrounds (Villegas & Lucas, 2002). Fostering digital literacy requires an understanding of how students develop the skills that are part of a widening definition of being literate (International Reading Association, 2009; National Writing Project, 2010). Collaborative action research "focuses on creating climates of inquiry in communities of practice, often with different stakeholders functioning as co-researchers" (Mitchell, Reilly, & Logue, 2009, p. 345) in order to foster meaningful interactions between teachers and university researchers and to offer teachers control over a process of systematic inquiry (Johnson & Johnson, 2002).

RESEARCH METHODOLOGY

This qualitative case study—a collaborative effort among the teachers and the researchers—involved classroom observation, interviews with the participating

Figure 1
The I-LEARN model

I: *Identify*	Choose a problem, topic, or question that can be addressed through information.
	• Activate a sense of curiosity about the world.
	• Scan the environment for a suitable topic within that world to investigate.
	• Formulate a problem or question about that topic that can be addressed with information.
L: *Locate*	Access information, either recorded or in the environment, related to the problem/topic/question through a variety of people and media.
	• Focus on what is to be learned.
	• Find the information potentially useful for that learning.
	• Extract the most relevant and salient information for that learning.
E: *Evaluate*	Judge the quality and relevance of the information found by ascertaining whether it has
	• Authority, as evidenced by the credibility of the source and/or author, internal logic, accuracy, etc.;
	• Relevance to the topic at hand, suitability in its level of depth for the question, and appropriateness to the topic; and
	• Timeliness, as evidenced by its currency or historicity (as appropriate to the topic) and its appropriateness in terms of its match with the learner's developmental level.
A: *Apply*	Use the information to generate a new understanding—that is, to learn.
	• Generate a new understanding that has personal meaning.
	• Organize that learning in an appropriate cognitive structure (e.g., chronological, hierarchical, etc.).
	• Create an appropriate product to convey that structure.
R: *Reflect*	Examine the adequacy of the process and product of learning, and revise as appropriate.
	• Analyze the quality of the process and of the product's form and content.
	• Revise the product as necessary, and determine how to improve the process for the next instance.
	• Refine the product, polishing it as appropriate.
N: *kNow*	Instantiate the knowledge gained so it can be used in the future.
	• Integrate the new learning into existing knowledge.
	• Personalize the new knowledge by recognizing it as a personal, individual construct.
	• Activate the new knowledge by drawing upon it as necessary and/or appropriate to generate and answer new questions.

---

teachers, and extensive analysis of students' work. All the members of the research team participated in the study's design and in the data analysis, and the two researchers with experience in urban elementary classrooms were also participant observers who actively helped the teachers implement the students' learning activities.

Research Questions

Three central research questions guided the study:

- How can the I-LEARN model be used to support problem-based, information-rich learning at Fairmount School?
- What dimensions of digital literacy are most salient for young urban students and teachers?
- How can these dimensions be taught and evaluated?

The project began with several professional development sessions at which (1) the researchers presented the I-LEARN model and the generic rubric created as part of its development; (2) the teachers decided to focus on the topic "What Makes Philadelphia Special," because it addressed the school district's existing social studies objectives and because several teachers had used it as the basis for previous projects and thought it would work well for this one; and (3) the researchers demonstrated several free digital-portfolio platforms that teachers might use for the project. Ms. A chose Little Bird Tales (https://littlebirdtales.com), which enables students to create digital tales using electronic tools designed for younger students. Ms. B selected Weebly (https://education.weebly.com), which allows students to create websites and digital portfolios.

As the planning continued, it became apparent that the researchers would have to provide the technology resources necessary for the project. At the time, Fairmount had no computers for its elementary classrooms and only one computer lab, which was designated for older students, in the building. The team was able to acquire discarded central processing units from one academic unit in Drexel University, while information technology specialists from another unit located used keyboards and screens and refurbished the machines and uploaded the software necessary to make the computers functional. A member of the research team, along with technical support staff from the University, delivered and set up the equipment.

Over the course of four weeks, individual students conducted their research in both digital and nondigital resources and ultimately presented the results in digital portfolios. The two research team members who worked most directly with the teachers helped Ms. A's 11 boys and 13 girls locate information on the internet, assisted them in preparing their drafts, and scribed their work into Little Bird Tales; they also typed Ms. B's 12 boys' and 13 girls' handwritten research into their individual Weebly sites. For both groups, this support was crucial in enabling the creation of these young students' digital projects. Finally, Ms. A, Ms. B, and several colleagues participated in a focus group interview at the conclusion of the project; the interview was recorded by the research team, transcribed by a transcription service, and verified by one of the researchers.

Data Analysis

First, the research team developed and applied a coding scheme based on the research questions to analyze the transcript of the focus group interview. Next, the team focused on the student data. To support this analysis, Ms. A provided students' self-assessments of their work along with records of the interviews she had conducted with them about the project. The research team created tables and Excel spreadsheets to organize all the nonelectronic student data and reviewed each student's completed portfolio in detail. Ms. B did not collect student self-assessment or teacher-assessment data.

FINDINGS

The teachers concluded that the I-LEARN model had been successful in supporting problem-based, inquiry learning for Fairmount's young students. Commenting on the clear, step-by-step nature of the model, they praised it as "a model for processing information [that] help[s] guide students in the research process. Instead of doing something because they are being told to do something, they are doing something based on a process where they are making decisions" (Ms. A). Ms. B reported that the process offered an opportunity for her students to have ownership over their research because it allowed them to "have control over what it is they are learning. It makes it interesting. It makes it kid-friendly."

Data related to Ms. A's and Ms. B's classes revealed that each teacher had taken a distinctive approach to the project—and each rested on that teacher's unique pedagogical style, understanding of her students' developmental levels and learning needs, technology fluency, and understanding of inquiry. While the students in both groups completed their projects successfully, the differences in the teachers' backgrounds and approaches seemed to lead to very different levels of in-depth understanding and achievement in relation to information/digital literacy. Ultimately, Ms. B's second graders were outshone by Ms. A's kindergarteners.

Ms. A's Approach

The "What Makes Philadelphia Special" project was typically done with first and second graders, and Ms. A had not previously completed it or any other research projects with her kindergarteners. However, she wanted to adapt the project so that she and her students could participate in the I-LEARN study. She quickly realized, however, that "a lot of kids don't even realize necessarily that they live in Philadelphia." So she engaged the class in talking about their personal community, the people who live and work there, and the places they had visited with their families; she read aloud books about activities people could do and places they could go in the city. She had students brainstorm possible foci for their projects, leaving the choice of what to investigate entirely to them rather than assigning specific topics. All these strategies primed students for their research by activating their sense of curiosity about the world, guiding them to scan for ideas within that world that they could investigate, and helping them formulate their own research topics—as described in the I-LEARN elements associated with the *Identify* stage.

Consistent with the elements associated with the *Locate* stage of the model, Ms. A brought in guest speakers to talk about topics of interest to the children, such as the important work that firefighters do for the city. She helped them understand that people—like the speakers and like the members of their own families—are important sources of information and explained that books and computer sites can be good sources as well. She had students draw pictures that represented three topics they might explore and identify three sources in which they might find useful information. For example, "Joan" identified as topics pizza delivery, murals, the post office, and Philadelphia's "restaurant week." Her sources were people with whom she spoke, murals, and a book. Students who wrote "computer" were assisted by one of the researchers in looking up topics on specific websites and in understanding the websites' information (which was generally written at a level beyond their independent-reading abilities).

Figure 2
Ms. A's responses about sources

Information sources used	Criteria for evaluating sources
• Books • Radio • TV • People (including family and teacher) • Neighborhood murals • Classroom materials (including "words on the chalkboard" and "centers") • The library • The "education store" • Places in the community (including police, fire, and train stations)	• "Using the computer because the computer goes faster than looking other places." • "The books we read tell us stories about where we live and the people who live there." • "Going to the park [because] you can see and look around."

As a result of her guided progress through the first two stages of the I-LEARN model, "Joan" ultimately chose to do her project about murals, which hold a special place in Philadelphia (see http://www.muralarts.org/). In terms of the *Evaluate* stage, she and her classmates generally relied on the teacher's and the researcher's expertise in determining authority, relevance, timeliness, and so forth—although they were able to articulate some "evaluation" criteria of their own. Figure 2 displays the sources they used and the criteria they cited.

For the *Apply* stage, students followed a model that Ms. A had developed by creating her own story on the Little Bird Tales platform about "What Makes Philadelphia Special." Technologically fluent, she first uploaded pictures of places she and her own family had visited in the city (doing this directly rather than using the platform's tools) and recorded a story about her family's adventures in Philadelphia (using the platform's recording tool). Next, she gave the students a specific structure that made the final "tales" easier to design and produce. Then, she guided each student through that structure's steps: creating his or her tale using clip art or the tools on the Little Bird Tales platform, writing a word at the bottom of the tale that described the illustration, and prompting each student to talk about what he or she had learned through the project about what makes Philadelphia special. She also had students identify the sources they had used and record that information with the platform's recording tool. Thus, she addressed all the elements of the *Apply* stage by helping each student (1) generate a new understanding that had personal meaning, (2) organize it in a structure that was appropriate to the task and the content, and (3) create a product that conveyed new knowledge in a creative and satisfying way.

Ms. A guided the students through the *Reflect* stage by asking each student three questions and recording the answers: What was your favorite part of the project? What part do you think you did the best? The worst? What is your favorite source that you used? Why is [that source] a good way to learn about Philadelphia? While this process didn't specifically address the "revision" and "refining" elements of this stage of I-LEARN, it clearly laid the groundwork for helping students understand the importance of stepping back and reflecting on their work.

Finally, Ms. A provided a formal assessment of her students' projects by scoring them according to a version of the generic I-LEARN rubric the teachers had adapted to meet the needs of their students (Figure 3). The teachers (primarily Ms. A) had simplified the elements of the rubric to reflect the kinds of tasks and levels of achievement they believed to be appropriate for their young learners. As with the generic rubric (Neuman, 2011b), the *kNow* stage is not included in this rubric because instructors would generally need another evaluation tool to assess the specific knowledge students displayed in projects, term papers, multimedia presentations, and so forth.

Analysis of students' scores on the rubric indicated that the overall mean score for the class was 11.5 out of a possible 15 points. Ms. A assigned all her students a score of 3 for *Identifies* a meaningful problem, and the mean scores for the other stages are as follows: 2.17 for *Locates*, 1.86 for *Evaluates*, 2.17 for *Applies*, and 2.17 for *Reflects*. These scores reveal that the students had relatively high and consistent achievement for most of the measures but seemed to struggle with *Evaluate*. These results confirm school librarians' well-known concern about students' ability to evaluate information and suggest that developing specific strategies within the I-LEARN framework is necessary to address that concern.

In sum, Ms. A's approach to the I-LEARN project represents a rich, detailed, and effective incorporation of the model into a project-based, inquiry approach to learning with information. While she intervened significantly at each step of the project, her intervention could be characterized as teacher guided rather than teacher directed. She carefully and systematically interwove structure and independence into a pattern that capitalized on students' developing skills and knowledge, while at the same time ensuring their success as researchers. In particular, she used the stages of I-LEARN to support them in *Identifying* their own topics, in *Locating* information about those topics in a variety of sources, in structuring both their conceptual and their technological development as they *Applied* their information to create well-structured digital portfolios, and in leading them to *Reflect* on their process and on what they had integrated into their kNowledge stores.

Ms. B's Approach

Early in the project, Ms. B determined that her second graders' limited knowledge and experience with the city of Philadelphia beyond their own neighborhood required her to adapt the model to meet their needs. Although she led them in some opening discussions to consider other areas of the city, in the end she "fed them different things" rather than promoting their own skills at *Identifying* questions. She limited their choices of projects to four famous sites—the Philadelphia Zoo, the Liberty Bell, Fairmount Park, and Memorial Hall—and printed out information on them (from a source that she never identified) and distributed it as a handout rather than allowing students to *Locate* information themselves. Students' comments about how they *Evaluated* their sources—for example, "It is good because my teacher gave it to me"—suggest that Ms. B also overlooked the opportunity to help students develop their *Evaluation* knowledge and skills. In addition, because she believed that many of her students' poor computer skills would lead them to take too long to create their portfolios, she asked the researcher to work with those who needed help in the *Apply* stage by uploading their notes and inserting stock photos of the sites that they had chosen. The researcher was also the one who asked the students to respond to the *Reflect* questions included in the I-LEARN template for their portfolios and typed their answers for them.

Figure 3
Fairmount I-LEARN rubric

Outcome	3	2	1	0
Identifies a meaningful problem	Chooses between given topics and writes a question that makes sense	Chooses a topic and writes a question that doesn't make sense or writes a statement (rather than a question)	Chooses a topic	Does not choose a topic
Locates information related to the problem	Finds 3 sources (ideally a mix of electronic, books, oral, pictorial)	Finds 2 sources	Finds 1 source	Finds 0 sources
Evaluates the information critically	Selects a preferred resource and explains why this is good info, using the I-LEARN criteria	Selects a preferred resource and explains why it's good using emotional criteria (e.g. , I like it.)	Selects a preferred resource but does not explain why	Does not select a preferred resource
Applies relevant information to the question	Answers question with info from identified source, using product criteria	Answers question with emotional or other irrelevant data	Partially answers question	Does not answer question
Reflects on the information process and product	Creates an accurate statement of what went well and what did not	Creates a statement but it is inaccurate, or just makes something up	Gives a broad or blanket statement with no detail	Does not create a statement

LESSONS LEARNED

Despite the difficulties that Fairmount faced, participating teachers were enthusiastic collaborators in this research. Their commitment to their students was evident; their eagerness to acquire new equipment, advance their own professional development, and become involved in a new way of doing things was especially admirable in light of the school's limited resources and highly stressful environment. The students, too, were generally engaged in the project—working in an under-resourced school in a deeply impoverished neighborhood to master unfamiliar technology as well as to learn new ideas about information and digital literacies.

Overall, the study's results indicate that the students of both teachers who used the I-LEARN model were successful in understanding and completing problem-based, inquiry-focused projects. Both teachers deemed the model a useful tool, and both groups of students profited from their I-LEARN experience. However, the counterintuitive finding that Ms. A's five- and six-year-old kindergarten students achieved higher levels of digital/information literacy than did Ms. B's seven- and eight-year-old second graders suggests that Ms. A's understanding of information, information resources, and information seeking and use provided significant advantages that the other students did not have. While she did not have a functioning library in her school, she was completing a library degree at the time of the research partnership. Drawing on this background, she was able to conceptualize meaningful research for her young students and to adapt each stage of the I-LEARN model in developmentally appropriate ways. Many of her five- and six-year-old students were able to discuss their information sources and share new facts, demonstrating an ability to learn with information that emerged from their participation in the project.

The project's collaborative research design also proved successful: teachers were able to reflect on their experience and to offer important insights into project successes as well as suggestions for improvement. During the focus group interview, Ms. A noted that—although her students had never before done an inquiry-based project—the model gave her an easy-to-use tool for guiding and supporting them in learning how to locate, evaluate, apply, and reflect on information related to specific questions. Ms. A also offered important feedback by identifying a challenging aspect of using the framework with young children: teachers must provide ample instructional support to equip students with knowledge they might not have had before, for example, the concept of "sources." Thus, while the model might be a useful tool for independent learning for older learners, younger ones need considerable scaffolding to be successful in its use.

CONTINUED I-LEARN RESEARCH

The research team has since enacted this collaborative research design with a variety of teachers and students, all in the Philadelphia area. These projects involved a high-performing city charter school's kindergartners and fourth graders; seventh graders at an under-resourced urban charter middle school; and tenth graders in an AP World History class at a private, suburban, all-boys Catholic high school. While all the students were able to use the I-LEARN model to support their learning, some students were markedly more successful than others. Productive student inquiry seems to require a key resource: teachers with strong information and digital literacy skills.

The research team offered professional development regarding the specifics of the I-LEARN model to all its research partners but accepted at face value the teachers' declarations of digital and information competence. Most teachers, however, did not have a rich information background—which is not surprising. Early childhood, elementary, and middle school teachers do not generally learn about libraries in their teacher-preparation programs; high school teachers seem to acquire their knowledge on the job because their students are often required to do research. In the study described earlier, Ms. A's preparation as a school librarian undoubtedly helped her cultivate her students' information skills. Our seventh-grade teacher partner, in contrast, was a strong instructor but taught his students to evaluate online information based only on a site's domain name, explaining that .org and .edu sites are more reliable than .com sources. The high school teacher—who divided his instructional responsibilities between teaching history classes and administering the school's well-stocked and well-staffed library—guided his students to create detailed and insightful multimedia presentations, some of which incorporated information they had found in online databases and through primary sources in the school's library (at his urging).

DISCUSSION

The challenges that face many teachers and students in Philadelphia are extreme, but they are not unique. Today, libraries in general and school libraries in particular face an unprecedented threat to their existence. Despite decades of compelling research that a library with solid resources and a certified librarian is highly correlated with student achievement (see, for example, Kachel & Lance, 2013), not enough decision makers have seen the importance of that key finding. Two persistent beliefs—that "everything is on the internet" and that all information is essentially equivalent in value—defy logic but undermine the idea that it is crucial for students to learn from well-trained experts how to access high-quality information, to evaluate it against established criteria, and to apply it efficiently and effectively to answer questions and solve problems.

These skills comprise the kind of learning with information that the students in all our studies—and their counterparts—will need throughout their lives to navigate our increasingly complex information world. The skills also comprise the core of the I-LEARN model, and our studies show that they can be mastered even by young learners as the basis for information-based learning. The studies also suggest that the model can be a helpful tool for fostering information competence at all school levels when used even by teachers with little "library" background.

Budgetary issues are likely to remain a significant issue for urban schools and school libraries far into the future, and the study's major implication for the school library field is a call to find a way to help teachers guide learners to develop information and digital literacies even as the spaces we call "libraries" disappear completely, become only reading rooms or story-telling venues, and rely more and more heavily on uncertified personnel. The consequences of this trend for the children of poverty who make up the majority of urban public school students are sobering. The question becomes, then, what can the field of school librarianship do?

NOTE

This chapter was previously published as Neuman, D., Allen, G., Lee, V., & Tecce DeCarlo, M. J. (2015). Information and digital literacy in a high-poverty urban school: An I-LEARN project. *School Libraries Worldwide, 21*(1), 38–53.

REFERENCES

American Association of School Librarians and Association for Educational Communications & Technology. (1998). *Information power: Building partnerships for learning*. Chicago, IL: ALA Editions.

International Reading Association. (2009). *New literacies and 21st century technologies: A position statement of the International Reading Association*. Newark, DE: IRA.

Johnson, B., & Johnson, K. (2002). Learning from warthogs and oxpeckers: Promoting mutualism in school and university research partnerships. *Educational Action Research, 10*(1), 67–82.

Kachel, D. E., & Lance, K. C. (2013). Latest study: A full-time school librarian makes a critical difference in boosting student achievement.*School Library Journal, 3*, 1–9. Retrieved from http://www.slj.com/2013/03/research

Mitchell, S. N., Reilly, R. C., & Logue, M. E. (2009). Benefits of collaborative action research for the beginning teacher. *Teaching and Teacher Education, 25*(2), 344–349. Retrieved from https://doi.org/10.1016/j.tate.2008.06.008

National Writing Project. (2010). *Because digital writing matters: Improving student writing in online and multimedia environments*. San Francisco, CA: Jossey-Bass.

Neuman, D. (2011a). Constructing knowledge in the twenty-first century: I-LEARN and using information as a tool for learning. *School Library Research, 14*. Retrieved from http://www.ala.org/aasl/sites/ala.org.aasl/files/content/aaslpubsandjournals/slr/vol14/SLR_ConstructingKnowledge_V14.pdf

Neuman, D. (2011b) *Learning in information-rich environments: I-LEARN and the construction of knowledge in the 21st century*. New York, NY: Springer.

School District of Philadelphia. (2012). *School progress reports [2012–2013 through 2017–2018]*. Retrieved from https://www.philasd.org/performance/programsservices/school-progress-reports/available-spr-reports/

Strauss, V. (2013, June 8). Philadelphia school district laying off 3,783 employees. *The Washington Post*. Retrieved from https://www.washingtonpost.com/news/answer-sheet/wp/2013/06/08/philadelphia-school-district-laying-off-3783-employees/?noredirect=on

Vargas, C. (2014, January 11). Obama names impoverished Fairmount [pseudonym] among first five Promise Zones. *Philly.com*. Retrieved from www.philly.com

Villegas, A. M., & Lucas, T. (2002). Preparing culturally responsive teachers. *Journal of Teacher Education, 53*(1), 20–31.

How School Librarians Contribute to Building Resilience in New and Beginning Teachers

Rita Reinsel Soulen and Lois D. Wine

ABSTRACT

School librarians can contribute to building resilience in new and beginning teachers, which may increase teacher retention in the early years, in turn improving student academic achievement. School librarians develop teaching skills by mentoring early career teachers. This qualitative study of first- to third-year teachers and school librarians investigated the contributions that school librarians made in building resilience of beginning teachers through a focus group of new teachers and interviews of school librarians. Findings show that school librarians may contribute to early career teacher resilience, especially during the first days of school, by encouraging perseverance, providing nourishment and empathy, and offering the library as a resource, especially for student research.

INTRODUCTION

Teacher retention is a problem in schools, especially among those teachers in their first few years. U.S. National Center for Education Statistics (NCES) data on public school teacher attrition show that among all beginning teachers in 2007–08, 10% did not teach in the following year. Just four years later, 17% had left the teaching field (Gray & Taie, 2015). High levels of teacher turnover are of concern as this relates to school cohesion and, in turn, student performance (Ingersoll, 2001).

Development of teacher resilience is critical to classroom success and teacher retention (Arnup & Bowles, 2016; Beltman, Mansfield, & Price, 2011; Bobek, 2002; Doney, 2013; Gu & Day, 2013). The American Psychological Association (APA) defines resilience as bouncing back from difficult experiences, or adapting well when faced with adversity (APA, 2017). Personal resilience of new teachers may be bolstered through caring and supportive relationships that create trust, provide role models, and offer encouragement and reassurance (APA, 2017). Psychological practice has moved toward building these positive qualities (Seligman & Csikszentmihalyi, 2000) as a means to promote resilience.

Many public schools in the United States currently provide a formal mentoring program to teachers new to the profession (Evertson & Smithey, 2000). Librarians working in K-12 public schools (students aged 5–18 years) stand in a unique position to offer guidance sorely needed by new educators as they enter the field (Morris, 2015). Anecdotal evidence indicates that many librarians reach out to their new and beginning teachers as a matter of practice, despite the lack of a standard model for the field. A plea on the listserv of a state professional association indicates that school librarians acknowledge this professional responsibility to support new teachers and seek input to develop a model that works in their school:

Hello fellow LibraryLanders! I am thinking ahead to next year and my school has an abundance of new teachers coming in. I am working on my welcome packet and wondered if any of you have a great one you wouldn't mind sharing? (Thompson, 2016)

First-year and beginning teachers may struggle on the front lines of the classroom. However, NCES research also shows that mentoring of new teachers does make a difference. The data show that the percentage of beginning teachers who continued teaching was larger (92%) among those who were assigned a first-year mentor than among those not assigned a first-year mentor (84%). In addition, four years later 86% of mentored teachers were still in the classroom, while 71% were not (Gray & Taie, 2015).

As leaders and professionals in the field, school librarians are primed to respond to this call to contribute to stabilizing a strong teaching force. Consideration of steps to prevent teacher attrition so that all children receive competent, continuous instruction in every community every year is essential for the success of our students as well as for our society as a whole (Sutcher, Darling-Hammond, & Carver-Thomas, 2016).

Recognition of the challenges new and beginning teachers face in the classroom and the role of a librarian as a leader in the school led to this case study, which explored the ways in which the school librarian can contribute to building resilience in early career teachers. The results of this study define how, as librarians and educators, our practice engages our entering professionals to promote their development. Results of this study show that school librarians have a unique opportunity to influence resilience of new teachers, which may affect faculty retention and, in turn, may relate to student achievement (Ingersoll, 2001).

BACKGROUND

O'Leary (1998) saw the development of strength through adversity as the ability to move beyond survival and recovery, to thrive in the face of profound challenge. Soon after O'Leary's observation, Seligman and Csikszentmihalyi (2000) first outlined a framework for positive psychology, which fosters positive attitudes through psychological interventions and a focus on building positive qualities. Powers (2010) developed an evidence-based framework of practice in schools in which positive and protective factors buffer the effects of risk factors to encourage resilience within the social environment. She defined resilience as a dynamic process of positive adaptation in the context of adversity with protective factors enabling functionality despite the risks. Organizations can influence their employees' resilience capacity, and thus should commit to fostering the resiliency of the employee (Ledesma, 2014; O'Leary, 1998). When applied at the school level, such supportive structures may lead to greater teacher resilience.

Castro, Kelly, and Shih (2010) described resilience for teachers as the ability to adjust to diverse situations and to increase competence in the face of adverse conditions. Resilience is influenced by sociocultural factors in the school, which build or erode the ability to perform as knowledgeable, committed, and enthusiastic teachers (Day & Gu, 2014). Several other researchers have developed models of teacher resilience. Tait (2008) focused on novice teacher resilience as an asset that relates to effectiveness and emotional competence. Doney (2013) looked at how stressors and protective factors affect resilience, and how resilience can be fostered to encourage teacher retention. Greenfield (2015) constructed a model to encourage supportive practices and policies that protect and promote teacher resilience. These models could provide a basis for a collaborative mentoring model to be used by school librarians.

By promoting a spirit of optimism and human agency (Johnson & Down, 2013), school leaders and colleagues can impact the school culture (Day & Gu, 2014)using a framework of support to include policies and practices, teachers' work, school culture, relationships, and teacher identity (Johnson et al., 2016). New teachers who develop characteristics of resiliency may be better able to combat the challenges of the first years of teaching.

Forming collaborative partnerships with teachers and other educators is a basic tenet of the role of the school librarian in the United States (American Association of School Librarians [AASL], 2009, 2018; AASL & Association for Educational Communications Technology, 1988, 1998). New and beginning teachers who are hungry for information, insight, and discreetly delivered assistance provide an opening for school librarians to encourage mentorships, build alliances, and connect to the newcomers' notions of success (Hartzell, 2003). Those librarians who offer their services may be pleasantly surprised at requests from new teachers (Freeman, 2014) who are "desperate for help and ideas" (Andronik, 2003, p. 45). The vulnerability of teachers in their first year (Hartzell, 2003) affords the opportunity to work together, provide resources, and share ideas in a professional learning community (Freeman, 2014).

Actions by school librarians for teachers appear on a continuum of collaboration, ranging from support to intervention, which directly impact academic achievement (Loertscher, 2000). Leaders in the field of school librarianship recommend tactics for building influence with teachers, such as creating an orientation program or video for new hires (Emery, 2008; Hartzell, 2003). Thomas (2002) suggests extending an invitation to collaborate, flexibly plan, stay actively involved, share responsibilities, and reflect on practice. Other recommended actions on the part of the school librarian include introducing best resources, booktalks, provision of websites and databases, and one-to-one instruction leading to more collaborative, innovative, and challenging lesson plans (Corrick & Amos, 2000). Such programs may also provide a social outlet for new teachers to temper the habit of isolation (Lindsay, 2005). The field encourages school librarians to welcome new teachers, provide collegial support, open doors to collaboration, and model effective teaching for student learning (Morris, 2015). As mentors and collaborators, the school librarian can help new and beginning teachers make sense of the uncertainties of the first years.

As instructional partners, school librarians "meet the learning needs of all learners, including other educators" and lead "professional-development opportunities that articulate the positive impact of the school library's resources, services, and programming" (AASL, 2018, pp. 89–90). School library program guidelines have historically identified building partnerships of teaching for learning that "promote collaboration among members of the learning community" (AASL, 2009, p. 19) and recommend that school librarians "model leadership and best practice for the school community" (p. 45). The importance of providing a welcoming environment, especially to new teachers, continues to be a recurring theme in the literature (Baker & Willis, 2016; Morris, 2015; Woeste, 2008). As school librarians, our professional practice engages our community of learners and assumes social responsibility for the development of their teachers, especially new and beginning teachers. As researchers we sought to describe how librarians support entering faculty in our school communities.

DESIGN OF THE STUDY

This case study used qualitative methods to investigate the contributions made by librarians to new and beginning teacher resilience in the natural school setting (Hays & Singh, 2012). Through a social constructivist approach, the researchers attempted to identify the building blocks of new and beginning teacher resilience and elucidate the lived experience of these teachers. With a strong bent toward critical theory (Creswell & Poth, 2018), the researchers strived toward empowerment of new and beginning teachers by defining the role of the school librarian in their professional development.

The researchers developed the conceptual framework for this study (see Figure 1) based on information gleaned from the literature, and drawing from models of teacher resilience (Doney, 2013; Greenfield, 2015; Tait, 2008). The collaborative role of the school librarian combines with the contributions of the school librarian to support new teacher resilient traits and behaviors. In turn, resilience of new teachers may influence teacher retention and student achievement.

Research Question: How do school librarians contribute to building resilience in new and beginning teachers?

Participants in this exploratory study consisted of 11 new teachers and school librarians ($N = 11$) from one urban school district in a mid-Atlantic state. The focus group consisted of six new and beginning teachers ($n = 6$) from one middle school serving students grades 6–8 (aged 11–14 years). New teachers were defined as those in their first contract year. Beginning teachers were defined as those in their second or third year of teaching under contract. Purposive sampling was used to select focus group

Figure 1
Conceptual framework

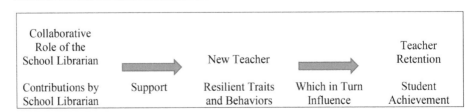

participants for the detail they could provide about development of resilience in new teachers. All were contracted teachers. Two were not yet certified, while four were certified in their subject area. Two participants were in their first year of teaching, three in their second year, and one in her third year. Two were music teachers, two were math teachers, and two were English teachers. The focus group was equally divided between male and female teachers. Five of the teachers were 30 years or younger, whereas one was over 50 years old. Self-reported race/ethnicity included White (2), Caucasian (1), Black/White (1), Black (1), and Black/non-Hispanic (1).

The interview population consisted of five librarians ($n = 5$) at separate schools in the same school district. Convenience sampling was used to select interview participants. All were White/Caucasian females who were certified, contracted school librarians ranging in age from less than 40 years to over 60 years. Three had less than 10 years of experience as school librarians, while two had more than 10 years of experience. Two practiced in elementary schools (students aged 5–11 years), one in a combined elementary/middle school (students aged 8–14 years), and two in high school (students aged 14–18 years).

It is important to note here that one of the researchers was the school librarian and lead teacher mentor at the school where the focus group of new teachers took place. She was also a school librarian in the district where the interviews of school librarians took place. These roles provided her with intimate knowledge of, and access to, the new and beginning teachers, and a professional relationship with the interview participants. This established insider relationship of one researcher to the study participants allowed for greater access to the new teachers and the librarians. However, this relationship may also have introduced bias into data collection and analysis. Additionally, since the research was performed in one school district using a small sample, generalization of the results would be inappropriate.

Data collection took place in two parts. First, the focus group of six new and beginning teachers centered on identifying resilient behaviors, especially those supported by school librarians over the course of the school year. In the second phase of the study, interviews of five school librarians focused on their contributions to resilience of new and beginning teachers. The researchers used the conceptual framework to create a blueprint from which they developed semistructured question protocols, which were adapted for each subgroup (see Appendix A). Questions included a personal definition of resilience, resilient traits and behaviors of teachers, importance of resilience for teachers, behaviors that evidence resilience, the role of school librarians in building resilience, examples of this role, mentoring new and beginning teachers, retention, and student achievement.

The researchers engaged in the process of memoing and summarizing (Hays & Singh, 2012) during the data collection process. The focus group and interviews were voice recorded, transcribed verbatim, and then coded to identify themes and patterns. Field notes also filled in details not captured in the voice recordings. The transcribed data were chunked and assigned descriptive tags, shortened into etic codes, and then developed into a digital codebook with patterns, themes, evidence, and quotes from new and beginning teachers and librarians. While some codes related directly back to the conceptual framework, blueprint, and protocol, others surfaced from participant discussion. Relationships, patterns, and themes emerged through this process. To establish trustworthiness, results were offered to participants for member checking, and the transcriptions and codebook were peer audited.

FINDINGS

Findings of this study outline the meaningful role played by school librarians in building resilience of new teachers. These include personal definitions of resilience from the perspectives of both the new teachers and the school librarians. This report focuses on the contributions of the school librarian in developing resilience for new and beginning teachers during the first days of school, and beyond. The researchers identified perseverance, nourishment, and empathy as foundations to building resilience for new teachers. Additionally, they recognized using the librarian and the library as a resource for ideas and materials in planning and for research as a contribution to building resilience.

Participants offered varied personal definitions of resilience. Both the new teachers and the school librarians pointed to being flexible and moving with the changes. One librarian saw resilience as the shiny side of perseverance: "Bright, shiny, it just has sparkles. The word resilience has sparkles around it in my vision." Another librarian saw resilience as crucial to survival in the field of education. One elementary school librarian even had her personal definition of resilience posted above her desk, "Resiliency: the act of recovering from hardship."

General Themes

Several general themes emerged from the data. Overall, both new teachers and school librarians described resilience as "huge" in the first years of teaching. Resilience is a necessary trait when dealing with difficult student behavior, and participants pointed out that student behavior and teacher resilience mutually impact each other. Perseverance was the practical side of resilience. The importance of teamwork as contributing to retention was influenced formally by administration and informally by other teachers and peers. Participants generally expressed that mentoring, both formal and informal, does make a difference. Although evidence arose that school librarians can contribute to new and beginning teacher resilience, retention of new and beginning teachers was also dependent on both district policies and the school environment in general. Participants responded that student achievement would be influenced more immediately by teacher resilience and long-term by teacher retention.

The data show that the opening days of school were a portal to establishing a relationship between the school librarian and new teachers. Other themes that emerged include persevering in the face of adversity, nurturing, empathy, the library as a resource, and guidance in teaching research skills. Together, these serve as building blocks of the contributions of school librarians to new teacher resilience.

The First Days of School

School librarians contributed to teacher resilience from the start of the school year. Orienting to the building during the first days of school ranged from a formal library orientation for new teachers to individual assistance with classroom setup. A high school librarian described a yearly event in her library during teacher preservice week where they hosted a casual presentation to the new faculty to let them know how librarians can assist them. In a middle school, a new teacher was appreciative of the librarian's attention when setting up her classroom. Another first-year teacher suggested a direct invitation to come to the library for assistance. One third-year English teacher appreciated a more balanced exchange of librarian visits to the classroom and teacher visits to the library to assess new teacher needs. A librarian in a combined elementary and middle school summed it up: "We've got to teach [new teachers] to learn how to navigate so they don't get burned out in the first five years ... latch onto the new ones and let them know what the library offers."

Perseverance

Perseverance was a recurring theme both in the general findings and more specifically as a trait that can be promoted by the school librarian. One second-year teacher identified the importance of the safety net provided by mentors of many kinds to build confidence. Reassurance from other faculty does make a difference. As one librarian affirmed, "Hey, you don't have to get it right the first time. Or the fifth time." One middle school librarian understood the contribution this encouragement made to teacher retention: "I would just work with them to try to, make things better for them, make them happier, make them want to stick around, so we don't lose them." As this confidence builds, teachers look to the future and begin to plan for the next school year. Librarians can support these plans by identifying resources, such as DVDs, databases, websites, and webquests, to be curated or even produced: "If we can't find one already made, we can create one."

Nourishment

The nurturing support of caring faculty, including the librarian, may lead to teachers who grow to be strong and flexible in the school community. One high school librarian compared the services of the school library to the food court at the mall. For new teachers, "it's a place you can come and get something that helps to hopefully nourish you." Another high school librarian imagined this support as "being a hand on their back," or, from another high school librarian, "to try to let them know they're not in it alone." One elementary school librarian saw this support as leading to comfortably approaching the school librarian for assistance for now, and for later in their teaching career.

Empathy

The profession of school librarianship combines the roles of both teacher and librarian, leading to a special professional rapport. A first-year teacher shared one moment of this empathetic relationship. "You told me your first-year experience, like you told me you went home for Christmas and you just had a breakdown. But then you came back ... It was good to know that everybody kind of struggles their first year." A third-year teacher confirmed that experience does lead to strength, "And people look so put together now. They've all had their time, their moments." As a former English teacher, a high school librarian further identified with the perspective of the teacher. She described the library as a "no judgment zone," a place of comfort and confidence, where new and beginning teachers are not alone. Just providing a listening ear and a comfortable environment may be enough. As one high school librarian said, "I can just be there to listen to them. And a lot of times they just need that."

Library as Resource

The school library serves as a resource for the community of learners and the development of their teachers. One third-year teacher recognized this deep connection, "I think you [the librarian] do have the pulse of the school because everyone uses your resources," which was supported by a high school librarian's statement, "Librarians are open to everyone." Another high school librarian referred to the notion of orienting to resources that bolster their lesson plans: "We will be here to help them as much as they need it." A librarian in a K-8 school recognized that librarians provide human, physical, and digital resources. She noted that librarians know the curriculum across all the content areas, match the curriculum to resources, and build classroom libraries and centers. Librarians also provide physical and digital resources in the forms of content area books, primary and secondary sources, reference resources, and websites and online resources. For a librarian in one elementary school, these baby steps lead to the big idea of collaboration. She expressed the idea that by providing resources, content, materials, and support, the next step would be collaborative lessons.

Research

In schools, one area of collaboration for librarians has traditionally been working with English teachers on research skills. One first-year English teacher spoke of his experience working as a long-term substitute with the school librarian who guided a research lesson with students. Another English teacher referred to the librarian supplementing lessons by working with her students in small groups on a focus area. However, convincing teachers in all content areas that the library has something to offer may be more challenging, while still possible. During the focus group interview, one geometry teacher expressed that she did not see an application for research in her curriculum. However, her close associate, who taught pre-algebra, replied that research would be worth looking into as an innovative strategy. In this exchange, the geometry teacher then responded more positively, with the caveat that such research would need to include understanding of concepts within the pacing of the curriculum.

DISCUSSION

As perceived by these participants, the school librarian contributed to building resilience of new teachers in several ways. During the first days of school, the librarian served in the role of orienting new teachers to their new careers. Later, she encouraged new and beginning teachers to persevere during difficult times, offering nourishment and empathy to build confidence. The school librarian provided the resources of the library and encouraged integrating research into the curriculum. These actions of the school librarian that augmented the resilience of these new teachers may, in turn, result in increased retention.

The beginning of the school year, when new teachers were feeling disoriented, provided the most concentrated opportunities for the school librarian to connect to the new teachers. Encouraging perseverance through nurturing and empathy led to the new teachers viewing the library as a resource, and the librarian as an expert in teaching research skills. However, the value of this expertise varied by the teachers' perspective based on the subject taught. Not surprisingly, the English teachers in this study were more connected to the school librarian, while math teachers had a more difficult time seeing the value of the librarian for their lessons. The opportunity was apparent, though, that with some convincing, all the new teachers in this study would be willing to work more closely with the librarian to build the collaborative relationship of a more mature professional practice.

CONCLUSIONS AND IMPLICATIONS FOR PRACTICE

For library and information science educators, this research provides evidence that the effective librarian can influence resilience of new and beginning faculty. By establishing relationships with those just entering the field, the librarian may create a safe zone, a retreat, and a place of replenishment for new professionals. The formation of a welcoming environment establishes the library as a useful resource and guide for new faculty to see the value of student research through opportunities for project-based learning. This investment by school librarians in mentoring of new and beginning teachers may result in teachers who are more comfortable with consulting the librarian as they gain more experience.

This research developed an initial description of the contributions that school librarians make to developing resiliency among new and beginning teachers, which may influence retention and in turn address student achievement. By affecting teacher retention, resiliency influences social stability both within and outside the school house doors. Parents, community, administrators, and other stakeholders rely on a stable, experienced, and highly qualified professional faculty to promote student achievement. With better definition of the role of school librarians as leaders and collaborators, we should feel compelled to take action to mitigate the escalating social problem of new and beginning teacher attrition in our school communities. Educators of school librarians can encourage preservice school librarians to consider new and beginning teachers as a special population with defined needs.

The AASL (2018) *National School Library Standards* recommend developing a personal relationship as best practice before attempting to collaborate. For new teachers, this may naturally take the form of mentoring. These standards suggest that sharing a table at lunch or attending department and grade level meetings opens the doors to opportunity to develop a friendly rapport. By listening for the special needs of new and beginning teachers, the librarian embraces the role of professional partner to recommend relevant resources and work together on instructional projects (AASL, 2018).

The findings show that the new teacher's subject area may influence their inclination to collaborate with the school librarian. Collaboration between the English teacher and school librarian appears to be an easy fit. However, school librarians must challenge themselves to step outside this comfort zone into other subject areas. Subramaniam and Edwards (2014) found that even the thought of collaboration between the librarian and math teachers requires a new interpretation of both roles. To strengthen the relationship between school librarians and teachers of mathematics, changes to the perceptions each has of the other are necessary, as well as changes to perceptions of technology integration in the classroom and collaborative relationships in general (Subramaniam & Edwards, 2014). Likewise, Green and Green (2014) found that interdisciplinary partnerships between school librarians and music educators demand a broadening of roles. Librarians and music teachers can mutually benefit in the equal exchange of technology integration and professional development support for creative advocacy ideas, marketing, and program planning (Green & Green, 2014). Educators of school librarians and school librarians in practice may need to consider massaging their approach to collaboration with new teachers, depending on the subject area taught.

EPILOGUE

This research has continued beyond the exploratory qualitative study to a quantitative study using interventions by school librarians for new teachers that provided supporting structures to promote resilience, reduce burnout, and increase retention. One of the researchers, Rita Soulen, received a grant of $10,000 from the AASL through the Causality: School Libraries and Student Success (CLASS) II initiative to support causal research in the field. Her recent study compared new teachers who received interventions from their school librarian ($n = 26$) to a matched sample who did not. For this study, the researcher developed a Continuum of Care, which was a calendar of interventions to support teachers in their first year. These interventions provided mentoring and collaboration by school librarians for new teachers under the Continuum of Care to increase resilience, reduce burnout, and increase retention.

The future of school libraries centers on innovative practices that deliberately develop the resilience of the school community. New and beginning teachers who may be more vulnerable to the uncertainties of the classroom can benefit from collegial support, especially from their school librarian. Collective impact initiatives, in this case, targeted mentoring and collaboration, solve specific social problems such as teacher retention, and contribute to the social cohesion of the organization (Aldrich, 2018). The unique role of the librarian in the school provides the opportunity to answer the immediate call to action to intervene in the working lives of new and beginning teachers for the betterment of our school communities.

REFERENCES

Aldrich, R. (2018). *Resilience*. Chicago, IL: American Library Association.
American Association of School Librarians. (2009). *Empowering learners: Guidelines for school library programs*. Chicago, IL: American Library Association.
American Association of School Librarians. (2018). *National school library standards for learners, school librarians, and school libraries*. Chicago, IL: American Library Association.
American Association of School Librarians & Association for Educational Communications Technology. (1988). *Information power guidelines for school library media programs*. Chicago, IL: American Library Association & Association for Educational Communications and Technology.
American Association of School Librarians & Association for Educational Communications Technology. (1998). *Information power: Building partnerships for learning*. Chicago, IL: American Library Association.
American Psychological Association. (2017). *The road to resilience*. Retrieved from http://www.apa.org/helpcenter/road-resilience.aspx
Andronik, C. (2003). *School library management* (5th ed.). Worthington, OH: Linworth Publishing.
Arnup, J., & Bowles, T. (2016). Should I stay or should I go? Resilience as a protective factor for teachers' intention to leave the teaching profession. *Australian Journal of Education, 60*(3), 229–244.

Baker, S., & Willis, J. (2016). When stars align: Teachers & students shine brighter. *Knowledge Quest, 45*(2), 56–63.

Beltman, S., Mansfield, C., & Price, A. (2011). Thriving not just surviving: A review of research on teacher resilience. *Educational Research Review, 6*, 185–207.

Bobek, B. (2002). Teacher resiliency: A key to career longevity. *Clearing House, 75*(4), 202–205.

Castro, A., Kelly, J., & Shih, M. (2010). Resilience strategies for new teachers in high-needs areas. *Teaching and Teacher Education, 26*, 622–629.

Corrick, G., & Amos, J. (2000). Packaged for success. *The Book Report, 5–6.*

Creswell, J., & Poth, C. (2018). *Qualitative inquiry & research design.* Thousand Oaks, CA: SAGE Publications.

Day, C., & Gu, Q. (2014). *Resilient teachers, resilient schools: Building and sustaining quality in testing times.* New York, NY: Routledge.

Doney, P. (2013). Fostering resilience: A necessary skill for teacher retention. *Journal of Science Teacher Education, 24*(4), 645–664. doi:10.1007/s10972-012-9324-x

Emery, A. (2008). *School library orientation: Introducing teachers to the roles and services of teacher librarians* (Unpublished master's thesis). University of Northern Iowa, Iowa.

Evertson, C., & Smithey, M. (2000). Mentoring effects on proteges' classroom practice: An experimental field study. *Journal of Educational Research, 93*(5), 294–304.

Freeman, J. (2014). Beyond the stacks. *American Educator.* Retrieved from http://www.aft.org/ae/winter2014-2015/freeman

Gray, L., & Taie, S. (2015, April). *Public school teacher attrition and mobility in the first five years (Research report no. 2015337).* National Center for Education Statistics Institute of Education Sciences. Retrieved from http://nces.ed.gov/pubs2015/2015337.pdf

Green, L. S., & Green, B. (2014). School librarians and music educators: Unique interdisciplinary partnerships. In K. Kennedy & L. S. Green (Eds.), *Collaborative models for librarian and teacher partnerships* (pp. 99–120). Hershey, PA: IGI Global.

Greenfield, B. (2015). How can teacher resilience be protected and promoted? *Educational & Child Psychology, 32*(4), 52–68.

Gu, Q., & Day, C. (2013). Challenges to teacher resilience: Conditions count. *British Educational Research Journal, 39*(1), 22–44.

Hartzell, G. (2003). *Building influence for the school librarian: Tenets, targets, & tactics* (2nd ed.). Worthington, OH: Linworth Publishing.

Hays, D., & Singh, A. (2012). *Qualitative inquiry in clinical and educational settings.* New York, NY: The Guilford Press.

Ingersoll, R. M. (2001). Teacher turnover and teacher shortages: An organizational analysis. *American Educational Research Journal, 38*(3), 499. Retrieved from http://proxy.lib.odu.edu/login?url=http://search.proquest.com.proxy.lib.odu.edu/docview/200409308?accountid=12967

Johnson, B., & Down, B. (2013). Critically re-conceptualizing early career teacher resilience. *Discourse: Studies in the Cultural Politics of Education, 34*(5), 703–715.

Johnson, B., Down, B., Le Cornu, R., Peters, J., Sullivan, A., Pearce, J., & Hunter, J. (2016). *Promoting early career teacher resilience.* New York, NY: Routledge.

Ledesma, J. (2014). Conceptual frameworks and research models on resilience in leadership. *SAGE Open, 4*(3).

Lindsay, K. (2005). Teacher/teacher librarian collaboration: A review of the literature. *School Libraries in Canada, 25*(2), 8–21.

Loertscher, D. V. (2000). *Taxonomies of the school library media program* (2nd ed.). Salt Lake City, UT: Hi Willow Research & Publishing.

Morris, R. (2015). You're hired! Welcoming new teachers to the school library. *Knowledge Quest, 43*(5), 38–41.

O'Leary, V. (1998). Strength in the face of adversity: Individual and social thriving. *Journal of Social Issues, 54*(2), 425–446.

Powers, J. D. (2010). Ecological risk and resilience perspective: A theoretical framework supporting evidence-based practice in schools.*Journal of Evidence-Based Social Work, 7*(5), 443–451. doi:10.1080/15433714.2010.509216

Seligman, M., & Csikszentmihalyi, M. (2000). Positive psychology. An introduction. *The American Psychologist, 55*(1), 5–14.

Subramaniam, M., & Edwards, A. (2014). The collaboration conundrum between school librarians and mathematics teachers. *Libri: International Journal of Libraries and Information Services, 64*(2), 185–209.

Sutcher, L., Darling-Hammond, L., & Carver-Thomas, D. (2016). A coming crisis in teaching? Teacher supply, demand, and shortages in the U.S. Retrieved from https://learningpolicyinstitute.org/product/coming-crisis-teaching-brief

Tait, M. (2008). Resilience as a contributor to novice teacher success, commitment, and retention. *Teacher Education Quarterly, 35*(4), 57–75.

Thomas, M. (2002). What is collaboration to you? In C. Andronik (Ed.), *School library management* (5th ed., pp. 47–48). Worthington, OH: Linworth Publishing.

Thompson, J. (2016, June 16). Welcome packet [electronic mailing list]. Retrieved from https://vassl.org/tabs/listserv/

Woeste, M. (2008). You've got a friend. *Library Media Connection, 27*(1), 32–33.

APPENDIX A FOCUS GROUP AND INTERVIEW PROTOCOLS

Focus Group Protocol

Building Resilience in New and Beginning Teachers: Contributions of School Librarians
Research Question:
How do school librarians contribute to building resilience in new and beginning teachers?

Sensitizing Concept:	Building Resilience
Participants:	New and Beginning Teachers
Expected Time:	50 minutes
Location:	Middle School Library Media Center Conference Room
Instructions:	Thank you for participating in this focus group today. Your participation is completely voluntary. I appreciate your taking the time to share your views on factors that contribute to new teacher resilience. Your identity will be confidential. Out of respect for your colleagues, please keep confidential the thoughts and experiences being shared here today. The session will be recorded then transcribed. Data collected will be reported out anonymously. You will have the opportunity to review the focus group transcript if the information is used for publication. Please be considerate of others in the group, and allow opportunity for all to share. For the purpose of this study, a new teacher will be defined as one in their first contract year while a beginning teacher will be defined as one in their first, second, or third contract year. Do you have any questions before we begin?

Demographics/ Background Questions:	How long have you been a contracted teacher? Do you have a mentor? If so, can you describe some of your experiences?
Key Research Questions:	How do you define resilience? Do you think resilience is an important trait for teachers? Please explain. What behaviors would you identify in new and beginning teachers that show evidence of resilience? What role do school librarians play in building resilience for new and beginning teachers? What factors would help you feel comfortable going to the school librarian for assistance in building resilience? What contribution(s) has the school librarian, either here or at another school where you have worked, given that has contributed to your developing resilience? What part do you think resilience plays in retention of new and beginning teachers? What part do you think resilience of new and beginning teachers plays in student achievement?
Probes (as needed):	Can you give me an example? Tell me a little more about that. What happened next? How did that happen? What was that like for you? Where were you? Who else was there? Can you elaborate on that?
Transition Messages:	Thank you for sharing your experiences with me today. In appreciation for your time, you will be entered into a drawing for a $50 Amazon gift card. Should any of the data collected be used for publication, I will give you the opportunity to review your contributions for accuracy in reporting.

Interviewer Comments:

Reflective Notes:

Interview Protocol

Building Resilience in New and Beginning Teachers: Contributions of School Librarians
Research Question:
How do school librarians contribute to building resilience in new and beginning teachers?
Sensitizing Concept: Building Resilience
Participants: School Librarians
Expected Time: 30 minutes
Location: School Library Media Center or Coffee Shop

Instructions:	Thank you for participating in this focus group today. Your participation is completely voluntary. I appreciate your taking the time to share your views on factors that contribute to new teacher resilience. Your identity will be confidential. Out of respect for your colleagues, please keep confidential the thoughts and experiences being shared here today. The session will be recorded then transcribed. Data collected will be reported out anonymously. You will have the opportunity to review the focus group transcript if the information is used for publication. Please be considerate of others in the group, and allow opportunity for all to share. For the purpose of this study, a new teacher will be defined as one in their first contract year while a beginning teacher will be defined as one in their first, second, or third contract year. Do you have any questions before we begin?
Demographics/ Background Questions:	How long have you been a school librarian? Do you now, or have you ever, served as a teacher mentor? If so, can you describe some of your experiences serving in this capacity?

Key Research Questions:

1. How do you define resilience?
2. Do you think resilience is an important trait for teachers? Please explain.
3. What behaviors would you identify in new and beginning teachers that show evidence of resilience?
4. What role do school librarians play in building resilience for new and beginning teachers?
5. How do you, as a school librarian, help new and beginning teachers build resilience? Please give specific examples.
6. If a new teacher came to you asking for help, what advice would you give her or him that would contribute to building resilience?
7. What part do you think resilience plays in retention of new and beginning teachers?
8. What part do you think resilience of new and beginning teachers plays in student achievement?

Probes (as needed):	Can you give me an example? Tell me a little more about that. What happened next? How did that happen? What was that like for you? Where were you? Who else was there? Can you elaborate on that?
Transition Messages:	Thank you for sharing your experiences with me today. In appreciation for your time, you will be entered into a drawing for a $50 Amazon gift card. Should any of the data collected be used for publication, I will give you the opportunity to review your contributions for accuracy in reporting.

Interviewer Comments:

Reflective Notes:

Voice and Identity: YA Urban Literature's Transformative Impacts on Youth

Sabrina Carnesi

ABSTRACT

In this qualitative study of collaboration between an eighth-grade English teacher and a school librarian, 14 urban youth from a suburban city in the mid-Atlantic region of the United States were interviewed on the impact they experienced from a yearlong study with young adult literature reflective of their lived experiences. Steeped in the language of social justice and inclusive of national school library standards and international school library guidelines, the findings bring attention to the impact that highly effective partnerships have on implementing literature discussion circles and Socratic seminars as a platform of expression for seldom heard young adult voices.

INTRODUCTION

Historically, school librarianship has focused on effective collaboration with classroom teachers for instructional implementation (Berkowitz & Eisenberg, 1989). Each American Association of School Librarians (AASL) *standard for learners (part of the AASL National School Library Standards https://standards.aasl.org)* (AASL, 2017) is achieved using this collaboration strategy to provide learners with the essential skills for today's world that are vital in providing resource equity and "a well-rounded education for every student" (AASL, 2016, p. 1). Providing literature for young adult urban youth of color is a priority, because this demographic is the fastest growing population in American society (Braun, Hartman, Hughes-Hassell, & Kumasi, 2014), and with the least amount of literature published annually (Cooperative Children's Book Center, 2017). It takes a purposeful move of inclusivity to provide the "particular resource needs and interests" (International Federation of Library Associations [IFLA], 2015, p. 8) that fit underrepresented youth who need to see their life mirrored in the text, "for when they can't see themselves, or they see a distorted image, they learn a powerful lesson about how they are devalued in society" (Bishop, 1990, p. 1).

Urban Youths' Disconnect

In the United States, a total of 4.9 million young adults are disconnected from school and not working; disconnection at this level ensures a future of low earnings, high unemployment, poor health, incarceration, and short lifespans (Fashola & Slavin, 1998; Jerald, 2006; U.S. Census Bureau, 2006). Statistics show that those most impacted are people of color and those from low economic urban areas (Belfield, Levin, & Rosen, 2012). Underrepresented youths show strong levels of pushback (Rauner, 2013; Todd & Edwards, 2004) due to poor support networks and unstable homes (Bridgeland & Milano, 2012). Maslow's (1943) hierarchy of needs reveals how basic psychological sustenance is a first priority for these youth, because they must feel they are safe, secure, and that they belong to someone or something if they are to succeed. Educators can help by providing environments that are communities of learning to aid these students in seeing possibilities of success (Christensen, 2009; Perry et al., 2003).

Identity begins to be "structured early in the lives" of youth (Van Ausdale & Feagin, 2002, p. 189), and strong identities are needed in order for youth to function competitively (Rauner, 2013). Reading books with diverse protagonists can facilitate positive identity development for underrepresented urban youth and also for those in the majority (Bishop, 1982, 1990), by presenting a balanced world vision "instead of [nurturing] conflict" (Larrick, 1965, p. 63). This balancing is required to understand what is needed to right systemic wrongs (Fricker, 2013) through a social justice lens (Froggatt, 2015; Rioux, 2010).

The Right to See Themselves on the Shelf

Rioux (2010) explained how, when viewing the world through a social justice lens, "each individual is important" and "deserves respect" (p. 12). Providing youth with the opportunity to access literature reflective of their own identity should be a fundamental consideration for school librarians to use in framing their policy for collection development and for developing effective library programming (AASL, 2010; IFLA, 2015). When youth from underrepresented groups can see themselves represented in the collection, because someone has purposely made the effort to provide literature about and for them and written by authors from their cultural groups, they are more able to feel that they are not being ignored and that their presence counts (Todd & Edwards, 2004; Van Orman & Lyiscott, 2013). When underrepresented youth cannot find themselves in the collection, they may feel invisible and unimportant. Taylor (1992) referred to identity misrecognition as something that "can inflict harm, [and] be a form of oppression [which could] imprison someone in a false, distorted, and reduced mode of being" (p. 25). From a social justice perspective, this can be viewed as a deliberate act of aggression (Birnbacher, 1984).

The social justice metatheory of Rioux (2010) is an emerging framework through which this study was viewed. Rioux's (2010) *Five Assumptions of Social Justice for Library and Information Science* states the following:

1. All human beings have an inherent worth and deserve information services that help address their informational needs.
2. People perceive reality in different ways, often within cultural or life role contexts.

3. There are many different types of information and knowledge, and these are societal resources.
4. Theory and research are pursued with the ultimate goal of bringing positive change to service constituencies.
5. The provision of information services is an inherently powerful activity. Access, control, and mediation of information contain inherent power relationships. The act of distributing information is itself a political act. (p. 13)

Termed as "nascent" (Rioux, 2010, p.13), these assumptions make allowance for research in the field of underrepresentation and resource availability related to school libraries that provide services to youths from underrepresented groups.

The School Library as a Site for Social Justice

The mission put forth in the AASL (2009) national guidelines is "to ensure that students are to be critical, effective, empowered, and ethical thinkers and users" (p. 8). Through the lens of Rioux's (2010) fifth assumption, this mission can be interpreted as the school library's "provision of information is an inherently powerful act" (p. 13), the provision of information that not only supports classroom curriculum, but the "everyday" realities that are pertinent for the "teen-to-adult maturation" process (Agosto & Hughes-Hassell, 2006, p. 1394). Focusing interpretations of this mission through Rioux's second assumption tells us that the lived experiences of youth from underrepresented groups should not be assumed to be the same as the lived experiences of youths in the majority, and underrepresented youths therefore require literature reflecting the issues specific to their reality. Tatum (1997) articulated the importance of racial identity for youth of color in our society by explaining how race and identity are very much part of a youth of color's maturation:

For teens of color and for Indigenous teens, the coming of age is integrally tied to the process of racial and ethnic identity formation. Although identity formation is a critical task for all, adolescent researchers have found that adolescents of color and Indigenous teens are more likely to be actively engaged in exploring their racial and ethnic identity than are white adolescents. (p. 1)

Tatum's research demonstrates how Indigenous and biracial youth, as well as Black, and Asian and Latin American youth, view themselves as part of a race or an ethnic group because of how society views them (Moule, 2010; Tatum, 1997).

Problem Statement

In the United States, the diversity demographics for young adults are rising; most youth "in the United States live in or just outside an urban area" (U.S. Department of Health, 2018, line 58). Research has been conducted related to urban youth and young adult literature in metropolitan settings (Brooks & Savage, 2009; Agosto & Hughes-Hassell, 2010; Morris, Hughes-Hassell, Agosto, & Cottman, 2006), and scholarly work for this same demographic group provides book lists by age (Morris, 2012) and subject (Guerra, 2012). Although young adult literature shows protagonists in nonmetropolitan settings experiencing urban social issues in their homes and on the streets (Hinton &

Carnesi, 2017), very little scholarly work concerning the reading preferences of youth from this demographic group has been done (Hinton & Carnesi, 2017).

Purpose and Research Question

Youth who are often silenced socially, misrepresented, and marginalized need to be provided with platforms that lend voice to their silence. In this study, I examined how young adult literature can affect the literacy experience of urban youth who see their own experiences and life issues reflected in the literature they read. I explored the question: "How does involvement in reading and discussing young adult (YA) literature about urban youth by urban youth shape their construction of their identity and epistemic outlooks?"

METHOD

Participants

The participants' school included 849 urban youth in a suburban area. Two-thirds of the students qualified as economically disadvantaged, making the school eligible for 100% free lunch. Fourteen students (3 females and 11 males) were interviewed in the yearlong study, within the last six days of school. Students' ages ranged from 13 to 15. Background information on each participant was collected, to develop deeper understandings of each student's literacy and classroom identities. Additional demographics on the group of participants are provided in Table 1.

Context of Study

As a school librarian in this school, I had an existing foundation of trust with these participants, which aided my role as a researcher. The study took place between October 2015 and May 2016 with cofacilitation in the class occurring two to three times a week. From the beginning of the academic year, I met with the classroom teacher, in the role of school librarian, to plan and schedule adjustments of the literature choices in the eighth-grade English curriculum. With the objective of identity development (Bishop, 1982) embedded in this effort, I wanted to form a "true partnership [with the students], in order to bring about a positive change and empowerment" (Rioux, 2010, p. 14).

To meet these students' independent reading needs, I began the year by collecting feedback on the students' preferred genres through an informal classroom discussion. This initial list of reading needs was followed up with an informal interest reading inventory for additional information on reading needs and an overview of the students' favorite titles, as shown in Table 2.

When students were introduced to the topics for each set of literature curriculum units, many were displeased with the outdated labels and wanted to create new ones. Students generated a new set of unit headings based on current social issues and values that directly correlated with their adolescent world experiences, as shown in Table 3.

From October through May, students met in literature discussion circles and Socratic seminars (Moeller & Moeller, 2015). The literature discussion circle was the method applied during reading, and the Socratic questioning method was applied at postreading. Each book was set in a diverse community, allowing the students to have exposure to working-class Whites, Blacks, and Latino/Latina (i.e., Latinx) storylines.

Table 1
Demographics for the Study Participants

Name	Race	Age	M/F	Household	Reading Level	Self-Described Disposition at Start of Study
Aeris	B	14	F	Single MC father	Above level	Says she cringes in the presence of some of her classmates, thinking they possess little in terms of intellect
Alex	W	15	M	Single WC grandmother	Grade level	An introvert who doesn't participate in class and rarely speaks in front of the class
Amani	B	14	F	Single WC father	Grade level	She feels it is not important to pass a test to show the teacher that she has command of skills
Ayanna	B	14	F	Single WC mother	Above level	Is always satisfied with producing minimal results, as long as it is a B or C
Charles	W	15	M	Both parents MC	Above level	Carries a negative view of Blacks in the school
Chris	W	15	M	Single UMC mother	Grade level	Self-identifies as a reluctant reader who is bored with books in the library and classroom
DeeJay	B	15	M	Single LI mother	Below level	Is very aware of his low reading and writing skills. Has little patience and low anger management
DeVonte	B	14	M	Single WC mother	Grade level	Prefers to read only books in graphic format
Elijah	W	14	M	Both parents WC	Grade level	Prejudges and stereotypes others based on their behavior
Kadin	B	15	M	Blended family MC	Above level	Bored and sometimes chooses to fail a test on purpose
Leon	B	14	M	Fostered to relatives LI	Below level	Doesn't participate in class because of low literacy skills
Mike	W	15	M	Single parent LI	Grade level	Not motivated. Accepts below average grades
Malik	B	15	M	Single Parent LI	Above level	Is trying to read 40 books but never gets to talk about what he is reading
Patrick	B	13	M	Both parents UMC	Grade level	Stutters badly when he is nervous, and speaking in class makes him really nervous

Abbreviations: B = Black American, W = White American, M = male, F = female, UMC = upper middle class, MC = middle class, WC = working class, LI = low income.

Table 2
Results of Informal Student Reading Interests Inventory

Reading Interests	Classroom Chats on Genre	Favorite Titles and Series
• Protagonists of color • Books should reflect the similar socioeconomic settings as students • Book protagonist should navigate through the same kind of daily urban social and urban street issues as students • Protagonists should use similar diction or vocabulary as the students • Protagonists should act like students	• Realistic fiction is not real or valid for students. • Students love horror and fantasy because it provides escapism from their realities, but there are very little to no Black people in the stories of the future. • Black writers don't write fantasy. • Fantasy writers that include people of color, such as Marissa Meyer and Suzanne Collins, are read over and over. • Authors do not like to identify the Black characters, which makes it difficult to find books with people of color in many fantasy titles.	• *Divergent series* (HarperCollins, 2011–2016) by Veronica Roth • *The Percy Jackson and the Olympians series* (Disney-Hyperion, 2005–2009) by Rick Riordan • *Cirque du Freak series* (Little Brown, 2002–2007) by Darren Shan • *Scary Stories to Tell in the Dark series* (Lippincott/Norton & Company/Harper, 1981–1991) by Alvin Schwartz w/Stephen Gammell or Brett Helquist (illustrators) • *First Part Last* (Simon & Schuster, 2003) by Angela Johnson

Data Collection

This study follows a single, embedded, exploratory case study approach (Yin, 2013), in which the 28 students from the same English teacher's class period were considered the case and each student participant was considered a subunit of the analysis. Data were collected at the end of the school year, via semistructured interviews of 14 student participants. The interviews were guided by five open-ended questions to elicit each student's perspective on their experiences with text engagement. The Appendix features book titles read by students.

My conversation was adapted to the cognitive and linguistic levels of my participants (Hill, Laybourn, & Borland, 1996), and I made sure that students understood the questions. I also attempted to ensure each student interviewee was motivated to talk with me during the interviews. Kortesluoma, Hentinen, and Nikkonen (2003) advise researchers that it is their responsibility to let the youth they interview know that they can choose to stop participating in the interview at any point and time, without any animosity. I scheduled the 14 individual interview sessions arranged within a 40-minute block of time during eighth-grade physical education and arts classes across five school days.

Data Analysis

I digitally recorded interviews and transcribed them within the NVivo 10 program, as it provided a more advanced means to classify, sort, and arrange the transcribed text.

Table 3

Book Titles in Their Final Student-Generated Categories

Curriculum Categories	Student Categories
Our History Ourselves	**The Mexican Presence in This Country**
• *Mexican Whiteboy* by M. de la Pena	**Should Not Have to Be Tested**
• *The Boy Who Carried Bricks* by A. Carter	• *Diego's Crossing* by R. Hough
• *So B. It* by S. Weeks	• *Mexican Whiteboy* by M. de la Pena
• *Orbiting Jupiter* by G. D. Schmidt	• *A Fighting Chance* by C. M. Salinas
• *Locomotion* by J. Woodson	
	Do Black Lives Really Matter? To Who?
Historical Moments	• *How It Went Down* by K. Magoon
• *The Rock and the River* by K. Magoon (References: Civil Rights, Black Panther movement)	• *Conviction* by K. L. Gilbert
	• *All American Boys* by J. Reynolds & B. Kiely
• *A Fighting Chance* by C. M. Salinas (References: Migrant Farm Movement, Immigration, and Alamo/Mexican Fight for Independence)	**Family Comes in Many Forms: So When You Find It Just Don't Let Go**
	• *Orbiting Jupiter* by G. D. Schmidt
	• *So B. It* by S. Weeks
Accepting Consequences for Civil Liberties and Disobedience	• *Locomotion* by J. Woodson
• *All American Boys* by J. Reynolds & B. Kiely	• *The Boy Who Carried Bricks* by A. Carter
• *Conviction* by K. L. Gilbert	• *Make Lemonade* by V. E. Wolf
• *Exposed* by J. Graves	
• *The Outsiders* by S. E. Hinton	**U Gotta Jus Meet the Challenge**
	• *The Rock and the River* by K. Magoon
Survival	• *Exposed: Retribution* by J. Graves
• *Diego's Crossing* by R. Hough	• *The Outsiders* by S. E. Hinton
• *Make Lemonade* by V. E. Wolf	• *Forged by Fire* by S. M. Draper
• *Forged by Fire* by S. M. Draper	

I coded the digital transcriptions and categorized the data within the software program to find underlying themes and ideas related to identity theory and the social justice assumptions for library and information science (Rioux, 2010). I compared the themes and codes emerging from the analysis to the themes presented in the literature. I grouped themes by the overarching perceptions by how the students' yearlong experience with literature had impacted each of them personally. Themes that were ambiguous or lacking in content were eliminated or integrated into related themes. I organized the final themes into four relevant groups that encompassed all of the students' responses. Although the software allowed for an easier means to select a word or phrase from the data, in addition to coding with NVivo 10, I also assigned codes by hand as necessary (Creswell, 2013).

Limitations

Researchers (Enriquez, 2006; Guerra, 2012; Ivey, 2014; Ivey & Johnston, 2013) have suggested that studying what students say about reading literature provides better opportunity to what to teach. In this study, I only interviewed members of one class session taught by one teacher; therefore, this study will not be generalizable to a larger education population.

FINDINGS

The emergent themes from the interview analysis were Finding Voice and Being Heard; Welcome to My World: The High Preference for Fantasy Is Finally Revealed; An Identity Within: "That Ain't the Way It Used to Be!"; and The Dissipation of Long-standing Misunderstood Images.

Finding Voice and Being Heard

For many of the participants, the study interview seemed to be the first time they were ever given a chance to express themselves and have those expressions be accepted as a truth. The opportunity to be heard and the empowerment of helping each other provided a platform that aided many participants in building the efficacy needed to help participants gain control of their own learning and improve in the skills needed to move forward academically. Evidence for how students were able to find their own voice and be heard is illustrated in Table 4.

Students shared responses on how the new classroom dynamics helped with processing, which aided in the building and strengthening of reading comprehension strategies and life lessons, due to their ability to gain ownership of their own learning. These students' comments illustrate how the failure to use one's voice can lead students into the habit of being a passive bystander, experiencing little to no progress due to their lack of interaction. For youth in particular, this restraint on their human spirit that keeps them from rising up and declaring they have something to contribute, or something to say.

Welcome to Our World: The High Preference for Fantasy Is Finally Revealed

Findings revealed a heavy interest in fantasy genre by every participant. The numbers causing fantasy books to dominate circulation seemed due to students' preference to check out entire fantasy series as opposed to the stand-alone single-titled realistic fiction and biographies. "I reread the entire Percy Jackson series (Riordan, 2005–2009) for the third time this year," Ayanna shared, while Aeris admitted to checking out all the ghost titles by Mary Downing Hahn; and Malik, who reads anything interesting, checked out all the titles in the Divergent series (Roth, 2011–2016) and The Mortality Doctrine series (Dashner, 2013–2016) when they were available.

Amani liked books about romance and spoke about the lack of available titles that interested her. "I want to read a book where the black girl is loved and she's not in the ghetto," responded Amani, "but there's not enough being written, so I find a good superhero title or fairies' series."

Table 4

Reports of Text Engagement's Direct Impact

Student	Quote	Activated Voice	Gained Learning Ownership	Improved Reading Skills	Increased Self-Efficacy
Kadin	*"I normally didn't get the opportunity to actively take part in talking with my classmates. [This year] we collaborated together ... with the people who are also reading [the same book] and talked about where they are at ... and if they didn't understand something, you explained it to them and they listened."*	✓	✓ ✓		✓ ✓
Elijah	*"Everyone could relate to Ponyboy [protagonist in* The Outsiders *(Hinton, 1967)], because ... he was more like the outsider. He inspired me to do better in school, to try my very best ... if I get something wrong."*		✓		✓ ✓
Leon	*"Like some students caught his mother's name in* The Boy Who Carried Bricks. *I didn't pay attention to the names of the characters. I didn't even know the main character's name. Everyone helped me in group ... the whole year ... nobody laughed at me ... I ... I ... they_ made it safe ... I feel like I'm a better reader."*		✓ ✓	✓ ✓	✓ ✓
Patrick	*"This year ... helped me with like public speaking, cuz I don't really like that. Socratic Seminars ... helped a lot ... and now ... and now ... I speak in public now." [Patrick overcame stuttering]*	✓ ✓	✓ ✓		✓
Amani	*"This year started off with others helping me through the readings, because I wasn't doing them, but then I saw others who couldn't do the reading cuz they didn't really know how ... and I began to help them and then I began to help me ... and I worked so hard this year, harder than before and I passed my standard tests. I passed ALL of them."*		✓ ✓	✓	✓ ✓

Table 5
Participants' Favorite Independent Reads

Fantasy Choices	Realistic, Informational, or Biographical Choices
1. *Percy Jackson and the Olympians series* by Rick Riordan	1. *Middle School series* by James Patterson
2. *Daniel X series* by James Patterson	2. Contemporary young adult biographies such as *The Boy Who Carried Bricks* by Alton Carter
3. *Divergent series* by Veronica Roth	3. *Schitzo: A Novel* by Nic Sheff
4. Anime and Manga series and single titles	4. *The Geeks Shall Inherit the Earth* by Alexandria Robbins
5. Ghost stories by Mary Downing Hahn	5. *All the Bright Places* by Jenifer Niven
6. *The Shadowshaper* by Daniel Jose Older	6. Anime and Manga series and single titles
7. The *Mortality Doctrine series* by James Dashner	7. *Augie & Me* by R. J. Palacio
8. *Naughts & Crosses* by Malonie Blackman	

When Leon was queried about this phenomenon, his response was more matter of fact, explaining that the reading preference types are due to real life experiences and the need to escape their day-to-day realities: "Our world is too intense. I prefer to read about something out of this world so I don't have to think. Most kids don't have the stamina to . . . read something . . . if they are dealing with it [themselves]."

DeVonte was an exception to the popular fantasy fandom, and normally he prefers realistic fiction. This year, however, he was introduced to young adult biographies through the memoir of Alton Carter, which brought to life conversations on how systemic the misunderstandings were between students that live in the more affluent and less affluent areas. He expressed how relieved he is that someone has finally written about what his reality is like and how hard it is to navigate through his world. He welcomed the conversations in the discussion circles: "This is what it's like in our world. Kids down here don't have money, [but] we all ain't thieves. You got one parent, one paycheck, and all these bills, and the lights ain't got first [choice], man."

Due to the participants' continued expressions on how the yearlong literary encounter caused their reading preferences to either change or remain the same, it was important to include this as a theme. Results from each participant's response revealed an even amount of interest in both fiction genres and nonfiction. Only titles mentioned by three or more interviewees are included in Table 5.

As Table 5 shows, the most popular fiction series were Rick Riordan's Percy Jackson and the Olympians series (2005–2009), Veronica Roth's Divergent series (2011–2016), and James Patterson's Middle School series (2012–2016). The most popular nonfiction informative title was *The Geeks Shall Inherit the Earth* (Robbins, 2011) and for biographies, it was *The Boy Who Carried Bricks* (Carter, 2015).

An Identity Within: "That Ain't the Way It Used to Be!"

School librarians and classroom teachers identify reluctant readers as students who are not necessarily missing skills that hold them back but lacking in motivation to read due to a disengagement that is not allowing them to connect with the textual content. The data in this case showed how students were motivated to read by connecting to their identities, as shown in Table 6.

Table 6
Student Identity Changes

Student Name	Current Academic and Reader Identity	Prior Reading Identity, Academics, and Social or Text Disengagement	Impact that Brought About Text Connection
Malik	Honor roll; reading identity based on his personal choice and reading curiosity	Recalls the absence of literature in his early years, low to fairly average grades in school, and a kind of dullness to his learning experience, until he found the book that he made a connection with, *"I won't never forget it because it had black children on the cover playing baseball and I liked to play baseball. I just started to read from there and my grades started getting better."*	The book that Malik is referring to was Walter Dean Myers's (1988) *Me, Mop, and the Moondance Kid*. Malik's comments on his success are significant to the research that says youth should be able to select their own literature, which is books they see themselves in and which allows them to build on their efficacy to succeed both in and out of school (Marshall, Staples, & Gibson, 2009).
DeeJay	Grades need improving; reading identity aligned with the quality of education he has been exposed to	*"In my past, it was all about the teachers. They didn't really help you."*	*"At this school, they care about you, like you they son. Like coming [to this interview] was something different."* DeeJay also admitted that he was one of the classmates that didn't like Aeris because her father was a police officer and actually apologized to her. He talked of his anger management issues and how he used to get into constant arguments. Deejay described how his encounter with Alton Carter's (2015) autobiographical memoir was a change factor, *"I used to catch a temp on everything. The author went through so much of the same as a child and he still succeeded."* DeeJay continued, *"That taught me to work harder. We have too much to do [and] this year showed me that I can do better."*

(continued)

Table 6
Student Identity Changes (Continued)

Student Name	Current Academic and Reader Identity	Prior Reading Identity, Academics, and Social or Text Disengagement	Impact that Brought About Text Connection
Alex	Average grades; identifies as reluctant reader	Alex looked at his literacy identity as one where he *"didn't get to share"* an *"opinion."* He remembers classes of students that *"just answered questions."* After overcoming his reluctancy to read, he then needed as chance *"to talk to other people about the books"* he read. Such an opportunity was not possible, for he shared a similar experience in classes where seldom chances were provided for dialogue.	The discussion circles in this study provided such an opportunity for him.
Aeris	Honor roll; reading identity based on her personal choice and reading curiosity	Aeris is the daughter of a police officer who harbored systemic issues of stereotypical misunderstandings of classmates. Up until this year, Aeris self-identified as one who did not accept the accounts of racial bias her classmates spoke of.	The books she read changed her perspective, viewing the world through a social justice lens, from their perspective. *"They made me aware of how important racism and inequality was to everyone,"* she reflected, *"We were talking about important topics like equality. You don't usually get to see intelligence like this in my class conversation, but we did it."*
Chris	Identifies as less reluctant and more eager to read	Average grades; typical reluctant reader who identified himself by saying, *"'I don't read not really."* Was afraid to reveal his weaknesses.	This year Chris's metamorphosis was supported by the safety net of daily dialogue with a peer group that allowed his vulnerabilities to be exposed for dissection without the loss of self-esteem. Describing the spark that ignited his desire to read, he says, *"Reynolds's book hooked me in the first couple of chapters! I said wow that really happens!"* Looking back on his year of growth, he reflectively admonishes, *"That ain't the way it used to be for me!"*

Many of the participants experienced reading identities that nurtured personal hesitancies to engage with literacy encounters; they felt marginalized at school and home. Many of these marginalized issues were systemic and out of their control, such as economic conditions that separated them from each other's daily lived experiences. Others were due to known or unknown learning development problems that made them feel different from their peers. Due to such vulnerabilities, the majority of participants expected negative responses from others in the class.

The Dissipation of Longstanding Misunderstood Images

In the fall of 2015, the school year opened with student participants having been bombarded by social media and news reports concerning fatal encounters of police with Black male youth, social media outcries for the validity of Black lives, social media outcries for the validity of police and/or all lives, Indigenous Nations' protests concerning land infringement at Standing Rock Reservation, and divisive political rumblings due to the approaching presidential campaign. With such current issues serving as backdrop, participants often tackled longstanding epistemic images of social injustices that could have turned into explosive confrontations outside the classroom setting, thus making the literature discussion groups the perfect setting in which to explore answers and work through misunderstandings of longstanding misrepresentations. Deeply embedded images of the Black Panther Party and the Civil Rights Movement were tackled during and after reading Kekla Magoon's *The Rock and the River* (2009). Misunderstandings of authoritative aggression and what underrepresentation and privilege looks and feels like were examined from Claudia Meléndez Salinas's *A Fighting Chance* (2015), S. E. Hinton's *The Outsiders* (1967), and Jason Reynolds's *All American Boys* (2015). Historical and contemporary news clippings that documented the subject were often used for additional support to the daily literature conversations. Results from the unpacking of these issues and more are summarized in Table 7.

Table 7 depicts specific misunderstood concerns based on social and historical misrepresentations. Each misunderstanding was corrected due to dialogue that was generated from the assigned literature, which acted as a change catalyst in the process.

DISCUSSION

Findings in the study support much of the literature regarding underrepresented youth of color's need for seeing their identities in literature (Bishop, 1990, 2012; Christensen, 2009; Van Orman & Lyiscott, 2013), in curriculum implementation (Camangian, 2015; Moule, 2010; Tatum, 1997), in library collection development and programming (Hughes-Hassell, Bracy, & Rawson, 2017), and in interpersonal development from social damage (Fricker, 2012, 2013; Froggatt, 2015; Larrick, 1965) and is in Table 8.

The responses from study participants correlated with the literature in relation to how voices of the underrepresented are "silenced and seldom heard" (Fricker, 2012, p. 287). Students were taught life lessons from their exposure to the controversies covered and learned to be less judgmental of other groups' truths (Fricker, 2013). By putting students into the lives of others, they began to develop understandings about people in history, in literature, and in media, whose culture, race, or gender identity is different from their own (Christensen, 2000).

Table 7

Misunderstandings Held and Changed Due to Dialogue with Peers and Novels That Served as a Catalyst for the Change

Student	Race/ Gender	Old Understanding	New Understanding	Change Catalyst
Charles	White/ Male	• Black Panthers as "radical" • Negative views of people of color in school and community	• Started out registering people to vote in Mississippi • Carried guns with no bullets to ward off attackers at Chicago programs • Broadening our reading selections helps us to understand things that are not in our textbooks	*The Rock and the River* by K. Magoon
Mike	White/ Male	• Racism doesn't still exist	• Racism is still here but exists in a different form in today's world	*All American Boys* by J. Reynolds & B. Kiely *A Fighting Chance* by C. M. Salinas
Aeris	White/ Female	• Felt there was no hope for the future • Thought Black youth were not intelligent • Physically cringed around other classmates of color	• Has restored "hope for humanity" • Realizes Black students are intelligent and have the same desires for success and hope for peace • No longer cringes	*The Outsiders* by S. E. Hinton *All American Boys* by J. Reynolds & B. Kiely
Leone	Black/ Male	• All middle-income families have two parents and live uptown • All lower income families have one parent and live downtown	• There are single parent households in middle income neighborhoods • There are two-parent families in lower income neighborhoods	*The Outsiders* by S. E. Hinton
DeVonte	Black/ Male	• Kids try to dress like the entertainers in the videos downtown • Only downtown kids steal clothes	• Uptown kids also dress like entertainers • Kids who steal are not limited to socioeconomic levels	*All American Boys* by J. Reynolds & B. Kiely *How It Went Down* by K. Magoon

Table 8

Missing Problems in Literacy Experiences for Underrepresented Youth

Category: Identity Needs in Literature and Platforms for Voice to Assist with Developing Agency

Explanation:

- *Youth from underrepresented minority groups are often misunderstood by their peers who are part of the majority or socioeconomic elite.* The youth who are members of these underrepresented groups may have little opportunity to share perspectives in verbal exchanges with others outside their social groups.
  - More literature should be made available that allows youth from all socioeconomic levels the opportunity to see their contemporary world in the stories they read.
- *More opportunities are needed in academic settings for student voices to be heard on the impact these stories have or have not made.*
  - When classroom teachers do not use literature that includes diverse characters in a variety of settings, they are denying their students opportunities to experience active engagement with literacy and limiting their student's chances to develop the efficacy needed for self-esteem.
- *Effective school librarians can provide platforms for voice and agency when they:*
  - foster more inclusive environments by ensuring underrepresented youths can find themselves in the library collection;
  - collaborate with classroom teachers, recommending diverse titles; and
  - work as coteachers on the reading skills lessons needed to better navigate and interpret the text. Having a "lower teacher-to-student ratios at point of instruction" (Moreillon, 2009, p. 28) is an additional benefit that produces two experts to support and facilitate learning in the classroom.
- *Provide resources reflective of the informational needs and wants of their patrons* (American Association of Schools Librarians, 2016). Hicks (1997) argued that marginalized youth need access to distinctive types of discourse and genres that serve as socially empowering tools of identities. This aspect of literary inclusion heightens student impact on reading proficiencies when they are engaged with literature and allows for real world alignment (Moreillon, 2009).

Category: Curriculum Implementation

Explanation:

- This study's findings illustrate how urban youth participants were able to reshape identities of themselves and others and form positive epistemic outlooks for their future when *young adult urban literature is implemented in the curriculum.*
- Including contemporary young adult urban literature in the curriculum provides vital opportunities for youth to discuss and work through their reactions to text in peer-generated dialogue, while
  - encouraging a conscious and purposeful move to include a broader range of readers' advisory dialogue in conversations.

(continued)

155

Table 8

Missing Problems in Literacy Experiences for Underrepresented Youth (Continued)

Category: Library Collection Development and Programming

Explanation:

One of the most compelling results from this study's findings reveals the new sense of empowerment gained by students who rarely took responsibility for their own learning. How does one look inwardly at personal flaws with open honesty, and learn from what they find?

- To look at what is needed to better yourself as a person is the first step toward change. However, to apply the effort it takes to change the paradigm you exist in so that you can succeed is empowerment.

- The five Social Justice Assumptions for School Library Information Programs play a crucial role in helping to understand feedback from youth who are searching to express not only their joys, but their pains, and puzzlements by:

  - *allowing youth from a cross-section of backgrounds to bond in dialogue for better understandings* (Assumptions 1 and 2);

  - *supporting findings that show a strong need for school library collections to include contemporary titles not only aligned with curriculum, but reflective of the life of the population the library serves* (Assumptions 3 and 5); and

  - *showing how important it is to carry out scholarly studies such as this to document the impact it has on student learning* (Assumptions 4 and 5).

Category: Interpersonal Development from Social Damage Is a Social Justice Move

Explanation:

Help to eliminate the problems of misunderstanding from the lack of empowerment by:

- removing the labels of race and class in our analysis of young adults,

- taking into consideration how young adults describe themselves within the scenario they are existing, and

- allowing today's them to explain the dilemmas based on their knowledge factors.

Almost all of this study's participants at one time or another addressed a misunderstanding they observed of their peers, basing previous perspectives on something either said to them by others or decided from a generalization of longstanding systemic misconceptions, as we saw in Table 8. Expressing surprise at the biases they held, many participants commented on how the opportunity to read and discuss the controversies in the young adult literature titles led to better clarity and improved interactions among the students (Moule, 2009). This is *a benefit of social justice in librarianship where the library program is purposely embedded into all aspects of their school's community in such a manner that it allows for selection efforts to reflect the community's wants and needs* (Mehra & Singh, 2016). Rioux (2010) notes that social justice concepts in the 20th and 21st, centuries have been "incorporated into discourses on human rights, government policy, public moral philosophy, and individuals' needs" (p.11).

- On a smaller scale, the opportunity to read, discuss, and learn from young adult titles allowed the titles to be used by the participants as guides and "enabling texts" (Tatum, 1997). To ignore the importance of implementing enabling texts in the classroom is equivalent to ignoring controversial texts in classroom curriculums; preemptive censorship practices exclude controversial texts in literature for classroom and school libraries.

CONCLUSION AND IMPLICATIONS

In this study, the implementation of the young adult titles within the weekly structured discussion changed students' perceptions of reading, themselves, and each other. School librarians and educators should consider adopting fresh perspectives about which factors determine the quality of good book, judging not necessarily by how well it is written, but by how it affects the reader, illustrating the life lessons and warning of the consequences of choices (Hill, Pérez, & Irby, 2008). School librarians who provide services to underrepresented groups should honor the cultural capital these diverse groups bring. Purposeful action toward inclusion and representation on the part of school librarians will encourage the presence of these underrepresented groups to positively affect collection and curriculum development decisions and provide opportunities for identity building (Bishop, 1990, 2012). Selection development policies with an emphasis on inclusion and representation can foster the type of learning environments that help students to "love themselves, love people" (Camangian, 2015, p. 448), and gain a better "sense of control over their collective lives" (Camangian, 2015, pp. 246–247).

From a social justice stance, school libraries can act as sites of learning where both literacy skills and student voices are "cultivated" (Hughes-Hassell, Bracy, & Rawson, 2017, p. 75). This type of efficacy building is reflected in the American Association of School Librarians' national commitment to provide equitable opportunities to "every child, regardless of race, income, or [culture]" (American Library Association, 2016).

School librarians and classroom teachers have an opportunity to learn more about how to use young adult fiction for middle school urban youth. By taking a social justice perspective and providing and using materials that represent the lived experiences of underrepresented youths in an instructional context, school librarians and teachers can foster an educational environment that can begin to address the educational issues facing underrepresented youths and empower them to engage in their own education. More research is needed on school libraries and social justice, to provide school librarians with the language they will need to effectively advocate. Rioux's (2010) social justice assumptions are grounded in the centrality of reading and information and are deserving of consideration to frame future studies.

NOTE

This chapter was previously published as: Carnesi, S. (2018). A platform for voice and identity: School library standards in support of YA urban literature's transformative impacts on youth. *School Libraries Worlwide, 24*(1), 99–117.

REFERENCES

Agosto, D. E., & Hughes-Hassell, S. (2006). Toward a model of the everyday life information needs of urban teenagers, part 1: Theoretical model. *Journal of the American Society for Information Science and Technology, 57*(10), 1394–1403.

Agosto, D. E., & Hughes-Hassell, S. (2010). *Urban teens in the library: Research and practice.* [Kindle for Mac version]. Chicago, IL: American Library Association.

American Association of School Librarians (AASL). (2017). *Standards framework for learners.* Retrieved from https://standards.aasl.org/wp-content/uploads/2017/11/AASL-Standards-Framework-for-Learners-pamphlet.pdf

American Association of School Librarians (AASL). (2009). *Empowering learners: Guidelines for school library media programs.* Chicago, IL: American Library Association.

American Association of School Librarians (AASL). (2010). *Position statement on the school librarian's role in reading.* Retrieved from http://www.ala.org/aasl/advocacy/resources/statements/reading-role

American Association of School Librarians (AASL). (2016). *Definition of an effective school library program.* Retrieved from http://www.ala.org/aasl/sites/ala.org.aasl/files/content/aaslissues/positionstatements/AASL_Position%20Statement_Effective_SLP_2016-06-25.pdf

American Library Association. (2016). Resolution on equity for school libraries for the DOE [U.S. Department of Education] making rules for ESSA [Every Student Succeeds Act] CD20.6. (2016). Retrieved from https://goo.gl/E65cuf

Belfield, C. R., Levin, H. M., & Rosen, R. (2012). *The economic value of opportunity youth.* Washington, DC: Civic Enterprises.

Berkowitz, R. E., & Eisenberg, M. B. (1989). The curriculum roles and responsibilities of library media specialists. ERIC Digest ED308880. Retrieved from https://www.ericdigests.org/pre-9212/roles.htm

Birnbacher, D. (1984). Social justice and the legitimation of aggressive behavior. In A. Mummendey (Ed.), *Social psychology of aggression: Springer series in social psychology* (pp. 157–170). Heidelberg, Germany: Springer.

Bishop, R. S. (1982). *Shadow and substance.* Urbana, IL: National Council of Teachers of English.

Bishop, R. S. (1990). Mirrors, windows, and sliding glass doors. *Perspectives: Choosing and Using Books for the Classroom, 6*(3), 1–2. Retrieved from https://scenicregional.org/wp-content/uploads/2017/08/Mirrors-Windows-and-Sliding-Glass-Doors.pdf

Bishop, R. S. (2012). Reflections on the development of African American children's literature. *Journal of Children's Literature, 38*(2), 5–13.

Braun, L. W., Hartman, M. L., Hughes-Hassell, S., & Kumasi, K. (2014). *The future of library services for and with teens: A call to action.* Chicago, IL: Young Adult Library Services Association (YALSA). Retrieved from http://www.ala.org/yaforum/sites/ala.org.yaforum/files/content/YALSA_nationalforum_final.pdf

Bridgeland, J. M., & Milano, J. A. (2012). *Opportunity road: The promise and challenge of America's forgotten youth.* Washington, DC: Civic Enterprises and American's Promise. Retrieved from https://www.serve.gov/new-images/council/pdf/opportunity_road_the_promise.pdf

Brooks, W., & Savage, L. (2009). Critiques and controversies of street literature: A formidable literary genre. *ALAN Review, 36*(2), 48–55.

Camangian, P. R. (2015). Teach like lives depend on it: Agitate, arouse, and inspire. *Urban Education, 50*(4), 424–453.

Christensen, L. (2000). *Reading, writing and rising up: Teaching about social justice and the power of the written word.* Milwaukee, WI: Rethinking Schools.

Christensen, L. (2009). *Teaching of joy and justice: Reimaging the language arts classroom.* Milwaukee, WI: Rethinking Schools. Retrieved from http://rethinkingschools.aidcvt.com/publication/tfjj/tfjj_intro.shtml

Cooperative Children's Book Center. (2017). *Annual multicultural statistics.* Retrieved from https://ccbc.education.wisc.edu/books/pcstats.asp

Creswell, J. W. (2013). *Qualitative inquiry and research design: Choosing among five approaches* (3rd ed.). Thousand Oaks, CA: Sage.

Enriquez, G. (2006). The reader speaks out: Adolescent reflections about controversial young adult literature. *ALAN Review, 33*(2), 16–23.

Fashola, O. S., & Slavin, R. E. (1998). Effective dropout prevention and college attendance programs for students placed at risk. *Journal of Education for Students Placed at Risk, 3*, 159–183.

Fricker, M. (2012). Silence and institutional prejudice. In S. L. Crasnow & A. M. Superson (Eds.), *Out from the shadows: Analytical feminist contributions to traditional philosophy* (pp. 287–304). New York, NY: Oxford Press.

Fricker, M. (2013). Epistemic justice as a condition of political freedom? *Synthese, 190*(7), 1317–1332.

Froggatt, D. L. (2015). The informationally underserved: Not always diverse, but always a social justice advocacy. *School Libraries Worldwide, 21*(1), 54–72.

Guerra, S. F. (2012). Using urban fiction to engage at-risk and incarcerated youths in literacy instruction. *Journal of Adolescent & Adult Literacy, 55*(5), 385–394.

Hicks, D. (1997). Working through discourse genres in school. *Research in the Teaching of English, 31*(4), 459–485.

Hill, M., Laybourn, A., & Borland, M. (1996). Engaging with primary-aged children about their emotions and well-being: Methodological considerations. *Children & Society, 10*, 129–144.

Hill, M. L., Pérez, B., & Irby, D. J. (2008). Street fiction: What is it and what does it mean for English teachers? *English Journal, 97*(3), 76–82.

Hinton, K., & Carnesi, S. (2017). On the street: A "radical change" in urban fiction featuring youth. *The Dragon Lode, 35*(2), 79–88.

Hughes-Hassell, S., Bracy, P. B., & Rawson, C. H. (2017). *Libraries, literacy, and African American youth: Research and practice*. Santa Barbara, CA: Libraries Unlimited.

International Federation of Library Associations and Institutions (IFLA). (2015). *IFLA school library guidelines* (2nd ed.). CH Den Haag, Netherlands: International Federation of Library Associations.

Ivey, G. (2014). The social side of engaged reading for young adolescents. *Reading Teacher, 68*(3), 165–171.

Ivey, G., & Johnston, P. H. (2013). Engagement with young adult literature: Outcomes and processes. *Reading Research Quarterly, 48*(3), 255–275.

Jerald, C. D. (2006, June). Identifying potential dropouts: Key lessons for building an early warning data system. Retrieved from https://www.achieve.org/files/FINAL-dropouts_0.pdf

Kortesluoma, R.-L., Hentinen, M., & Nikkonen, M. (2003). Conducting a qualitative child interview: Methodological concerns. *Journal of Advanced Nursing, 42*(5), 434–441.

Larrick, N. (1965, September 11). The all-white world of children's books. *Saturday Review*, 63–65, 84–85.

Marshall, E., Staples, J., & Gibson, S. (2009). Ghetto fabulous: Reading Black adolescent femininity in contemporary urban street fiction. *Journal of Adolescent and Adult Literacy, 53*(1), 28–36.

Maslow, A. H. (1943). A theory of human motivation. *Psychological Review, 50*(4), 370–396.

Mehra, B., & Singh, V. (2016). Library leadership-in-training as embedded change agents to further social justice in rural communities: Teachers of library management subjects in the ITRL and ITRL2. In N. A. Cooke & M. E. Sweeney (Eds.), *Teaching for justice: Implementing social justice in the LIS classroom* (pp. 247–286). Sacramento, CA: Library Juice Press.

Moeller, V. J., & Moeller, M. V. (2015). *Socratic seminars in middle school: Texts and films that engage students in reflective thinking and close reading*. New York, NY: Routledge.

Moreillon, J. (2009). Reading and the library program. *Knowledge Quest, 38*(2), 24–30.

Morris, V. I. (2012). *The readers' advisory guide to street literature* [Kindle for Mac version]. Chicago, IL: American Library Association.

Morris, V. J., Hughes-Hassell, S., Agosto, D. E., & Cottman, D. (2006). Street lit flying off teen fiction bookshelves in Philadelphia libraries. *Young Adult Library Services, 5*(1), 16–23.

Moule, J. (2009). Understanding unconscious bias and unintentional racism: Acknowledging our possible biases and working together openly is essential for developing community in our schools. *Phi Delta Kappan, 90*(5), 320–326. Retrieved from http://www.jeanmoule.com/wp-content/uploads/2013/02/MouleKappan.pdf

Moule, J. (2010, March). Changing our minds (and theirs): Understanding vs. empowerment. Keynote address at NAACP Annual Conference. Eugene, OR.

Perry, C. L., Komro, K. A., Veblen-Mortenson, S., Bosma, L. M., Farbakhsh, K., Munson, K. A., . . . Lytle, L. A. (2003). A randomized controlled trial of the middle and junior high school D.A.R.E. and D.A.R.E. Plus Programs. *Archives of Pediatrics & Adolescent Medicine, 157*(2), 178–184.

Rauner, D. M. (2013). But what does caring accomplish? In D. M. Rauner (Ed.), *They still pick me up when I fall: The role of caring in youth development and community life* (p. 78). New York, NY: Columbia University Press.

Rioux, K. (2010). Metatheory in library and information science: A nascent social justice approach. *Journal of Education for Library and Information Science, 51*(1), 9–17.

Tatum, B. D. (1997). "Why are all the Black kids sitting together in the cafeteria?" *Brown University Child & Adolescent Behavior Letter, 13*(10), 1.

Taylor, C. (1992). The politics of recognition. *Multiculturalism: Examining the Politics of Recognition, 25*(25), 25–73.

Todd, R. J., & Edwards, S. (2004). Adolescents' information seeking and utilization in relation to drugs. In M. K. Chelton & C. Cool (Eds.), *Youth information-seeking behavior: Theories, models, and issues* (pp. 353–386). Lanham, MD: Scarecrow Press.

U.S. Census Bureau. (2006). Income, earnings, and poverty data from the 2005 American Community Survey. Retrieved from https://www.prb.org/theamericancommunitysurvey-2005/

U.S. Department of Health. (2018). *The changing face of America's adolescents*. Retrieved from https://www.hhs.gov/ash/oah/facts-and-stats/changing-face-of-americas-adolescents/index.html

Van Ausdale, D., & Feagin, J. (2002). *The first R: How children learn race and racism*. New York, NY: Rowman & Littlefield.

Van Orman, K., & Lyiscott, J. (2013). Politely disregarded: Street fiction, mass incarceration, and critical praxis. *English Journal, 4*(102), 59–66.

Yin, R. K. (2013). *Case study research: Design and methods*. Thousand Oaks, CA: Sage Publications.

APPENDIX: YOUNG ADULT TITLES REFERENCED IN STUDY

Individual Titles

Blackman, M. (2005). *Naughts and crosses*. New York, NY: Simon & Schuster.

Carter, A. (2015). *The boy who carried bricks*. Stillwater, OK: Roadrunner Press.

de la Pena, M. (2008). *Mexican whiteboy*. New York, NY: Delacorte.

Gilbert, K. L. (2015). *Conviction*. New York, NY: Hyperion.

Graves, J. (2015). *Exposed: Retribution*. Victoria, BC: Orca.

Hinton, S. E. (1967). *The outsiders*. New York, NY: Viking.

Houch, R. (2015). *Diego's crossing*. Toronto, ON: Annick Press.

Johnson, A. (2003). *First part last*. New York, NY: Simon & Schuster.

Magoon, K. (2009). *The rock and the river*. New York, NY: Aladdin.

Magoon, K. (2014). *How it went down*. New York, NY: Henry Holt.

Myers, W. D. (1988). *Me, Mop, and the Moondance Kid*. New York, NY: Delacorte Press.

Niven, J. (2015). *All the bright places*. New York, NY: Random House.

Older, D. J. (2015). *The shadowshaper*. New York, NY: Scholastic.

Palacio, R. J. (2014). *Auggie & me*. New York, NY: Knopf.

Reynolds, J., & Kiely, B. (2015). *All American boys*. New York, NY: Atheneum.

Robbins, A. (2011). *The geeks shall inherit the earth*. New York, NY: Hachette Books.

Salinas, C. M. (2015). *A fighting chance*. Houston, TX: Pinata Books.

Schmidt, G. D. (2015). *Orbiting Jupiter*. Boston, MA: Clarion Books.

Schwartz, A. (1984). *More scary stories*. New York, NY: Norton & Company.

Schwartz, A., & Gammell, S. (1981). *Scary stories to tell in the dark*. New York, NY: Lippincott.

Schwartz, A., & Helquist, B. (1991). *Scary stories 3: More tales to chill your bones*. New York, NY: Harper.

Sheff, N. (2014). *Schitzo: A novel*. New York, NY: Simon & Schuster.

Weeks, S. (2007). *So B. it*. New York, NY: Harper Collins.

Wolff, V. E. (1993). *Make lemonade*. New York, NY: Henry Holt.

Woodson, J. (2009). *Peace, locomotion*. New York, NY: Putnam.

Series

Dashner, J. (2013–2016). *The mortality doctrine series*. New York, NY: Random House.

Patterson, J. (2008–2015). *Daniel X series: Books 1–6*. New York, NY: Little Brown.

Patterson, J. (2011–2016). *Middle school series: Books 1–10*. New York, NY: Little Brown.

Riordan, R. (2005–2009). *Percy Jackson and the Olympians series: Books 1–5*. New York, NY: Hyperion.

Roth, V. (2011–2016). *Divergent series: Books 1–3*. New York, NY: Harper Collins.

Shan, D. (2000–2006). *Cirque du freak series: Books 1–12*. New York, NY: Little Brown.

Practicing a Critical Stance to Research Ethics in Global Contexts: Challenges and Ways Forward

Marlene Asselin and Ray Doiron

INTRODUCTION

The International Association of School Librarianship (IASL) has a reputation for supporting and disseminating research informing school librarianship around the world. Since the organization serves a multinational and multicultural library community, it has the responsibility to promote sound ethical procedures for all research. This can raise serious dilemmas for researchers planning to work in Global South countries with different ethical standards for conducting research when members of the Global North academic community are bound by strict guidelines covering ethical procedures. These dilemmas can include (1) differing views on what counts as research; (2) differing values and policies on gender, religion, inclusive practices, and other social and cultural areas; (3) the insider/outsider phenomenon (white privileged researchers working in nonwhite communities); and (4) developing research instruments that are culturally sensitive. These dilemmas present serious challenges to Western-oriented researchers with research sites in remote/rural areas and large urban centers where frontline staff have little or no experience with, nor knowledge of, ethical considerations of educational research. Researchers are charged then to pay serious attention to issues of positionality, paradigms of what is "truth," and iterative methods and analyses, as well as an overarching awareness of their reflexivity throughout the research process. Research in this context becomes a continuous process of examining relationships with collaborators and research participants, the dynamics of those relationships, and their relationship to the research that is undertaken. Without a self-critical lens through which to engage in the research process, researchers run the risk of placing themselves in the position where "ethical research guidelines [as imposed by universities] could be yet another western construct that creates a global discourse of 'our way' is the 'right way' to do things" (Skelton, 2008, p. 29). In this chapter, we as authors, researchers, and IASL members direct attention to the complexity of expanding IASL research into non-Western contexts.

Over the past two decades, the ethics of research involving children and youth has become a prominent topic in the literature (Powell, Fitzgerald, Taylor, & Graham, 2012), sparking a proliferation of resources for researchers (Alderson & Morrow, 2011; Childwatch International Research Network, n.d.; Graham, Powell, Taylor, Anderson, & Fitzgerald, 2013; UNICEF Office of Research www.unicef-irc.org/office/; Young Lives Project www.younglives.org.uk/). Spurred by the UN Convention on the Rights of the Child (1989) and the emergence of the sociology of childhood (Mayall, 2002), accordant rights-protecting procedures were instituted and methods of research designed to enable voices of children and youth to be heard in various degrees throughout the research process. However, from an international perspective, this paradigm of research with children and the knowledge generated by it are unbalanced as "only a little more than 10% of the world's children live in the developed countries of Europe, North America and other European outposts . . . yet the research is heavily concentrated on children from these places" (Pence & Nsamenang, 2008, p. 14).

How then should researchers working with children in school and community libraries develop research that assures fair and respectful ethical procedures? What role do children play in the research process—subject, informant, or participant? How can Western researchers approach research in developing countries where expectations for ethical research may or may not exist? This chapter takes a critical perspective on these issues by (1) reflecting on the various stances that researchers take in approaching new research, (2) comparing expectations for ethics in developed/Global North and developing/Global South countries, and (3) identifying the position children are placed in before, during, and after research projects. We begin our discussion by examining some of the current political, economic, and ethical challenges facing all researchers, especially those from Western contexts, wishing to work in international contexts.

RESEARCH CHALLENGES

All research is influenced by the political climate in which it is generated and then conducted. In Canada, we see several examples of what could be called "political interference" when we see major research organizations issue calls for proposals usually framed within specified themes, such as gender, aboriginal cultures, fragile economies, or adult/workplace literacy. Often these themes come with expectations that partnerships and collaborations will be developed, outcomes and deliverables will be achieved, and some economic impact will accrue from the research. This becomes a pressure for "real" results and "real world" applications that can stifle some forms of research and leave researchers chasing projects that meet the criteria of the themes outlined by the governing research bodies. Similarly university research offices frame their research directions within the same thematic frameworks as major funders, and review proposals with key national criteria in place.

In international contexts, political and economic pressures are also exerted on researchers, nongovernmental agencies, and government departments of education and health as well. Many African countries, for example, are currently being supported by large international aid organizations (e.g., US AID, British Council, Australia AID), who bring new energy, reform, and money to help emerging-economy countries meet

Millennial Development Goals (MDG) and achieve "literacy for all." These initiatives are also closely monitored through large-scale assessments and mostly quantitative program evaluations. Since within-country researchers have limited research experiences, these major "outside" initiatives dominate the research landscape. In similar ways, local governments set their educational priorities with many countries emphasizing secondary and postsecondary initiatives that see new universities and colleges being established and priority being given to science and technology programs.

FUNDING CHALLENGES

Tied closely to the political agendas of governments, foundations, donors, and international aid agencies are issues related to research funding. It takes financial resources to be able to develop research projects and, in the Canadian context, funding sources are closely tied to the political and long-range goals outlined by these organizations. A "corporate" model has emerged with funders expecting results that will further their agendas. Most universities and colleges in Canada have clear statements outlining the research foci that will be supported—collaborative, interdisciplinary, focused on marginalized groups, and with increasing expectations for researchers to find international partners for their projects. It would be fair to say that without attention to these criteria, a researcher would likely not get funded.

Most universities in Canada have also developed large research offices with a growing staff for managing and leading research in each faculty, searching for new funding sources, supporting grant writing, and leading efforts at research dissemination. Strategic vision statements have been written in most institutions, and these documents guide the types of funding grants that will be supported.

In the international context, the links between political agendas and research funding are just as obvious. With most of the funding for major literacy initiatives coming from outside the country (such as from international aid, donor- and faith-based organizations), researchers in many African countries are attracted to these funding sources. With little or no internal research funding and many university-based researchers being largely self-funded, their research remains isolated from their continental and global colleagues and lacking in a cohesive strategy over the long term. Adding to the difficulties facing these researchers is the lack of funds for research dissemination or travel for conferences in most developing countries. The rise of open access journals has started to have some impact on increasing access to the research from these countries. However, the advent of "predatory publishing" could be seen to counter this progress.

ETHICAL CHALLENGES

Most universities in the Global North are advocating for researchers to develop international research projects by forming university-to-university academic agreements that include program sharing, faculty and student exchanges, and research collaborations that also increase the challenge of aligning ethical standards between the two (or more) institutions. In Canada, the *United Nations Convention on the Rights of the Child* and the Canadian *Charter of Rights and Freedom* dominate the contexts in which all research must be done. The Canadian government through its Tri-Council agencies (Canadian Institutes of Health Research, Natural Sciences and Engineering Research Council of Canada, & Social Sciences and Humanities Research Council of

Canada, 2014) sets policies, guidelines, and procedures for conducting research within the country (with additional guidelines for marginalized individuals and communities) and gives special attention to international research (see *Tri-Council Policy Statement of Research Involving Humans*). Local universities and colleges refer to the Tri-Council directives and guide their implementation through their own in-house research policies/procedures led by Research Ethics Boards (REBs) established at each postsecondary institution. All of these regulations affect the research context in Canada and must be addressed faithfully in order to receive and maintain research funding. These regulations cover such issues as the privacy and safety of research participants, gaining access to populations, the use of recording equipment and data, internet access, and informed consent/assent, to name a few. Researchers are advised to follow regulations for involving community members in the research and to make plans for ongoing communication with participants, as well as plans for reporting back to participants as part of their dissemination plans. All of these regulations are even more stringent when researchers are working with vulnerable populations.

In the international context, few countries of the Global South have instituted comprehensive processes for conducting educational research. In many cases with educational research, no formal ethical approval is needed. Researchers (often a male authority figure) enter a school assuming children and teachers will participate in whatever projects they are undertaking. Parents are rarely asked for permission to involve their children, and children are not asked to give assent to take part. In addition, there is little reporting back to participants once results have been analyzed.

DILEMMAS ARISING

With this brief look at the political, economic, and ethical challenges facing researchers in Canada and some developing countries, we turn now to examine some of the dilemmas arising out of these challenges. The dilemmas can be briefly stated in the following way:

Differing views of what counts as research. Within our country and beyond its borders, researchers are faced with meeting the needs of those who expect research to be quantitative in design yielding results that "prove" what works and those who expect research to be more qualitative giving a richer and more robust sense of a phenomenon and those affected by it.

The qualitative/quantitative dilemma is particularly prevalent as the Global North view of research meets the emerging research culture in countries like Ethiopia, Kenya, Uganda, and other developing countries in Africa. In these countries the quantitative research culture is deeply entrenched, while increasing numbers of "outside" researchers view research from a sociocultural, more qualitative perspective, thus immediately running into competing "worldviews."

Role of the child in the research. Research in international contexts exposes variance in the position of the child in the research process. There is a range of views of the child from simply being a passive subject acted upon through to being a competent participant in the research with important perceptions on matters that affect their lives (Asselin & Doiron, 2016). Should researchers provide children with the opportunity to give informed consent or at least assent?

Insiders and outsiders. The majority of Western researchers are White, privileged academics who are attempting to move into cultural situations very different from their own. These differences include not only cultural and linguistic differences but differences in previous research experiences, access to a wealth of resources unknown to many emerging researchers in developing countries, and expectations of the language of research and partnerships (English).

Differing inclusive policies and practices. In Canada researchers are governed by strict policies and common beliefs/values about diversity, equity, and inclusion (Canadian Institutes of Health Research, Natural Sciences and Engineering Research Council of Canada, & Social Sciences and Humanities Research Council of Canada, 2014). These values extend into all vulnerable communities, differences in gender roles, religions, sexual orientation, and the myriad of developmental and physical limitations common in any society. However, such policies and practices around inclusion are just emerging in many developing countries, and there are underlying differences in how people perceive gender roles, diverse religions, and equal rights for all.

Western requirements for ethical procedures. How do Western researchers proceed, and what can be done with data collected outside of the standards established by Western national agencies and local university REBs? Can Western researchers analyze and then disseminate findings if the data were not collected following national procedures? Are participants in research truly giving informed consent or merely going along with authority figures? The data collection process may seem appropriate and "legal" in the local context but would likely be disqualified without following the ethical standards established by Western researchers' parent institutions.

Developing/adapting culturally sensitive instruments. Coupled with issues of the ethical collection of data are those related to the development of data tools that are culturally sensitive, reflective of how "locals" would address the issues and written in a language that is accessible to all participants. In our own experiences as Western researchers in the Global South, we have been in the situation where we are developing instruments in our first language (usually English) when this may be the second or even third language of local users of such an instrument. How we say things in English may not be easily translated into Amharic, Swahili, or Luganda, for example.

RESEARCH "HEADWORK"

Faced with these challenges and ethical dilemmas, researchers wishing to work with colleagues in developing countries need to approach their research with a new set of lenses through which they initiate, conduct, analyze, and report research in these international contexts. Sultana (2006) emphasizes that "fieldwork is always contextual, relational, embodied, and political" (p. 374). What emerges then is a complex iterative research process that folds back into itself repeatedly, relying on deep listening, ongoing communication, reflection, re-visioning, and attention to ethics in both the originating context and the local situation in which the research is carried out. It follows that library researchers need to become less reliant on traditional data collection and analysis methods and instead develop a more generative, iterative, conceptual process focused on building research capacity and new understandings of educational research. All of this should be developing with the ever-present trepidation about imposing values and shades of postcolonialism on the people and contexts in which research could be carried out.

On the other hand, these dilemmas could provide researchers with a rich space in which to build collaborations around exploring mutual issues, finding common ground, and focusing on what Chiseri-Strater and Sunstein (2006) call the "headwork" in doing research. This headwork involves critical "habits of mind" such as (1) the nature of "truth"; (2) reflexivity; (3) positionality; (4) emergent methods, analysis, and findings; and (5) dissemination.

The nature of "truth." Competing paradigms for research as exemplified by the qualitative/quantitative debate really represent differing epistemologies and a concern with the nature and scope of knowledge. One approach to research is based on the notion that "truth" is simply "out there" and it just has to discovered, while another approach assumes that all meanings are interactively and socially constructed by all participants including the researcher. Most researchers see benefits in these different approaches but tend to lean philosophically to one or the other. How researchers see the world and how they understand the purposes and processes for doing research, and how they understand how the formation of new knowledge are all factors in determining what is seen as the "truth." When attempting to develop research with new colleagues, researchers need to be cognizant that they may be coming from a different paradigm and that a negotiation needs to take place to ensure each worldview is recognized, respected, and employed to achieve a balance in the relationship.

In our own past experiences with school library research, we have learned that nonpragmatic research (such as case study, ethnography, hermeneutics, narrative, and qualitative approaches in general) holds little resonance with politicians and decision makers. This realization forced us to more clearly articulate the goals, value, and impact of our research. The need for impact is particularly critical in countries faced with extreme challenges in health and education brought on by poverty and slow economic growth.

Reflexivity. Reflexivity involves making the research process itself a focus of inquiry where researchers lay open preconceptions to become aware of situational dynamics and recognize that all participants are jointly involved in knowledge production. Research then becomes a continuous process of examining our "personal baggage" (Kirby & McKenna, 1989), our personal assumptions and preconceptions, and how they affect all research decisions. In our own work with international colleagues, we enter into a continuous process examining our relationship, the dynamics of that relationship, and its impact on the research.

Moving into research in school and community libraries in global communities requires awareness of that our particular vision for how a school library operates may be vastly different than those of colleagues in small, underdeveloped libraries. Our experiences of working in such libraries have taught us that while the quantity and quality of resources is wanting, and the training and sophistication of library programs is still emerging, the very essence of what a library is and how it contributes to learning and the culture for reading in a community is very strong in all of these libraries.

Positionality. All researchers are positioned by factors of age, gender, race, class, nationality, religion, institutional affiliation, historical and personal circumstances, and intellectual disposition. The extent to which such influences are revealed or concealed is circumscribed by the paradigms and disciplines under which they train, work, and publish. Recognizing positionality and using it as a lens through which research is carried out will shed light on (1) the power relations that would affect the kinds of relations with the people involved in the research, and therefore the kinds of information observed; and (2) the effect one's own subjectivity might have on how "results" are interpreted (Chiseri-Strater, n.d.; Ganga & Scott, 2006; Kapoor, 2004).

As we began our work with libraries in Ethiopia, we felt very much like O'Leary (2012) who expresses her reflections about the position she experienced:

At the outset of a research or consulting project, my social identification by others as an outsider and an "expert" has generally meant that I have been invested with power by others in the group. Yet the philosophy that underpins my worldview and the ways in which I engage in research is a collaborative and participative one which is based on sharing power. (p. 2)

This means that researchers need to take the time to listen, engage respectfully with counterparts, and take small steps toward a mutual position regarding what questions to explore, how they will be explored, and ultimately what will be done with any insights attained.

Emergent methods, analyses, and findings. Jones (2006) warns researchers that "the processes of coding, analysis, interpretation and reporting of data can be coloured by the researcher's conceptual framework to the exclusion of the informants, placing the researcher in a supreme position of control over the research process" (p. 171). This forces the reexamination of the traditional research model where questions are generated, data are collected, analysis is completed away from the informants, and findings are reported in isolation. The entire process must become an iterative one where the research team develops the research focus that becomes a starting point for the study. Research tools are adapted, revised, and responsive to the context and the feedback from participants. By using different contextually sensitive methods of data collection, such as storytelling, community dialogue, talking circles, music, and proverbs, cultural ways of knowing can be incorporated into data collection methods

Findings/insights emerge throughout the process and not only at the end. Participants verify and add input to the analysis, helping to keep the richness of the situation. In other words, context and sociocultural factors influence the development of research methods and analysis. Our own experiences with a family literacy program led by community library staff brought home many of these issues as we set out to adapt a literacy assessment instrument to the languages, cultural contexts, and informed consent procedures most of which were nonexistent. Our partners in the work were unfamiliar with such instruments and worked along with us to translate the questions not only into local languages but also into recognizable situations familiar to those who would do the assessment.

Dissemination. In a traditional research model, researchers wait until their data have been collected, analyzed, and a set of findings is developed. Too often, Western researchers share their work in journals and conference venues where global perspectives and participants may be limited. In a reflexive model, dissemination is seen as part of the ongoing collaborative, participatory process where one cycle of collaborative work leads into the next, where established relationships can grow and deepen as respect is building and collaborators trust each other more easily. It is not seen as a "take the data and run" process. This has led to Western researchers looking for new venues in which to share research results, ones that are closer to the global community where the work took place. In addition, it has led to opportunities to facilitate local researchers getting their work shared at in-country and international conferences (see CIES at http://www.cies.us, for example) and having articles published in peer-reviewed journals (see the *IFLA Journal* and *School Libraries Worldwide,* for examples).

RESEARCH "ALERTS"

Western researchers are familiar with the concept of "alerts," those messages (sometimes annoying) alerting them to some new ideas, resources, or innovations. An alert is also seen as a warning, a "heads-up" about potential problems or issues to be aware of before venturing out on a new project in the hopes of avoiding them or preventing them from happening. Western researchers need to be on the alert for situations, ideologies, and new understandings that will challenge what they have been doing traditionally in research while leading the way to new research landscapes where true collaboration and meaningful new insights into school and community library effectiveness can be identified and disseminated in a global and democratic exchange of ideas. Taking a more critical approach to research will be challenging and will increase the time it takes to get a research agenda established, one based on mutual respect, true collaboration, and mutual benefit. With this vision in place, we offer several research "alerts" that colleagues need to be aware of and prepared to accept.

1. As more Western academics move into research partnerships with nongovernmental organizations, university collaborators, and frontline library leaders, they need to embrace a more critical research paradigm where research is understood as "the co-production of new understandings and solutions that tap the expertise of non-academic partners" (Sharrock, 2007, p. 10).
2. Skelton (2008) warns us that "ethical research guidelines (as imposed by Universities) could be yet another Western construct that creates a global discourse of 'our way' is the 'right way' to do things" (p. 29).
3. The lack of regulatory mechanisms in some majority world contexts places the onus on researchers and the institutions to which they belong (Leach, 2006). Part of our role is to help local researchers develop the ethical principles that will enhance their research and ensure participants of fair and respectful treatment.
4. Ethical codes that are restrictive and binding need to become more iterative and responsive, which does not fit the standard format of knowing in advance what will happen and how it will be managed, as is generally required by ethics boards in Western universities and colleges.

Be knowledgeable of local policies concerning education and research. For example, although the UN Convention on the Rights of the Child may be supposed universal, Africa has its own Charter of the Rights and Welfare of the Child (https://www.un.org/en/africa/osaa/pdf/au/afr_charter_rights_welfare_child_africa_1990.pdf).

A CHALLENGE FOR IASL IN MOVING FORWARD

Many professional associations, including the International Association of School Librarianship (IASL), originated in Western countries. IASL has worked diligently to build international membership and encourage school library development globally. This has included disseminating current research at its annual conference, through research grants, and by publications in *School Libraries Worldwide*. However, as research and collaborations are encouraged by government, funders, and the academy to become more global, the persistent dominance of Western perspectives is uncomfortable for present and future members. In IASL, by far the majority of research remains carried out and published by colleagues in Western countries (Asselin, 2011). Is the Association doing enough to support and disseminate school library research being conducted by the global school library community? Is some of that research being done but not reaching an international audience? How can IASL show leadership in gathering and disseminating that research? As Western school library academics move into more global research, could IASL offer guidelines for conducting that research in ethical and respectful ways?

In Canada, as in all Western countries, institutions and organizations are composing visions, guidelines, and principles for the current reality of researching in an international arena (Association of Canadian Deans of Education, 2014; Canadian Bureau for International Education; 2013; Ethics of International Engagement and Service-Learning Project, 2011). The potential of principled, collaborative, international research includes "increased intercultural understanding and dialogue through a realization of interdependence" . . . and "building partnerships based on reciprocity, social accountability, and sustainability" (Association of Canadian Deans of Education, 2014, p. 5). From such potential, enormous opportunities for supporting economic and social justice are afforded.

Internationalization offers an opportunity to establish collaborative, ethical partnerships that foster the ideals of economic and social justice and that take us beyond the ethnocentric, hegemonic, depoliticized, and paternalistic historical patterns of engagement. In turn, increased understanding may result in a reciprocal improvement of educational research and practices (Association of Canadian Deans of Education, 2014, p. 5).

As an international association representing libraries supporting teaching and learning for children and youth throughout the world, IASL needs to seriously take renewed responsibility to ensure ethical research for their global membership and for the larger library community. In this chapter, we have identified key issues and challenges, have provided concepts that can undergird formation of ethical international research, and pointed to exemplary documents by relevant institutions and associations. It is time for IASL to step forward for the global school library community.

NOTE

This chapter was previously published as Doiron, R., & Asselin, M. (2015). *Ethical dilemmas for researchers working in international contexts. School Libraries Worldwide, 21*(2), 1–10.

REFERENCES

Alderson, P., & Morrow, V. (2011). *The ethics of research with children and young people: A practical handbook.* London: Sage Publications.

Asselin, M. (2011). Internationalism as leadership in IASL research: Accomplishments and directions. *School Libraries Worldwide, 17*(2), 13–24.

Asselin, M., & Doiron, R. (2016). Ethical issues facing researchers working with children in international contexts. *Journal of Childhood Studies*, 41(1), 24–35.

Association of Canadian Deans of Education. (2014). *Accord on the Internationalization of Education.* Retrieved from https://csse-scee.ca/acde/wp-content/uploads/sites/7/2017/08/Accord-on-the-Internationalization-of-Education.pdf

Canadian Bureau for International Education. (2013). *Code of ethical practice of the Canadian Bureau for International Education* (CBIE). Retrieved from http://www.cbie.ca/members/code-of-ethical-practice/

Canadian Institutes of Health Research, Natural Sciences and Engineering Research Council of Canada, & Social Sciences and Humanities Research Council of Canada. (2014, December). *Tri-council policy statement: Ethical conduct for research involving humans.* Retrieved from http://www.pre.ethics.gc.ca/pdf/eng/tcps2-2014/TCPS_2_FINAL_Web.pdf

Childwatch International Research Network. (n.d.). Retrieved from http://www.childwatch.uio.no/

Chiseri-Strater, E. (1996). Turning in upon ourselves: Positionality, subjectivity and reflexivity in case studies and ethnographic research. In P. Mortensen & G. E. Kirsch (Eds.), *Ethics and representation in qualitative studies of literacy* (pp. 115–133). Urbana, IL: NCTE.

Chiseri-Strater, E., & Sunstein, B. S. (2006). *What works? A practical guide for teacher research.* Portsmouth, NH: Heinemann.

Ethics of International Engagement and Service-Learning Project. (2011).*Global praxis: Exploring the ethics of engagement abroad.* Vancouver, BC. Retrieved from http://ethicsofisl.ubc.ca

Ganga, D., & Scott, S. (2006). Cultural "insiders" and the issue of positionality in qualitative migration research: Moving "across" and moving "along" researcher-participant divides. *Forum Qualitative Sozialforschung/Forum: Qualitative Social Research, 7*(3), Art. 7. Retrieved from http://nbn-resolving.de/urn:nbn:de:0114-fqs060379

Graham, A., Powell, M., Taylor, N., Anderson, D., & Fitzgerald, R. (2013). *Ethical research involving children.* Florence: UNICEF Office of Research—Innocenti. Retrieved from http://childethics.com/

Jones, M. (2006). The guest from England: Exploring issues of positionality in a foreign and yet familiar setting. *European Societies, 8*(1), 169–187.

Kapoor, I. (2004). Hyper-self-reflexive development: Spivak on representing the Third World "other." *Third World Quarterly, 25*(4), 627–647.

Kirby, S., & McKenna, K. (1989). *Methods from the margins: Experience, research, social change.* Toronto, ON: Garamond Press.

Leach, F. (2006). Researching gender violence in schools: Methodological and ethical considerations. *World Development, 34*, 1129–1147.

Mayall, B. (2002). *Towards a sociology for childhood: Thinking from children's lives.* London: Open University Press.

O'Leary, D. (2012). Outsider positioning in action research: Struggling with being on the outside looking in. Retrieved from http://arcolloquium.weebly.com/uploads/6/9/2/5/6925239/doleary_final_presentation.pdf

Pence, A., & Nsamenang, B. (2008). A case for early childhood development in sub-Saharan Africa. Working Paper No. 51. The Hague, The Netherlands: Bernard van Leer Foundation. Retrieved from https://files.eric.ed.gov/fulltext/ED522731.pdf

Powell, M. A., Fitzgerald, R. M., Taylor, N., & Graham, A. (2012). *International literature review: Ethical issues in undertaking research with children and young people,* for the Childwatch International Research Network, Southern Cross University, Centre for Children and Young People, Lismore NSW and University of Otago, Centre for Research on Children and Families, Dunedin, NZ.

Sharrock, G. (2007) After Copernicus: Beyond the crisis in Australian universities. *Australian Universities Review, 49*(1 & 2), 2–4. Retrieved from http://files.eric.ed.gov/fulltext/EJ802269.pdf

Skelton, T. (2008). Research with children and young people: Exploring the tensions between ethics, competence and participation. *Children's Geographies, 6*(1), 21–36.

Sultana, F. (2006). Reflexivity, positionality and participatory ethics: Negotiating fieldwork dilemmas in international research. *ACME: An International E-Journal for Critical Geographies, 6*(3), 374–378.

UN Convention on the Rights of the Child. (1989). Retrieved from https://www.unicef.org/sites/default/files/2019-04/UN-Convention-Rights-Child-text.pdf

Index

About the Editors and Contributors

MARLENE ASSELIN, University of British Columbia, Canada. Marlene is an associate professor in the Department of Language and Literacy Education at the University of British Columbia. Her research encompasses local and international studies of school and community libraries, early childhood education, digital literacies, information literacy, and ethical issues in conducting research.

SABRINA CARNESI, Old Dominion University, USA. Sabrina researches secondary education, teaching methods, marginalized youth, and YA literature. She is a middle school teacher librarian in Virginia (USA) and leads committees for intellectual freedom and books for youth in custody. Her book reviews and articles are frequently published in professional literature for educators and school librarians.

GAIL DICKINSON, Old Dominion University, USA. Gail is associate dean for Graduate Studies and Research in the Darden College of Education and Professional Studies at Old Dominion University in Norfolk, Virginia. Her research encompasses issues of school library management and curriculum.

RAY DOIRON, University of Prince Edward Island, Canada. Ray is professor emeritus in the Faculty of Education at the University of Prince Edward Island, Canada. He has taught courses in early literacy, kindergarten, and school librarianship, and his research interests include early childhood, digital/print literacies, and how libraries support literacies in schools and communities.

DEBORAH LANG FROGGATT, Director of Library Services, Boston Public Schools, Massachusetts, USA. Dr. Froggatt's school library career and public school advocacy spans 25 years, serving in Boston, Danvers, and Beverly, Massachusetts, and in Brookfield, Ridgefield, and Woodbury, Connecticut. She earned a bachelor's in history from Miami University, a master's of Christian education from Princeton Theological Seminary, a master's in library science from Southern Connecticut State University, and a PhD from Simmons College. Her work with urban high school students prompts her investigation of the impact of the lack of school library access on academic success. Public school libraries and issues of equity are a professional and personal passion.

ALLEN GRANT, Drexel University, USA. Allen is an associate clinical professor at the Drexel University School of Education. He holds a bachelor's degree in history, a master's degree in curriculum and instruction (early childhood education), and a PhD in educational leadership and research (educational technology). He has a particular interest in exploring the pedagogy of the I-LEARN model.

LUCY SANTOS GREEN, University of South Carolina, USA. Lucy is an associate professor at the University of South Carolina, where she teaches graduate courses in library and information science. Green's research centers on technology integration in teacher education, instructional partnerships between school library professionals and other educators, and the design and development of digital learning environments.

MEGHAN HARPER, Kent State University, USA. Meghan is a professor and serves as the Coordinator of the School Library program, teaches courses in the school library and youth program of study, co-directs the Virginia Hamilton Multicultural Literature Conference, and presents at numerous state, national, and international conferences.

DANIELLE HARTSFIELD, University of North Georgia, USA. Danielle is assistant professor in the Teacher Education Department at the University of North Georgia in Dahlonega. She teaches children's literature and other courses in the elementary education program. Her research interests include controversial children's books and promoting students' right to read.

RENEE F. HILL, University of Maryland, USA. Renee is a senior lecturer and Director of the School Library specialization. Her research and teaching focus on LIS and cultural competence, diversity, inclusion, and service to underrepresented populations.

MICHELLE HUDIBURG, Pittsburg State University, Kansas, USA. Michelle is a professor in the educational technology program at Pittsburg State University in Kansas. Hudiburg holds a PhD in instructional design and technology from Old Dominion University, Norfolk, VA. She has been part of realigning professional library training standards in the state of Kansas. Current research includes best practices for online teaching, as well as the role of librarians in school redesign.

SANDRA HUGHES-HASSELL, University of North Carolina, USA. Sandra is a professor and coordinator of the School Library Media Program in the School of Information and Library Science at the University of North Carolina at Chapel Hill. In her current research, she focuses on social justice issues in youth library services, connected learning, and the role of school librarians in education reform.

MELISSA P. JOHNSTON, University of West Georgia, USA. Melissa is an associate professor at the University of West Georgia, where she teaches graduate courses in the school library media certification program. Johnston's research and publications focus on school librarians as leaders, the school librarian's role in technology integration, and school librarianship on a global level.

SUE KIMMEL, Old Dominion University, USA. Sue is an associate professor at Old Dominion University's Darden College of Education. She teaches children' literature and school librarianship. Her research interests include school librarianship and selection and access to materials for children.

KAFI D. KUMASI, Wayne State University, USA. Kafi is an associate professor and she teaches in the areas of school library media, urban librarianship, multicultural services and resources, and research methods. Her research centers on literacy, and equity and diversity in urban educational environments, spanning primary, secondary, and tertiary educational contexts.

VERA LEE, Drexel University, USA. Vera is an associate clinical professor of literacy studies at the Drexel University School of Education. She holds a bachelor's degree in English, a master's degree in reading/writing/literacy, and an EdD in reading/writing/literacy. Her current research focuses on information/digital literacy development of K–12 urban teachers and students and on fostering the home/school literacy practices of immigrant families.

KATY MANCK, International Association of School Librarianship. Katy is president of the International Association of School Librarianship and "librarian-at-large" from Gilmer, Texas. During the past 40 years, she has worked in academic, corporate, public, and school libraries. She is a founding member of IASL's GiggleIT Project for global student writing through school libraries and recommends young adult books beyond bestsellers on her BooksYALove.com website.

MARCIA A. MARDIS, Florida State University, USA. Marcia is a professor and an associate dean for research at Florida State University's College of Communication & Information. She codirects the Information Policy, Management, & Use Institute where her team investigates professional identity development among information and technology technicians and professionals. Marcia is also the coeditor of *School Libraries Worldwide*, IASL's peer-reviewed research journal.

ELIZABETH MASCHER, Pittsburg State University, Kansas, USA. Elizabeth is a professor in the educational technology program at Pittsburg State University in Kansas. Mascher holds an EdD in educational leadership from the University of Arkansas, Fayetteville. Current research includes ensuring quality in online instruction and the role of technology in supporting student learning.

DELIA NEUMAN, Drexel University, USA. Delia is professor emerita at Drexel University, where she directed the School Library Media (SLiM) program in the College of Computing and Informatics. She holds bachelor's and master's degrees in English and a PhD in education (instructional systems design). The I-LEARN model is based on her years of research into students' use of information resources and her extensive experience designing instructnal materials.

DIANNE OBERG, University of Alberta, Canada. Dianne is professor emerita, University of Alberta, Edmonton, Canada. Her research has focused on school library education and on the implementation and evaluation of school library programs. She has served on the IFLA School Libraries Standing Committee for 12 years and has been an active member of IASL since 1982. She was the founding editor of the peer-reviewed international journal, *School Libraries Worldwide*.

ALICE SAGEHORN, Pittsburg State University, Kansas, USA. Alice is a professor and chairperson of the Department of Teaching and Leadership, College of Education, Pittsburg State University, Kansas. She teaches ESOL and curriculum courses and works with preservice and in-service teachers. She is a Fulbright-Hayes Scholar and has presented in 25 states and 7 countries.

RITA REINSEL SOULEN, Old Dominion University, USA. Rita is a lecturer in the library science program at Old Dominion University in Norfolk, Virginia, USA. She is a member of the NxtWave leaders for 21st Century Libraries. Her research is focused on the role of the school librarian in developing new and beginning teacher resilience through mentoring and collaboration.

JULIE STIVERS, Mt. Vernon Middle School, Raleigh, NC, USA. Julie is the librarian at Mt. Vernon Middle School in Raleigh, North Carolina. Her research interests are inclusive youth literature, graphic novels, and equity in the library.

M. J. TECCE DECARLO, Drexel University, USA. Mary Jean is an associate clinical professor of literacy studies at the Drexel University School of Education. She holds a bachelor's degree in elementary education and a master's degree and EdD in reading/writing/literacy. She conducts research in a variety of literacy-related fields, including digital and information literacy and brain-based-reading comprehension assessment.

JANICE UNDERWOOD, Old Dominion University, USA. Janice is the director of diversity in the Office of Institutional Equity and Diversity at Old Dominion University. As a national expert in the cultural contexts of K-20 public education reform, Dr. Underwood spearheads initiatives to recruit and retain a diverse workforce, leads integrated diversity campaigns and community-wide professional development related to teaching, learning, and overall diversity, and partners with faculty and policy leaders interested in advancing reforms, research, and grant initiatives that proactively create and sustain affirming workplace and learning environments.

DIAN WALSTER, Wayne State University, USA. Dian is a professor and her research interests are autoethnography and attitude-behavior consistency models; instructional design in online teaching and learning; everyday decision making; school librarians' collaboration and management skills; and media for children and young adults 9-14 years old.

LOIS D. WINE, Old Dominion University, USA. Lois is a doctoral candidate and NxtWave scholar at Old Dominion University. She is a practicing high school librarian and library lead in her district in Williamsburg, Virginia, USA. Her primary research areas are the impact of school librarians within the school ecosystem and the implementation of school librarians' roles as described by the National School Library Standards.